SOUFFLES-ANFAS

SOUFFLES-ANFAS

A CRITICAL ANTHOLOGY

FROM THE MOROCCAN JOURNAL OF CULTURE AND POLITICS

Edited by OLIVIA C. HARRISON

and TERESA VILLA-IGNACIO

STANFORD UNIVERSITY PRESS

STANFORD, CALIFORNIA

Stanford University Press
Stanford, California

Abdellatif Laâbi, "Doldrums," trans. Andrew Zawacki. *Chicago Review* 58:1 (Summer 2013): 116–23. Reprinted with the permission of the *Chicago Review*.

Etel Adnan's "Jebu" from *To look at the sea is to become what on is: An Etel Adnan Reader* (Nightboat Books, 2014). Reprinted by permission of the author and Nightboat Books.

The translations of Mohammed Khaïr-Eddine's "Bloods," Abdelkebir Khatibi's "The Street," "Becoming," and "Riot," Mohammed Ismaïl Abdoun's "Palma," Mostafa Nissabouri's "Untitled," Tahar Ben Jelloun's "Planet of the Apes," and Abdellatif Laâbi's "We Are All Palestinian Refugees" were first published in *Aufgabe* 13 (2014): 121–45. Reprinted with the permission of the translators.

Parts of the introduction were originally published in Olivia C. Harrison and Teresa Villa-Ignacio, "*Souffles-Anfas*," *Literary Encyclopedia*; http://www.litencyc .com/php/stopics.php?rec=true&UID=19351; published September 17, 2013. Reprinted with the permission of the *Literary Encyclopedia*.

Printed in the United States of America

Library of Congress Cataloging-in-Publication Data

Souffles-Anfas : a critical anthology from the Moroccan journal of culture and politics / edited by Olivia C. Harrison and Teresa Villa-Ignacio.
    pages cm
  Translated from French and Arabic.
  Includes bibliographical references and index.
  ISBN 978-0-8047-9470-1 (cloth : alk. paper)--ISBN 978-0-8047-9615-6 (pbk.
)--ISBN 978-0-8047-9623-1 (eBook)
  1. Postcolonialism--Literary collections. 2. North African literature.
3. Literature, Experimental. I. Harrison, Olivia C., 1980- editor, writer of introduction. II. Villa-Ignacio, Teresa, 1975- editor, writer of introduction.
III. Souffles (Rabat, Morocco) Excerpts from: IV. Anfas (Rabat, Morocco)
Excerpts from:
  PQ3989.2.S62S654 2015
  840.8'0964--dc23

                    2015026357

Typeset by Bruce Lundquist in 10/14 Palatino

CONTENTS

FIGURES

IT HAS BEEN AN IMMENSE PLEASURE to prepare this anthology for publication, from the first machinations of two eager graduate students nearly ten years ago, to the much slower and infinitely rewarding work of soliciting, editing, and assembling the beautiful translations collected here. Our first thanks go to our translators, who gave unsparingly of their time and energy to bring this collaborative project to fruition. Though the translations speak for themselves, much of the labor of translation remains invisible, and we wish to acknowledge it here. In addition to providing us with their meticulous translations, our translators graciously accepted several rounds of often exorbitantly detailed comments, which we felt were necessary to ensure that our translational choices remained consistent without sacrificing the originality of texts and translations. The extensive conversations we had with translators about the fine points of transposing French and Arabic texts into English very much shaped our editorial choices. In this sense the anthology is the product of a multi-year, virtual translation workshop in which each member played a key role. We are also indebted to our translators for their invaluable assistance in identifying secondary sources and finding the contextual information that was needed to produce accurate translations. We could not have produced a scholarly translation of this ilk without our translators' research efforts. Of course, we take responsibility for any translational or citational inconsistencies or errors contained in these pages.

Souffles-Anfas' editor-in-chief Abdellatif Laâbi lent us his support from the beginning stages of this project, and we are immensely grateful to him for allowing us to translate the texts included here and reproduce artwork from the journal. Publishing this anthology with his blessing, we have felt all the more motivated to do translational justice to the groundbreaking works presented here. We also thank Abdellatif Laâbi and Jocelyne Laâbi for so generously sharing their personal memories of the journal's production and for pointing us in the right directions for recent biographical information about many of the *Souffles-Anfas* contributors. Etel Adnan, who contributed a poem to *Souffles* and was an early supporter of the journal, has also been a source of inspiration for the project. We are grateful to her for giving us permission to reprint parts of her self-translation of "Jebu." In the past few years, we have had the pleasure of being in touch with several *Souffles* contributors and their family members, and wish to thank them here for their responses to our inquiries: Mohammed Ismaïl Abdoun, Tahar Ben Jelloun, Mostafa Nissabouri, and Colette Bennani.

We were able to present our translation project at several venues during the years leading up to its publication. Our editorial and translational choices were informed and enriched by conversations held at our special session on *Souffles-Anfas* at the Modern Language Association convention in Los Angeles, a symposium on translating North African literature at the University of Southern California, the PXP Poetry Symposium at Tulane University, and a workshop with the Tulane University Morocco Group as well as by countless conversation with friends, colleagues, and students who gave us invaluable advice, feedback, encouragement, and critique. We wish to thank particularly Omar Berrada, Homi Bhabha, Fayçal Falaky, Forrest Gander, Marilyn Hacker, Pierre Joris, Felicia McCarren, Panivong Norindr, Valérie Orlando, Kenza Sefrioui, Keith Waldrop, Rosmarie Waldrop, and Eliot Weinberger.

We are indebted to Thomas Spear, Anne George, and Carole Netter for uploading the content of *Souffles* to the Web in HTML, and the Bibliothèque Nationale du Royaume du Maroc for uploading the PDF versions of *Souffles* and *Anfas* to its website. The existence of the electronic versions of the journals made it possible to complete this project in a fraction of the time it would have taken otherwise. We are also grateful to the many individuals and institutions who assisted us at various stages of this translation project: the staff of the Bibliothèque Nationale de France and of the library of the Alliance Israélite Universelle, in particular Rose Lévyne, who was of precious assistance in identifying secondary sources; David Easterbrook of Northwestern University's Melville J. Herskovits Library of African Studies; Michael Bonnet of the University of Southern California's Dornsife Technology Services, who prepared the images for publication; Gina M. Allen of Tulane University Technology Services, who helped us brainstorm cover image ideas; and the Office of Research of the University of Southern California as well as the Department of English at Tulane University for the material support that enabled us to see this project through.

We feel very lucky that this anthology has received the expert guidance of our editor at Stanford University Press, Emily-Jane Cohen, and her indomitable editorial assistant Friederike Sundaram. We are grateful to the SUP production team, under the leadership of Mariana Raykov, and to our diligent copyeditor, Charles Trumbull, for bringing the manuscript into its print form. Last but not least, Ammiel Alcalay and Brian T. Edwards, the then anonymous readers of the manuscript, provided excellent suggestions for making the anthology more user-friendly. We hope the book in its current form meets their expectations, and those of the reader.

SOUFFLES-ANFAS

SOUFFLES-ANFAS FOR THE NEW MILLENNIUM

Olivia C. Harrison and Teresa Villa-Ignacio

IN THE SPRING OF 1966, ten years after Morocco gained independence from France, a small group of poets and artists—Abdellatif Laâbi, Mostafa Nissabouri, Mohammed Khaïr-Eddine, Bernard Jakobiak, Mohamed Melehi, Hamid El Houadri, and Mohammed Fatha—published the first issue of *Souffles* (in French, literally "breaths," figuratively "inspirations"), a poetry and culture review that would serve in the late 1960s and early 1970s as a conduit for experimental art and progressive politics in Morocco and beyond. *Souffles* was founded after the March 23, 1965, student protests in Casablanca, a violently repressed demonstration that marked the beginning of "the years of lead," as the regime of King Hassan II (reigned 1961–1999) is known in Morocco. The founding members of *Souffles*—teachers, artists, and poets who came of age during the transition from French tutelage to national sovereignty—corralled their talents, energies, and revolt into this iconoclastic and incendiary cultural review. They imagined this publication as a lightning rod for what, deploying a global Marxist lexicon, they called *revolution*. In Laâbi's words, something was "about to happen in Africa and in the rest of the Third World" and *Souffles* planned to be the vanguard of this cultural and political effervescence.[1] In 1971 the editorial team founded a parallel Arabic-language journal, *Anfas*, which became a tribune for the Moroccan left.[2] Laâbi and several other contributors were arrested the following year, putting an end to the *Souffles-Anfas* adventure.[3]

A repository of seminal 1960s texts from across the colonized and postcolonial world, *Souffles-Anfas* provides a window onto the transnational cultural and political movements that mark the heyday of Third Worldism and anticolonial theory. The journal was instrumental in establishing transnational dialogues between writers, artists, and activists from Africa, Asia, and the Americas. It published seminal works by tricontinental writers and political activists, such as the Haitian writer René Depestre, the Syrian poet Adonis, and Amilcar Cabral, the leader of the struggle for independence from Portugal in Guinea-Bissau, as well as key revolutionary and postcolonial texts, such as the ten-point program of the Black Panthers or the Argentine manifesto for a Third Cinema. Frantz Fanon, the theorist of decolonization and prophet of postcolonial disillusionment, was a particularly important interlocutor for the journal's founding members. Heeding Fanon's call to leave Europe behind,[4] Laâbi advocated for what he called "cultural decolonization," a process by which Moroccan writers and artists would break with stagnant French models and Arabic canons in order to forge new artistic forms and literary languages in dialogue with the rest of the decolonizing world.[5]

Given the brief lifespan and meager resources of *Souffles-Anfas*, it is remarkable that it has had such an enduring impact, both nationally and internationally. Entirely self-funded and run out of Laâbi's modest apartment on a pro-bono, part-time basis by its contributors, the journal was printed in Tangier and distributed in kiosks in major Moroccan cities as well as to a small number of foreign subscribers for the symbolic sum of three dirhams. The modest print run averaged three to five thousand copies per issue, and barely covered production costs.[6] In all, twenty-two issues of *Souffles* (including five double issues) were published from 1966 to 1971 (the final issue appeared only in January 1972). All eight numbers of *Anfas* (including two double issues) were published in 1971.

While the first issues of *Souffles* primarily published experimental poetry and essays on Moroccan literature, popular culture, art, and film, the journal gradually expanded its focus to cultural production and political developments across the Third World. At the same time, it became increasingly outspoken in calling for anticolonial and Marxist revolution throughout the Arab world, especially after the June 1967 war, which placed the Palestinian cause front and center on the pages of *Souffles-Anfas*. In 1969 the journal published "Pour la révolution palestinienne" (For the Palestinian revolution), a special issue (*Souffles* 15), which, though it continued to feature poetry, marked a sharp political turn in the journal's editorial line. Subsequent issues adopted a more legible format and an explicitly Marxist-Leninist tone. In addition to publishing poetry, essays on culture, and literary criticism, the journal began to feature commentary on domestic and international affairs, including continuing coverage of the Palestinian-Israeli conflict, liberation struggles in the Portuguese colonies of Africa, and the independence movement in the western Sahara.

Souffles-Anfas is an important archive of global Marxist and Third Worldist thought and an early example of opposition to authoritarian regimes in the formerly colonized world. In 1968 the engineer and leftist militant Abraham Serfaty joined the editorial board, bringing with him a fresh group of leftist contributors even as several founding artists and poets left the journal.[7] Two years later, Laâbi and Serfaty founded a clandestine Marxist-Leninist political party, Organisation Alif (A), which would subsequently adopt the name Ilal Amam (Forward), while their comrades from the new left formed Organisation Ba (B), which would later be renamed 23 Mars in memory of the thousands killed in the March 1965 Casablanca student protests.[8] *Souffles* and, from 1971, its companion Arabic-language journal *Anfas*, became the de facto mouthpieces for the radical Moroccan left. In 1972, Laâbi and Serfaty were arrested, tortured, and summarily condemned to life sentences. Laâbi was released in 1980, while Serfaty, who had remained in hiding until 1974, was freed only in 1991.

Souffles-Anfas is also one of the most fascinating and varied repositories of postcolonial Moroccan poetry and cultural criticism. The journal's collection of texts ranges from experimental poems, literary manifestos, and abstract art to political tracts, open letters, and interviews. Alongside its short-lived publishing house, Atlantes, *Souffles* was the first publication to feature the work of some of the most important postcolonial Moroccan and Maghrebi writers: Laâbi, Nissabouri, Khaïr-Eddine, Abdelkebir Khatibi, Tahar Ben Jelloun, and Malek Haddad, among others. *Souffles* was also one the first journals primarily devoted to literary criticism and cultural critique in the Maghreb.[9] Critical of some early Francophone writers such as Ahmed Sefrioui, considered to be an "ethnographic" writer—that is, a documentarian of Moroccan society writing for the benefit of the colonizers—*Souffles* enthusiastically revived the work of predecessors such as Driss Chraïbi and Kateb Yacine. Chraïbi had been accused by his contemporaries of betraying the Moroccan independence struggle because his 1954 novel *Le passé simple* (*The Simple Past*) took aim at Moroccan customs in a way that the anticolonial movement felt was complicit with French Orientalist scholarship on the Maghreb. Judging that Chraïbi's critique of tradition had come too soon, Laâbi reinstated him as a suitably iconoclastic writer, critical of both colonial and traditionalist narratives. In another article he unreservedly praised the Algerian writer Kateb Yacine, one of the few elders to have successfully "decolonized" history, to use an expression coined by the historian Mohamed Sahli.[10]

Souffles nevertheless marks a rupture with previous literary traditions. The journal's founding manifesto, published as the prologue to the first issue, declares a decisive break with literary forms and idioms derived from the French and Arabic literary canons and calls for writers to establish a new Moroccan literature in both French and Arabic. In an important editorial ("Realities and Dilemmas of National Culture," *Souffles* 4), Laâbi parts ways with two writers from the previous generation who had famously predicted the imminent death of French-language literature: the Tunisian theorist Albert Memmi and the Algerian novelist Malek Haddad. For Laâbi, these writers' preoccupation with language choice had been detrimental to the emergence of a national culture. Unlike his elders, Laâbi seeks to move beyond the binary opposition of colonizer and colonized, emphasizing the importance of elaborating national culture in any language. While cautioning writers to remain suspicious of whichever language they used, "whether French, Arabic, or any other," Laâbi defends Maghrebi intellectuals writing in French and advocates for the emergence of Moroccan culture in all its languages.[11] *Souffles* began practicing a politics of bilingualism and translation from the ninth issue, which includes a French translation of a manifesto by the Syrian poet Adonis, whose journal *Mawaqif* (Positions) was lauded by the editorial team as an example of avant-garde Arabic literature.[12] *Souffles* 10–11, 12, and 13–14 went even further, featuring new Maghrebi literature in both French and Arabic.

The poems published in the journal's first issues share a common investment in provoking the reader and upsetting the political and aesthetic status quo through what Marc Gontard calls "the violence of the text."[13] Laâbi characterizes this new literature as a "terrorist literature": "a literature that on all levels (syntactic, phonetic, morphological, graphical, symbolic, etc.) shatters the original logic of the French language."[14] This literary terrorism is aimed at both stultified Moroccan culture—what "colonial science" dubs tradition, according to Laâbi—and contemporary forms of neocolonialism and cultural imperialism.[15] Peppering their texts with scatological, sexual, iconoclastic and even blasphemous figures and themes, the *Souffles* poets suggest new discursive modes through which to explore, valorize, and debate the meaning of subjective experience in colonial and postcolonial contexts.

While *Souffles* sought to demonstrate Moroccan and Maghrebi literature's independence from, and alterity to, French literature, it also maintained a dialogue with the avant-garde in Western aesthetics. As critics have noted, the journal made frequent reference to literary and artistic movements outside Morocco, including the *nouveau roman*, the theater of the absurd, Russian futurism, American beat poetry, and abstract expressionism in painting.[16] Yet it remained wary of overdependence on Western culture and guarded itself against Western "paternalism-vampirism."[17] Several articles testify to this growing distrust of cultural imperialism, particularly through French publishing and distribution circuits. In his review of Rachid Boudjedra's debut novel, *La répudiation*—like Chraïbi's *Le passé simple*, a scathing critique of Maghrebi family and class structures—Laâbi celebrates its iconoclasm while warning that it may be recouped by French critics eager for Arab denunciations of "stifling ancestral traditions."[18] In *Souffles* 13–14, Noured Ayouch interviews the French theater director Jean-Marie Serreau who produced, for French audiences, plays by Aimé Césaire, Kateb Yacine, and René Depestre. While deeply sympathetic to Serreau as an anticolonial director who took risks staging Kateb's plays during the Algerian war, Ayouch takes issue with the disparities between the conditions of theatrical production in France and its former colonies.[19]

The journal's commitment to cultural decolonization led the editorial team to revise its position on language in the final issues of *Souffles*. Despite earlier claims that Moroccan writers and artists were to forge national culture in all the languages available to them, *Souffles* ultimately opted to transition to the Arabic language—despite the fact that its editorial team wrote in French. Written without any foreknowledge of his impending imprisonment, Laâbi's foreword to what would be the last issue of *Souffles* declared that henceforth the journal would focus primarily on issues pertaining to the Arab world, and announced the launch of the Arabic-language monthly *Anfas*, which would become the principal organ of the *Souffles-Anfas* team.[20] This choice signaled *Souffles'* increasing identification with ongoing liberation struggles in the Maghreb and Mashriq. It also marked a shift to

Arabic, seen as the sole legitimate national language and a weapon against continued cultural imperialism.

The eight issues of *Anfas* feature opinion pieces on education reform, foreign control over the financial sector, and mining strikes in Morocco alongside essays on class struggles in Egypt and the Palestinian resistance. Articles devoted to cultural themes were few, and only a small number of poems made their way into the pages of *Anfas*. One of these, by Sudanese poet Muhammad al-Fayturi, is included here.[21] The comparatively large press run (5,000 copies) and extremely modest price of *Anfas* ensured a sizeable following in both the Maghreb and Mashriq.[22] As the Arabic-language mouthpiece of the Moroccan opposition, *Anfas* ostensibly posed a greater threat to the regime than had *Souffles*, precipitating the violent crackdown on the editorial team. *Souffles* 22 and *Anfas* 7–8 were to be the journal's final issues.

Reading *Souffles-Anfas* Today

Souffles-Anfas has enjoyed increasing visibility in the past few decades. Recent scholarship on contemporary Moroccan literature credits the journal for validating popular culture at a time when cultural production in Darija, the colloquial Moroccan Arabic dialect, and in Tamazight ("Berber") had been marginalized.[23] The journal dismissed "folklore" as an Orientalist invention and condemned nativist or traditionalist attempts to value Islamic art and classical Arabic texts over popular theater and poetry, "naive" art, and crafts that had evolved over the course of centuries. The editors also insisted on recognizing Morocco's ethnic and religious plurality, including not only Imazighen but also Jews. Abraham Serfaty contributed several important essays to the journal on the historical importance of Jews in Moroccan society and political life, and argued against French colonial and Zionist claims that Jews had always formed a disenfranchised class in Morocco.[24]

Yet if *Souffles-Anfas* was a trailblazer in heralding Moroccan diversity and popular culture years before the 1980s Berberist movements, it remained focused on anticolonialism, class struggles, and cultural decolonization and adopted an unapologetically militant tone in advocating them. The journal is characterized by the populist, masculinist, and militarist imagery typical of radical leftist and pan-Arabist discourses of the era, as evidenced in the tone and iconography of the journal: posters

of Kalashnikov-bearing Palestinian fedayeen (resistance fighters, literally "martyrs"; figs. 11–13, 16, pp. 189, 190, 206, 216) and of the assassinated Congolese political leader Patrice Lumumba (fig. 18, p. 235), or
a cartoon of a European general who looks suspiciously like Charles
de Gaulle being served a ticking time bomb by an African and an Arab
waiter, for example (fig. 19, p. 236). It is thus not surprising that women
played only a small role in *Souffles-Anfas*. In all, the journal published
only one poem by a female writer, "Jebu," by the Lebanese writer and
artist Etel Adnan, one review essay on scholarly works by Maghrebi
women, and one article by the art critic Toni Maraini.[25] In a spirited
interview conducted by Laâbi, Chraïbi insists on an issue that appears
nowhere in the pages of the journal: women's rights ("isn't woman,
wherever she happens to be, the last remaining colonized being on
Earth?"). Gender equality was never a top priority for *Souffles-Anfas*.[26]

The journal did set the stage for more inclusive movements in
Moroccan cultural politics, however. Several scholars see in *Souffles-
Anfas* the harbinger and predecessor of the Moroccan human rights
movement, which took the struggle initiated by the radical left in the
1960s and 1970s into the domain of Moroccan and international law.[27]
Safoi Babana-Hampton argues that *Souffles'* aesthetic practices formed
a new space in which civic discourse and citizen agency became
possible, one in which Moroccans might engage with their cultural
heritage and history as well as with questions regarding the nation's
future.[28] Valérie Orlando finds that by advocating for social justice
and political change in Morocco, Laâbi and his colleagues at *Souffles*
and *Anfas* set the tone for the politically engaged literature produced
in the 1990s and 2000s by former prisoners of Tazmamart.[29] She further notes that the new generation of Francophone Moroccan authors
demonstrate a particular commitment to the inclusion of marginalized
citizens, a commitment that finds its roots in *Souffles-Anfas'* policies of
inclusivity.[30]

Translating *Souffles-Anfas*

This anthology takes part in a movement for greater inclusion of
Maghrebi literary texts in English translation, including an anthology of Laâbi's poems, the compelling collection of Moroccan poetry
published in the fifth issue of the journal *Aufgabe*, and a monumental

anthology of North African literature that spans twenty-seven centuries of Maghrebi literature and covers a wide range of oral and written traditions composed in Tamazight, Phoenician, Hebrew, Latin, Arabic, Turkish, and French.[31] This growing interest can be attributed to Western curiosity about North African cultures following the recent upheavals in the region as well as the burgeoning market for "world literature." It also betokens a profound engagement with the vast and varied repertoire of Maghrebi literature and its political and historical contexts. As more of these texts become available in translation, we can expect a rise in critical scholarship that explores how the exigencies of these texts speak to the concerns of Anglophone readers today.

In selecting and presenting the texts included in this anthology for an English-language audience, we focused on three defining threads of the journal's evolution: (1) its journey from experimental poetics to experimental political engagement; (2) its emphasis on the role of the arts, especially literature, in postcolonial societies; and (3) its shift in focus from Moroccan to global postcolonial struggles and engagement with Maghrebi and Mashriqi politics and culture. Rather than grouping texts together by genre or theme, we have chosen to follow the chronology of the journal's publication history. Moreover, while we accentuate the global reach of *Souffles-Anfas'* editorial vision by including such texts as a public talk by the Haitian writer René Depestre on Negritude and an interview with the Senegalese writer and filmmaker Ousmane Sembène, our selection focuses on North Africa and the Middle East.

Due also to the constraints of space and our editorial vision, we chose not to include several features of historical interest, such as numerous book reviews, art exhibition reviews, readers' correspondence, several vividly militant Marxist-Leninist documents (e.g. reports from international activists' meetings) that appear in the later issues, and even advertisements for cigarettes and the like. While such features contribute to the uncannily local-yet-global qualities of the *Souffles* and *Anfas* print issues, the diverse and dynamic texts and works of visual art presented here convey these same qualities with boundless creative ferocity. The anthology includes twenty-three illustrations, placed in the order in which they appeared in the journal: reproductions of contemporary Moroccan artwork, posters commissioned for special issues of the journal, cartoons, and facsimiles of issue covers and particularly visually striking poems. We selected a broad and representative sample of images to give the reader a sense of the diversity, range, and quality of the artwork reproduced in the journal, as well as a visual representation of the formally experimental poetry it published.

Finally, we have chosen to call *Souffles-Anfas* a *journal* rather than a *review* or *magazine* (all options for translating the French term *revue*) in order to emphasize the quality of the peer-reviewed scholarly work that appeared in it, as well as to highlight its place among seminal journals such as *La Revue du Monde Noir*, *Tropiques*, and *Présence Africaine* that galvanized decolonizing and postcolonial movements around the globe. That being said, the dire material conditions in which *Souffles-Anfas* operated meant that its contributors had limited access to research facilities, with the consequence that their citations of source texts are occasionally incomplete, erroneous, or simply missing. We have tried to make up for these lacunae and provide complete or partial citations whenever possible. Without burdening the texts with cumbersome translators' and editors' notes, we do indicate when a quotation departs from the original in a meaningful way or when a citation or page number could not be found.

The diversity of *Souffles-Anfas* texts presented here is matched by the diversity of styles our translators have employed. The texts often presented us with a difficult choice between anachronistic terminology and a historically accurate expression that might be misinterpreted in the current context, thus distorting the original intent of the French and Arabic originals. In most cases, we chose to err on the side of fidelity to the original so as to preserve the historical character of *Souffles-Anfas* as a Marxist-Leninist, pan-Arab, Third Worldist revolutionary journal with all its virtues and shortcomings. The journal's consistent use of male pronouns as neutral, compounded in French and Arabic by the tendency to use the singular (e.g. "the writer" becomes "he"), may strike the reader as outdated if not offensive, but we felt it was important to keep the singular in these cases. Similarly, we retained locutions such as "Negro" and "Negro-African" in, for example, Haitian writer René Depestre's scathing critique of Negritude, though we capitalized them to make clear their historical significance.[32] Instead of creating a blanket policy for these kinds of translational issues, we worked with translators one-on-one to determine the choices that best fit within each text.

Each text also presented its own unique translational challenges. In translating it is impossible to give equal attention to every aspect of a text, and this is especially true in the case of literary texts: lexical choices, tone, register, form, and sound all compete for the spotlight, and through it all the translator must resist the temptation to rewrite the work—unless of course the translator is also the writer of the original text. Etel Adnan's self-translation of "Jebu," a text she originally published forty-five years ago (in *Souffles* 15, 1969) features many revisions that represent her vision of the poem as a mature poet and (self-) translator. While we considered including an English-language version of the poem that more closely reproduces the text as it appears in *Souffles*, we felt that Adnan's self-translation belonged with the rest of the translations presented here, which were all newly produced for this volume. The seventeen other translators whose work appears here, all of whom are poets and/or scholars with intellectual and creative investments in Maghrebi literature, also came to the project with a diversity of translational philosophies. Jennifer Moxley explains that in her view, which was formed through her participation in the translation workshops held by Emmanuel Hocquard and Juliette Valéry at la Fondation Royaumont in the 1980s and 1990s, "the goal of the translator is to create a work that can become part of the literature of the target language." She seeks to create a text that "reads wonderfully in English—in part because the reader . . . does not have access to the source."[33] Other translators have preferred to emphasize their translations' disruptions of English.

Our ultimate aspiration has been to translate the tone and tenor of this iconic journal. The quality that unites the many modes of the *Souffles-Anfas* texts—their rage against injustice, revolutionary fervor, razor-sharp erudition, potent urgency, and emotive solidarity—is the authors' conviction that the power of the written word and their work as a community of writers could effect political change for the greater good.

Legacies of *Souffles-Anfas*

The political and cultural legacies of *Souffles-Anfas* are far-reaching. In Morocco the journal's significance is twofold. On the one hand, it constitutes a testament to early opposition to the regime, and a crucial document in contemporary Moroccan political history. On the other, it carries great literary and historical significance as one of the most important platforms for poetic and artistic expression in the post-independence period. Outside Morocco and the Maghreb, *Souffles-Anfas* is synony- mous with the cultural and political effervescence of the late 1960s, and an example of tricontinental aesthetic praxis. With the renewed critical interest in pan-Arabism, pan-Africanism, and global Marxism, as well as the recent rise of media studies and literary journal studies in the academy, *Souffles-Anfas* has gained new currency and relevance, par- ticularly in light of recent phenomena such as the Arab Spring.

In his preface to Kenza Sefrioui's monograph on *Souffles-Anfas*, pub- lished in 2013, Laâbi characterizes the global effervescence of the late 1960s, in which *Souffles-Anfas* played a non-negligible role, as the "in- augural spring" that paved the way for today's revolts against authori- tarian regimes.[34] The journal's revolutionary goals constitute, at the discursive level at least, an early example of the protean pro-democracy movements that have swept across the Arab world since late 2010. The transnational character of the upheavals—which extend far beyond the region if recent protests such as *los indignados* in Spain and the Occupy demonstrations in the United States are included—also harkens back to the Third Worldist discourses of the post-Bandung era. Moroccan left- ists drew inspiration from the Black Panthers, Africans rising against their Portuguese colonizers, and the struggles of the Vietnamese and Palestinian peoples. This strong sense of historical and political affili- ation with today's youthful protestors has led Laâbi and a few other Moroccan intellectuals, such as the historian Abdelahad Sebti, to sup- port the fledgling February 20 movement, which protests against cor- ruption, crony capitalism, and the enrichment of the few and advocates for economic opportunity, social justice, and political rights.[35]

It is impossible to gauge if democratic change and economic justice are indeed "inevitable" in Morocco, as Laâbi maintains.[36] Economic and other development indicators such as literacy rates and access to healthcare—according to Gilbert Achcar, these are the principal fac- tors that triggered the revolts known as the Arab Spring—remain dis- mal, and yet the mainly urban protests in Morocco have failed to rally massive popular support.[37] Nor were the protests directed at remov- ing the king or abolishing the monarchy. Some critics speculate that this is because the "years of lead" have given way to a lighter touch under Hassan II's successor Mohamed VI, who has deftly adopted the discourse of human rights and democratic reform and implemented a series of highly visible measures: the Equity and Reconciliation Commission of 2004, which seems to have turned the page on arbitrary arrests, trials, detention, and torture—though no perpetrators were held accountable, and though some of these methods continue to be deployed against presumed Islamist and Sahraoui terrorists; a new family code greatly enhancing women's rights; the recognition of Tamazight as a national language; and a series of constitutional reforms initiated and supervised by the monarch.[38] It remains to be seen if these incremental political reforms will outweigh widening economic disparities in successfully preempting the kinds of popular upheavals that led to the ouster of authoritarian rulers in Tunisia, Egypt, Libya, and Jordan—upheavals that have not delivered on the promise of economic justice or even political transformation, as most of these cases make cruelly clear.

Whatever the afterlives of the recent protest movements in Morocco, reading *Souffles-Anfas* in the wake of the global revolts that began in 2010 is simultaneously thrilling and chilling. Thrilling by virtue of the journal's uncompromising advocacy for democratic transformation across the region. Chilling in that its endeavors were so abruptly put to an end—or suspended, if we agree with Laâbi that the fight continues today. The aspirations and inspirations (*souffles*, *anfas*) of the poets, artists, and militants collected in this anthology resonate with particular acuity in the first decades of the new millennium.

PART ONE

SOUFFLES 1–3 (1966)

IN CONFIDENT, PASSIONATE TONES, and brilliant, exuberant poetry and prose, the contributors to *Souffles'* first three issues announce the beginning of a new phase of Moroccan literature and culture. Abdellatif Laâbi's prologue to the first "manifesto-issue" describes its young writers as poised at a threshold. Wholeheartedly rejecting the cultural stagnation brought about by colonial acculturation and the subordination of Moroccan cultural production to the whims of imperial French tastes, these writers confront the social and political issues facing their newly independent country to produce a critically grounded Moroccan national culture. Laâbi envisioned *Souffles* as a nonpartisan venue for a new poetry and literature, open to a global authorship and intended for Moroccans and other decolonizing peoples around the world. In the second issue he reaffirms *Souffles'* distance from Moroccan old-guard pseudoliterature—emblematized by *Le petit Marocain* (*The Little Moroccan*), an ultraconservative daily and holdover from the colonial period—and invites the reader to engage directly with intellectuals' and artists' works. Abdelkebir Khatibi's essay on the Maghrebi novel echoes Laâbi's observations and exhortations. Acknowledging the indispensable politicization of Moroccan, Algerian, and Tunisian literatures during these countries' struggles for sovereignty, Khatibi questions the legitimacy of writing literature in French for a largely illiterate, non-French-speaking population, and demands a clearer relationship between aesthetic and political practices in the postcolonial context.

The essays in this section vividly demonstrate *Souffles'* simultaneous rejection of the old submission to European frameworks and enthusiasm for new forms of decolonized culture. Abdallah Stouky's scathing review essay on the 1966 World Festival of Negro Arts in Dakar, Senegal, protests the festival's multiple objectifications of African culture and the use of venues such as museums and Italianate theaters that tend to divorce African cultural objects from their contexts. Stouky further reveals the downfall of Negritude: while for the preceding generation it was an aesthetic and political rallying cry, in 1966 it appears to him as an essentialist colonial anachronism that must give way to an independent African identity ready to face contemporary challenges. Ahmed Bouanani's "An Introduction to Popular Moroccan Poetry" explores the traditions of indigenous Moroccan oral literature, detailing the history of its itinerant singers, sacred poets, and regionally diverse musical instruments, song forms, and poetic subgenres. Drawing attention to Moroccans' centuries-old practice of orally transmitting history, Bouanani calls for a comprehensive study of these rapidly vanishing oral traditions.

Showcasing the range of contemporary experimental poetic production was the primary mission of these first three issues; the selections translated here highlight the stylistic diversity through which *Souffles* approached poetry as cultural critique. Laâbi's "Doldrums," invoking poisonous scorpions and scatological offenses, recasts his essayistic critiques of cultural stagnation in terms of human-embodied experience at its most chaotic. Mohammed Khaïr-Eddine's "Bloods" overwhelms the reader with its turbulent stream of unpunctuated, uncapitalized prose and rejoices in blood's long history of cultural significance as an ancient symbol of life and marker of identity, while simultaneously succumbing to a modern-day, paranoid view of blood as a biological vector for disease. The plural "bloods" of the title also testify to the literal and figurative pooling of the blood of those who disappeared during the years of lead, calling on this collective experience of loss to critique the boundaries that define family, community, tribal, and national allegiances. The speaker alternately rages with and against his realization that the coursing of blood and his attempts to contain it ultimately lead, through violence, to its corruption and loss. Although Khatibi's tightly controlled verses recall the poetic innovations of Western modernism, they are most notable for the critical tact and subtlety that would become his trademarks. The "twilight dance of a dead leaf" in "Becoming" is reminiscent of Poundian imagism, while "The Street" and "Riot" pay homage to the street as a primary site of encounter with language and history, recasting the Baudelairean *flâneur*'s paradoxical solitude-within-a-crowd. However, these poems emphatically reconstitute these modernist commonplaces as vehicles for latent memories of the violence of colonization and decolonization.

FIGURE 1. Front cover of the first issue of *Souffles* with painting by Mohamed Melehi and logo by Mohamed Chebaa. *Souffles* 1 (Rabat, 1966). Reprinted with permission.

PROLOGUE

Abdellatif Laâbi

Translated from the French by Teresa Villa-Ignacio

The poets who have authored the texts of this, the manifesto issue of the journal *Souffles*, are unanimously aware that publishing in this venue means they are taking a stand at a moment when issues pertaining to our national culture have attained a degree of extreme tension.

The current state of literary affairs is not characterized, as some might believe, by a proliferation of creativity. The cultural disturbance that some individuals or groups are hoping will pass for a literary growth spurt is, in fact, only the expression of our ongoing stagnation or a certain number of misunderstandings about the deeper meaning of literary activity.

Petrified contemplation of the past, sclerosis of forms and themes, shameless imitation and forced borrowings, and the misplaced vanity of false talents constitute the adulterated daily bread with which the press, journals, and the greed of our rare publishing houses bludgeon us.

Even when we leave these multiple prostitutions out of the discussion, literature has become a form of aristocratism, a rosette on display, a force of intelligence and cunning.

This is not a quarrel between the ancients and the moderns. In fact, the literature ravaging the country today most often conceals a shocking eclecticism of heritages and borrowings from hearsay. It would even be possible for an objective critic to study outdated literary trends here where they are still in vogue. And since the tourist brochures speak of a "land of contrasts," one will find in this literature whatever is needed to satisfy all curiosities, all nostalgias: the residue of classical medieval poetry, Oriental poetry of exile, Western romanticism, symbolism from the turn of the century, social realism, not to mention the results of existentialist indigestion.

As a result, "representatives" of "Moroccan literature" occupy a special place at international gatherings, and congresses of writers are held in our country. The reader is at once disoriented and nauseous. His dis-

satisfaction is all the more justified in that he can find some of his problems echoed in foreign literatures, those that various "missions" have
benevolently placed at his doorstep. We can explain the oft-commented
complex of our national literature by its current incapacity to "touch"
the reader, to gain his attachment, or to provoke in him some kind of
reflection, a wrenching away of his social or political conditioning.

On an entirely different level, Maghrebi literature in French, which
at one time gave birth to so much hope, is currently stalled and seems,
according to some observers, to belong to the domain of history. This
literature must, however, be called into question today.

Two of its most brilliant representatives prematurely celebrated its
demise with touching funeral ceremonies.[1] Analyzing the situation of
the colonized writer, his linguistic dramas, his lack of true readers, they
concluded that this literature was "condemned to die young."[2]

Others have abstained from falling into this pathetic determinism.
But they are all ready, despite their lucid self-critique, to entertain the
paradox of a suicidal literature that keeps going, in spite of everything,
albeit in slow motion, along its path.

A glance through the most recent publications in French reveals
that that those who have pronounced the imminent death of this literature have come to this conclusion too quickly. Although we should
in no way ignore the issue of the very status of Maghrebi literature in
French. This is a delicate issue, and we must approach it prudently
while excluding all tendencies toward generalization. In fact, the situation of writers of the previous generation (Kateb Yacine, Mohammed
Dib, Mouloud Feraoun, Mouloud Mammeri, Albert Memmi or even
Driss Chraïbi), reveals itself to be closely tied to the colonial experience in its linguistic, cultural, and sociological implications. From the
pacifist autobiographies of the 1950s to the protestatory and militant
works from the period of the Algerian War, we may remark that despite the diversity of talents and creative power, this production was
entirely inscribed within the framework of acculturation. It perfectly
illustrates the relationship between the colonized and the colonizer
within the cultural sphere. Thus, even when a Maghrebi was represented in these works or when autochthonous writers spoke up to
denounce abuses, this literature almost always remained a one-way
street. It was conceived for the public of the "Métropole" and des-

tined for foreign consumption. That was the public it aimed to move to pity, in which it sought to awaken solidarity; that was the public to whom it needed to demonstrate that the fellah in Kabylia or the factory worker in Oran were not so different from the farmer in Brittany or the dockworker in Marseille. Today one has the impression that this literature was a kind of immense open letter to the West, or something like a list of Maghrebi grievances. Of course this enormous deposition has proven its usefulness. These Maghrebi works caused a scandal and accelerated a coming-to-consciousness among progressive milieux in France and elsewhere. In this sense they were revolutionary.

In order to avoid making generalizations of our own, we should point to the exceptional work of two or three writers who surpassed all the limiting frameworks of their time, even if their work initially arose from these common preoccupations.

We must admit that this literature now only concerns us in part; in any case it is hardly able to satisfy our need for a literature that bears the burden of our current realities, of wholly new problematics in the face of which disarray and savage revolt are gripping us.

Writers have had to attain a certain level of putrefaction, or maturity, if you will, in order to be able to formulate what you will read in these texts.

The poets who clamor here have not been able to avoid their elders' agonies, but it has fallen to them to rigorously delineate the limits of the arduous task they have inherited. They intend to demonstrate that they are less continuers than they are initiators.

Amidst the chorus of insults about our underdevelopment and current humiliations, these poets have seen with the eyes of peace the mutations of a society that has too often been taken for a testing ground or a storehouse of legends. They are its witnesses and its leading actors. Despite the kaleidoscope of tones, their voices come together in fierce alarms.

Hypotheticals remain to be leveed, contradictions to be sealed up and surpassed, but complexes are being swept away, a new circulation is gaining momentum.

At this point we can already guess what charges will be made against us, notably our choice of language.

Without wading into the murky waters of false issues, let us respond for now that four of these poets discovered their literary vocation through the French language. There is no drama or paradox there. This situation has become too common in today's world. The priority is to arrive at a correspondence between written language [*langue*] and the poet's inner world, his intimate, emotive language [*langage*]. Some are not able to achieve this. Others, even those who write in the national written tongue remain at the surface of their selves and of the reality they wish to theorize and put into question.

Despite their linguistic disorientation, the poets in this collection succeed in communicating their most profound feelings through a language filtered through their history, their mythology, their anger—in short, through their very selves.

The issue of communicating this poetry remains. On the one hand, and this has already been said (but strangely never taken seriously), there is the possibility of translating these works if one even briefly considers that they have their place and their role to play in the context of our national literature. On the other hand, the particular issue of communicating our literature in its entirety is not as simple as one might think. Putting aside questions of appreciation, interpretation, or critique of literary works, the Moroccan public that is even capable of reading such works is exceedingly limited. Illiteracy on the one hand and a superficial culture on the other has limited this readership to a nearly derisory residue.

Another paradox, but one that derives from a global social situation that can't be overcome through reasoning or some kind of magic trick. Why then resign ourselves to an even more overwhelming, sterile silence? The poet's language is first of all "his own language": the one that he creates and elaborates in the heart of linguistic chaos, the manner also by which he re-imagines the veneer of his world and the dynamics that coexist in him.

Why should we be distressed about this situation, as if we suffered an infirmity, when we must by all means make up for the delay we have incurred and respond to the urgencies of the moment?

Perhaps the next generations will resolve this issue, though they will already bear witness to their own world, a world that will no longer be ours though we are self-consciously striving toward it.

What is most important is that the one-way communication of past works is abolished. The era of managers and masters of thought is finished. We can no longer tolerate limitations due to favoritism or territorial taboos.

Something is about to happen in Africa and in the rest of the Third World. Exoticism and folklore are being toppled. No one can foresee what this "ex-pre-logical" thought will be able to offer to us all. But the day when the true spokespersons of these collectivities really make their voices heard, it will be a dynamite explosion in the corrupt secret societies of the old humanism.

We have had to exercise strict patience and rigorous self-control in order to produce this journal, which above all views itself as the vehicle of a new poetic and literary generation.

Souffles is not here to swell the ranks of ephemeral journals. It responds to a need that we can no longer ignore. If the journal finds its public, as we are hoping it will, as long as resources are available, it will become a flashpoint for debates on issues in our culture. All the texts that come to us will be examined with objectivity and, if they are accepted by our editorial board, published.

Souffles is not sponsored by any niche nor any minaret and does not recognize any frontiers. Our Maghrebi, African, European, and other writer friends are fraternally invited to participate in our modest enterprise. Their texts will be welcome.

It is still necessary to juggle with words tarnished by dint of being dictated. The act of writing cannot depend on any tabulations of income, nor concede to fashion, nor to the tear-jerking needs of wealthy demagogues hungering for power.

Poetry is all that is left to man to reclaim his dignity, to avoid sinking into the multitude, so that his outcry forever carries the imprint and attestation of his inspiration [*souffle*].

DOLDRUMS

Abdellatif Laâbi
Translated from the French by Andrew Zawacki

Surrender
small pledge of allegiance
and the earth goes pale

safe but not sane

the splinter plunders
this tadpole accuses
and for starters who will I stick up my toe or thumb to

I accuse yet again
this time surrender
small pledge of allegiance
it's too much
vast vast the fire vast
and the vast bombs
and this cursed Archimedes at the window
turns turns a vast seism
blows up the baobab's greening
turns turns the scorpion dance
and the arachnid's suicide
black like my face
or this crow watching over me
turns turns the axis turns
double
the crowd of sharded abysses
double facet
you die
but your place is an electric chair
there will be no letting up

Into the garbage poem
Into the garbage rhythm
Into the garbage silence

the word thunders

its first victim is me
nevertheless I extract it
and chuck it
at you

I accuse yet again
and myself to start with
of being your social animal
your strapped for cash cow
this dry moolah
amid the soil
the tree
where I lay myself down
and the centuries' crank handle turns turns
the weapons' brew turns
MINED
our globe is mined
terrestrial life is mined
our human voices are polluted
when the equations turn turn
the cube roots of missiles
Stop you airlift of ruins
bastard Shem
blow your nose
you also look pekid
and my face is afire
like dry cilantro
my face that no longer resembles me
my face
falls
cluster of ants and spit
my face cries out

*

My body lifts up
a poem wrings me
I jack it off
like a rancid fetus
I detach it

place it under your gills
your haywire lenses
it's no vaccine I serve you
hocus pocus or lighthearted truths

Lord give us our share of the daily absurd
and shield us from our overwhelming freedom

I emasculate you
in your husbandly pride
your strident culture
your floor level babble
you make my text ugly
you snuff me out
you soften me up
you dissect me in mini ceremonies
how-are-you-doing and health-is-what-matters
you fling your blandness
your single-storey manners at me
your flatlined familiarity
you dumb me down to a blueprint my brothers
but barely sully my torso
I've roots
a route of subterranean signs
a breath of unknown elemental stuff

Get out my body
scar furred hyenas
empty my bilgewater blood from your biles
begone
for good saltpeter and trash
I've slammed my life shut
on alms
to your oblivion
I'm going
I leave you my carapace
my appetite and my everyday talk
I exile myself among you
I hold my tongue

I pull my anger in
my brotherhood that takes you aback
my words worn down by othering you
freeze beneath your gaze
poems stalk me
foment
      the charges
              my putting to death

                    *

It's freezing
someplace inside my brain
a glass wall shatters in my temples
a people gnashes its teeth
let's say children die
a woman aborts
a man sells his body
a cry stops me cold
blasphemy hurled
at the entrails of heaven
the cemetery repopulates
with hands
It snows on the graves
somewhere there
in my brain

                    *

strong wind
people united
you explore my history
you exclude yourself from my rigid perception
walks
hanged or guillotined
wanks
squatting
      your stride
but shuttle body
sweats
      walks
           wears out

walks
        hush the horizon
the pillory
            undo the language
                        form the word
return to me
sarcophagus down in the dungeon
take my hand
suck in your tummy
heave your heresies
                drool
I don't like your blue Tuareg moon
stomp on the recipe
wind body mellowed
citadel's crenels
horde of convicts
hide your gripes
disguise your hunger
your fag ends of hope
your round the bend headwind from hand to mouth
coarse and mine own
                morsel
mundane
you come from out the stunted dawn
from the clanking of centuries
and give your name up
Pubescent
tallying of ages
you affect nothing but my freedom
you seize only my freedom
you don't know me
but stay
don't pity me
don't plead me not guilty
don't lie to the crowd
to clear me

                        *

You
you've got but a day
haze from the levees
edges of towns
you should speak
ducking out after would be easy
they'll stone you
so say what a dagger can conjure
between the eye and the wound
speak of this blood
boils off in your breath
tell them
if your reach exceeds your grasp
or else what
dream of paradise
of butterfly houris
or flitting angels all ambrosial
you stand guard
your torch is the word
exploding in your arteries
don't titter
I'm serious
a serious swollen with gas
I bloat myself
to erupt at the crossroads
                    at the pits
                        at water's source

Once polluted
                my life sterilized of the world

I accuse yet again
surrender
small pledge of allegiance

but this humanity I couldn't care less
its copulations
its thin-skinned skin
its coitus between two cuts of meat

Peoples with no memory
                              none
peoples of slag and hail
mine are muscular
dark skinned
with a callused hide
and turns turns the noria
to a null tempo
turn the seasons at random turn
the colossal gusts of locusts turn
rags
typhus
trachoma
the buildings hold back
when death turns turns
in the alleys
mucky
like my face
dispossessed of this face
a mole has muddied by night
my face
multiplied in all the faces
that shout
voice of the gut
of sex
and of a sickly dignity
unwritten
that pussyfoots
through a bombing
by catapults

READ *THE LITTLE MOROCCAN*

Abdellatif Laâbi

Translated from the French by Lucy R. McNair

The creation of a literary journal in a country like ours should respond to a necessity. It should not be a stopgap, as some would have it, but rather bear witness to a "reality in action," open up perspectives that will ultimately define a path and impose a new vision. This amounts to saying that a journal is above all the materialization of a certain number of choices and considered options. If we do not clarify our demands from the outset, any effort risks becoming a collection of possibly illegitimate interests or mere filler.

But demand is a corollary to creation and creation is the culmination of awareness, an acute perception of national and universal problems.

Souffles arose from diverse motivations. Firstly, we needed to oppose an inflationary literary and cultural trend that has taken root in the country since independence, a trend that not only ridicules its representatives, who were overcome by events, but even more so our own country in the eyes of the world, for this official pseudo-literature happens to be relatively well read and even translated. Secondly, we did not want to give too much importance, in the interim, to a group nostalgic for a Casablanca-based cultural hegemony that attracts young Moroccan poets in flocks to its cosmopolitan gatherings and readings and operates under the pretense of guiding them and teaching them to write poetry. This kind of malodorous outgrowth of the old regime will wither away once these young poets have gained greater awareness of themselves and of the problems facing their country. We must nevertheless condemn the paternalistic agitations of these poetry-craving old men.

Faced with the impatience of the press and national opinion, we felt the need to take a stand. We have thus responded by making our presence known in our manifesto-issue, which is devoted to five poets (who also write novels, short stories, and drama) and is intended, above all, to put the reader in direct contact with their works, not their ideas or beliefs.

We felt impelled to attest to the productivity and creative vitality that current circumstances had condemned to vegetate in forgotten corners.

Souffles was thus a vital move forward, the only combat tool we could find to make our voices heard. For the record, I want to remind the reader that poet friends of ours such as Nissabouri and Khaïr-Eddine, lacking better outlets, first published their poems in the Casablanca *Revue de l'Automobile*, and that the author of this article published prose, poetry, and nonfiction in anachronistic foreign reviews.

Finally, *Souffles* was conceived in the beginning as a tool or organ permitting all those who had something to say in the field of literature and culture to express themselves in total liberty. The sole form of censorship we will allow being the quality of the writing, its degree of relevance, and its contribution to our national literature, whose first milestones we are seeking to establish. We stressed in our first Prologue that the *Souffles* Group does not constitute a school or an autocratic clique and that the writing published in this first issue had the simple goal of formulating a tone and defining a few basic principles and perspectives.

The letters and essays we received and the contacts we established in response confirmed that our intentions were not misjudged. The editorial board has already attracted new friends in the Maghreb, Africa, and abroad. But those were the first, collective goals that motivated the creation of this journal. Now each writer is responsible for his writing and pursues his creative adventure within his own context and according to his own means. *Souffles* should not impede that individual destiny, but rather witness it and be of help in a spirit of fraternity, of warm friendship, and with the awareness of shared goals.

We leave to those who are not interested in our undertaking—either because they suffer from academic or idiosyncratic biases and refuse to look reality in the face, or because they are dried up or bloated with illusions—we leave to such people the indescribable columns of *The Little Moroccan*. A cup of coffee, a crossword puzzle, the sports page, and the daily horoscope never hurt anyone. For the "intellectuals" there are always family planning issues, Karsenty cabarets, and the film club.

To all regular and involuntary readers of *The Little Moroccan*, we hope you aren't hungry for much.

The only way to cut through this darkness and deal with our true problems, to find a way out of our current doldrums, is to deploy all our energy. Each of us is responsible and each gesture, each word, each piece of writing we present will hold serious weight. Petty speech, charlatanism, and concessions should not stop us. No one has the right to shirk their role.

Intellectual avarice that revels in its own contradictions ends up becoming a kind of sterility. The trick is to stay honest and not hide one's impotence or tepidness behind pretentious palaver. Decolonization and national culture will remain empty slogans as long as we fail to take possession of ourselves, as long as in-depth analysis of our current problems remains a mere spinning on the surface of things, a vague inclination in so-called serious discussions. Every struggle is based on conscientious stocktaking motivated by hard-won experience and apprenticeship in local and distant realities.

Western science has held the monopoly on all research until now. Our history, our sociology, our culture, and our art have been studied and interpreted in the function of an externally motivated curiosity and rigor that fundamentally do not correspond to our perspective, our needs, or even our strict realities. While we can more or less objectively profit from the work that has been done, our role is to put everything into question, to reorient these analyses in light of new data and according to our own perspective. As for the scandalmongers, they agitate for immobility and do nothing but perpetuate the constraints we now urgently need to loosen. To do so, we need great lucidity and great courage. Mohamed Sahli's essay, *Décoloniser l'histoire* (Decolonizing history), is significant in this regard and allows us to hope for a new departure.

Our journey has only just begun. We have not yet come up against the cyclical butchery of values, against the impasses that lead certain civilizations towards apathy or absolute skepticism. We are at the stage of reconsolidation, of rediscovery. We are on the threshold of speech that has not lost its meaning for us.

In this regard, the violence of the *Souffles* Group is no longhaired marijuana dealer's shoulder shrug. Stop berating us with beatniks and other war-and-peace mongers. We are too anchored, too pure for that. We have not yet killed either the individual or the collective in these parts. If elsewhere man has done away with himself through his own speech and his own creations, we want to show that the only reason he has bogged himself down is because he wanted to play the game, because the socioeconomic machine he created has outpaced him, domesticating him while he tried to domesticate and direct it. We do not know whether other men are capable of refusing this conditioning and by which path they may rediscover true authenticity.

In this sense we owe it to ourselves to deflate such forms of hegemony and passive conquest, which are replacing traditional methods of assimilation and depersonalization before our very eyes. Hegemonies that present themselves as sincere dialogues. But we have not reached the stage of any dialogue. We have barely reached the stage of clearing house. Dialogue is only possible once we have satisfied certain demands. It will not be accepted in the name of tolerance alone.

Our role is to show that we were not born yesterday. It will no longer be possible to ignore these new vitalities. Soon they will ask to see the balance sheets.

FIGURE 2. Untitled painting by Mohamed Bennani. *Souffles* 2 (Rabat, 1966), p. 14. Reprinted with permission.

BLOODS (EXCERPT)

Mohammed Khaïr-Eddine

Translated from the French by Teresa Villa-Ignacio

i eschew myself and it's not inadvertently that blood extradites me i go to the clashes in the cities that have no real name and everywhere i trudge along atom-sized clouds on all the telephone lines dishonorably intentioned stars and downpours are placed i only address these words to you because we remain unseparated you say we are inseparable we are separable i retort on oath at the very hour that i was assassinated i constructed you according to my sense of propriety according to the agility of traps without omitting anything of the magic of voodoo dethroned by the european with teeth so sharpened with hands so long with the science of a smiling reptilian the father of fathers of the old fish fabricated by the old sacred tarantula before the father of fathers and the mother of fathers i have not made you to measure up to God have not raised you to the height of the globe i gave you my voice we are even you say and i object i claim to be from a civilization of mongooses and anarchic vipers i do not know Asia hearsay and fat books sentences rhymes coups d'état stirrings of the heart blood like a rosary dedicated to political insurgencies of my blood cutting off breath and rations from whoever wants to be drenched in it of course i'm disappearing blood-pyre blood-oil blood-bath blood believe me i see clearly the bad conduct of bloods and leukemic eyes i don't pass by without noticing the barrages of blood the blood and the black sardine of blood i was present at bleedings operated on the nape of the neck and the pubis it was on a throne of schist and on the adjoining void of delirium the old maid embittered by the work in the fields and by all the wells she had dug sinking down until only her head appeared above the rock and laughing half asleep while above her and at her level the *doctoresse* sketched the deluge smoke snow war death was present i said to myself does she have a heart of blood a body capable of enchanting me it was not true death had long gray hair rather death was all black very sharp hair death not described death of invisible blood crouching in the store-room of our sorrows of our devastations i held her against my soul i gave her my heart she made a bird of it a bird who accompanies her everywhere she assassinates and undresses where she eats and gets

drunk death has favorable intentions death justifies without punish-
ing and we made sacred love without my knowing why i made her
an excellent cake with my sperm and my floury blood she will not
forget my caresses my stay-don't-leave-i-am-your-spouse-you-are-
my-Great-Chosen-One not soon in any case she will return perhaps
one night and it is not from my viscera that she will spring she will
applaud will hail me oh Master like Caesar oh Owl like the filibuster
or the Tornado come so that i may poison you come so i may dress
you in a white and delirious toga ah forgetting no longer believing
loving dying sparingly milestones pedestrians automobile drivers cy-
clists kings but you logical writers customs raids the evening opens
cafés light bulbs eat sun man rots his liver they patch up my blood it
hurts where i glow red they see me running under the draperies and
the tables in a flow of magma i infect the mosaic i lacerate the couches
i destroy the flowers block the toilets i don't respect money that falls
from the holey pockets of these poor fellows who are afraid of you my
iguana blood and me always calling into question my blood which i
treat as a garbage dump as rats pestilent with an epidemic of malodorous moons of negation as all that makes one happy and avid to
hold on to during the rain when coal costs as much as blood my vom-
ited blood my blood that does not go to the lobsters of two ingots'
worth of incense up my nose and the Italian hairstyle my blood that
wobbles chips ages my scoundrel blood my ordinary blood my tergal
winter blood in which i learn to hide myself to better count the black
ice and hail my sidewalk blood my bastard blood docile and devi-
ous not a salon dog not for the ladies with the copper red smiles the
real smile of the helianthus it's you proper blood that always skids
toward the roots of disorder my leper blood my blood like Saint-Just
on the scaffold my blood you tremble my blood you consecrate a real
evildoer my blood you gun down my blood you have the eye of a
terrorist my blood you fled from the protuberance on the bejeweled
hand of a master my blood in which clang chains and real palace bells
my blood which spends a bad afternoon and will spend a bad night
and a monday of wrinkles my blood you do not win the lottery my
blood you drag your juicy spurting sauce from a base of sap of stars
whose throats were cut by flint and the carob tree on the last scrolls
of vertigo and from a renunciation deferred my blood you listen to

the abyss and the veterans who know well how to pronounce the words factory tin and money order my blood you have not understood that you must perform your ablutions like a good muslim my blood i must croak one day i slam the doors of my blood i lose in its doldrums the Ruby of rubies the Blood of bloods and the worst of the worst my blood editor my blood i exile myself with tons of turtle doves and ivory.

POEMS

Abdelkebir Khatibi

Translated from the French by Lucy R. McNair

The Street

expands in my blood
extends its roots
its tombs, its memory
to the body's limits.

The street is invincible,
irreducible
all revolt is an avalanche of rocks
doors blown off in the whirling night
avalanche of dust winged with lines
piercing geometries

Standing, in the violent street
man is the first to speak

Becoming

The trees cast their frail shadows
interlocked
They persist like a childhood worry

The twilight dance of a dead leaf
builds a geometry
of time
my act becomes an axe in the night

Riot

You must cross the street
Body suspended
That colorful point
Between my throbbing gaze
And a city open to death.

You must cross the street
Body suspended
Before a wall knifed with cries.
In the street my back is dying
Straight as a line.

The sidewalk sporadically rushes up
To cross the horizon of my eyes
Then cracks almost ear-splitting
Like a cat's last wail.

THE WORLD FESTIVAL OF NEGRO ARTS, OR
THE NOSTALGICS OF NEGRITUDE

Abdallah Stouky

Translated from the French by Laura Reeck

Making use of all modern methods of propaganda—as is to be expected—a great Senegalese leader epitomizing the Greco-Roman Negro, along with a group of tired ethnologists and unverified champions of decolonization and emancipation, has long called for a mobilization of Negro efforts the world around. This mobilization was meant to lead to the first World Festival of Negro Arts, a gigantic and colossal event, the first of its kind, whose goal was to "show the fundamental unity of the Negro spirit."

Before this festival was inaugurated in the whitewashed city of Dakar on April 1, 1966, the convincing scientific argument was made that the festival aimed to illustrate "the immense contribution Negro art has made to universal civilization" and to transform Africa, a consumer of culture, into a producer and exporter of culture.

So the representatives of all the world's Negro peoples are supposed to meet in Dakar, where the most well-known storefront sign reads "À Saint-Germain-des-Prés" and on certain street corners elegant white mannequins invite well-behaved Negroes, who had never been ashamed of their nudity until the Christian missionaries arrived, to use "Eminence" underwear or "Scandal" bras.

But is this really the general assembly of Negritude? No, because despite the assertions of the poet-president Léopold Senghor, neither Guiana, nor Cuba, nor Paul Robeson, nor Miriam Makeba, nor many other progressives are participating in the festival. And they have no shame in saying loud and clear that the festival is being held under the patronage of General de Gaulle and the president of another country currently enacting one of the most atrocious genocides in history while continuing to deny American Negroes the most basic rights.

When you get off the plane at the magnificent Dakar-Yoff International Airport, you're right in the thick of things. Even before you have completed passport formalities, you're privy to a quaint show of Senegalese folklore. All the while you slowly inhale a light sea breeze, coming perhaps from Gorée Island, where every evening Jean Mazel presents a magical sound and light show whose pretention and didactic nature brings a quizzical smile to your face.

Whether you want to or not, the Senegalese authorities, who have, by the way, given very strict orders about hospitality to the Senegalese population, insidiously suggest that you be a good little tourist and leave your critical senses on the other side of the border. You will only be taken seriously if you appreciate the exoticism of this part of Africa located two hours by plane from Paris.

After having spent a night at a terribly expensive hotel in Dakar—U.N. statistics indicate that the cost of living in Dakar is the highest in the world—you set off in the morning, happy to discover a country you do not know. And its people—Africans like you. The only thing separating you from them is a vernacular language that is foreign to you. As a result you find that you can only talk with the French-speaking Senegalese. You'll be denied direct access to modest folk, who have an intense inner life, who work, produce, and continue to be exploited, and who think about serious issues.

Because you can't communicate with them, for advice you refer back to the brochures that have so kindly been left at your bedside.

It's morning, and there's nothing to do but visit the museums.

Awaiting you are thousands of pieces of artwork tragically exiled to these tombs called "museums" and guarded protectively by soldiers armed to the hilt. It's already heretical enough to put works of Western art, expressions full of life and creative energy, in the "Louvre" or the "British Museum." As regards African art, such museums are thoroughly nonsensical because these objects are an integral part of everyday life, essentially of a functional or religious nature. It's not the Negro who sees an aesthetic value in them, but the European ethnologist or colonial administrator of refined taste. This is not to say the Negro is not familiar with beauty, because in the end the artisan, the Negro-African artist, could not conceive of anything without beauty. The African object has several functions, among them utility and beauty. And when this artisan creates a mask or a statuette, he not only represents a more or less figurative face or body, he also puts all his faith into it and believes he is endowing it with a soul, a spirit bad or good. So a Bantu statuette with two faces signifies something very different than a Cubist painting by Picasso in which only a formal aesthetic concern exists.

Instead of representing this common and functional aspect of Negro art, the exhibits in Dakar and even "Living Artisanry in the Village of Soumbedioune," give the impression of being at an exhibit of dusty sarcophagi, especially since no real care has been put into the objects' presentation. There is practically no difference between the exhibit from Nigeria, the guest of honor at the festival, the "Black Greece of Africa," and Dakar's funeral parlors.

Only the Musée Dynamique attempts to give meaning to the objects' presentation. And in case you don't understand the exhibit, they take pains to explain the museum's purpose in a few handouts they give you. In them, President Senghor, father of Negritude, is not afraid to cite a Greek tragic author, thereby showing the great depth of his literary knowledge. But let's hear what he has to say: "*Some claim that if works of art could speak, they might say these words that the tragic Greek author confers to Helen*: 'So he [the son of King Priam] thinks that he has me—an empty thought!—he doesn't. . . . And yet I was not the cause of the Trojan War, a prize for Greek spears, but my name was.' *Some claim that Negro works of art have taught Europe or America nothing, or at most a few technical points. I don't share that opinion. To speak in the same terms as André Malraux, Negro art has entered into the living museum of the soul.*"[3]

I have no intention here of denying Negro art's contribution to Western civilization, a unanimously accepted fact. However it would be a monumental error or mystification to consider Negro art of precisely the type shown in the Dakar museums as anything other than a simple point of reference, as irrefutable proof of Negro creativity and personality. To see it as more than this—to return to the beginning of time, dwell there, and extrapolate from it—just reproduces folkloric Negro art, the junk produced for tourists. Indeed Dakar is overrun with such "exotic" products. For, as Frantz Fanon admirably put it, "Exoticism is one of the forms of this simplification. It allows no cultural confrontation. There is on the one hand a culture in which qualities of dynamism, of growth, of depth can be recognized. As against this, we find characteristics, curiosities, things, never a structure."[4]

Africa needs art. Not because the Negro is pure emotion and does not understand discursive reasoning, as some people mired in Negritude continue to reiterate, but because, as the poet Aimé Césaire has shown, "*Africa has definitively entered into the orbit and forward move-*

ment of Western civilization, whose impact has been enormous all around the world. That's why Africa needs African art—in order to resist accul-turation and avoid depersonalization."[5] So the African intellectual or art-ist must not fall prey to the pointless aestheticism of André Malraux, writer and French minister of culture, and lament the fact the Negro-African artist can no longer reproduce the magnificent masks of the past. The French minister received the pertinent response that no one ever thought to ask European artists to recreate the equally beautiful medieval cathedrals.

Once you have visited the museums, you wonder about the shows. And you imagine that in these concert halls of European design where African shows are to be staged, it will be obvious if Negro-Western cul-tural symbiosis has been successful or not.

Obviously, a show is designed above all else to entertain. To this end a certain number of attributes are necessary, including beauty and the talent of the performers. Unfortunately, with few exceptions, Afri-can national troupes offer only a poorly plagiarized version of Western theater with no particular attempt to do anything original. If you let yourself get carried away by the soft purr of classical French declama-tions in the vein of Mounet-Sully, you might think yourself in one of the numerous charity events, where you can find a bit of affectation, a bit of grandiloquence, and a lot of awkwardness.

Thus several plays, "Lat Dior's Last Days" (Senegal), "Guikafi's Passing" (Gabon), and "Hannibal" (Ethiopia), offer the terrible spec-tacle of realist sets in the style of Antoine, uninteresting scripts, lack of preparation, *trompe l'oeil* backgrounds . . .

The largely white audience leaves the theater quickly, and with every performance, more audience members are to be found in the presidential and honorific boxes than in the general seating area.

And since we're talking about the audience, we should not forget that the audience's reactions—if it's a sensible audience—help a theater find its way. This has certainly not been the case during the festival in Dakar. In the very attractive Daniel-Sorano theater, it isn't unusual to see Africans and Europeans in tuxedos whistling at the bosom of a beautiful young girl as if at a striptease show at Pigalle.

In the same domain of theater, the African artist must separate him-self from anything resembling exoticism, go beyond old themes, be authentic, and find inspiration as much in the contemporary, living reality as in ancestral rites. On the technical level he must try to innovate on stage and in the play's very structure.

Only one play is worthy of mention as a success: *La tragédie du roi Christophe* [*The Tragedy of King Christophe*] by Aimé Césaire, which is presented at the French gala evening by the troupe "Le Toucan." In conjuring up the problems that Africans must unequivocally and unconditionally face today, this play is bound to shake up the gala guests, Senegalese and *pieds-noirs* in their most sophisticated attire, who come to hear the illustrious French deputy Monsieur Aimé Césaire speak. So great is their disappointment to hear the unexpected language of hard truth, realism, and demystification.

And then there's folklore, in which many vague populists or mystifiers have wanted to circumscribe national culture, claiming that therein lies the truth of the people. Here too it is disappointing to note that were it not for the natural beauty of the dances and costumes, one would have been thoroughly disgusted by the poor scenic transposition of what naturally took shape on public squares and in the fields. It is all the more difficult to overcome this deficit because, instead of mingling with the public, the performers confront it in accordance with the principles of Italianate theater, preventing the free flow of spontaneity and instead relying upon rigid staging and even, at times, choreography.

All of these problems are only surmountable if the director does not get hung up on false problems he has culled from the mouths or the writings of so-called ethnologists, zealous interpreters of ancestral or biblical myths existing only in their minds.

To present folklore successfully to an audience that is neither national nor populist, we must avoid mixed messages and pretention, we must successfully communicate some pure and simple emotion to the audience.

Having endured three or four failed theatrical and folkloric evenings, you fall back on the eternal and very useful program in the hopes of finding something good. And you're delighted to learn that you can see African films or films about Africa (among them, Yves Ciampi's incomparable *Liberté I*). You get a taxi and head to the Palace movie theater. Once there, you are kindly told that the films you want to see—often short films—are only shown once a week. What do you do now? Try your luck with Monsieur Gabin in *The Upper Hand* or Belmondo in *Crime on a Summer Morning* in the theaters where smoking is at least permitted? No, you didn't come to Dakar during the World Festival of Negro Arts to see such silliness.

With nothing better to do, you walk around the city with its beautiful, clean, well-planned avenues leading to the gigantic shantytowns where little Negro children with distended stomachs play.

But you have been warned you might see such things in Dakar. Moreover, a Senegalese man points out that these native quarters are very clean because they are built on sand, which absorbs all filth and never turns into the awful mud common to Casablanca's shantytowns.

If you try to inquire about the poverty of the Senegalese people, you're told: "You know, the Lebanese own almost all the small businesses, so the natives are left with shining shoes or smuggling."

As you look for your street, you stop a passerby. He very amiably points you in the right direction and even shows you the way. Over the course of your conversation, he tells you he is a civil servant, a Christian, that he likes the president a lot—in fact, his son is named Léopold Senghor—that Senegal is a secular democratic country . . . And if you ask him why the African Independence Party has been banned, the civil servant responds with a hint of consternation, "But they aren't even communists. Just opportunists. If the president—yes, him again—cites Teilhard de Chardin, he doesn't exclude Marx and Engels, or even Lenin. Yes, it's true."

Tired out by this nighttime jaunt, you return to the hotel, a little exasperated by the fact that a festival of Negritude is taking place in the capital of a country whose current president thought it best to support French ideas about Algeria. But then again perhaps things have changed. Or maybe not. The following day, Foccart, de Gaulle's top spy, is welcomed with all the pomp and ceremony of a head of state, and you learn that students are on strike, much to the disapproval of all civil servants.

The following question arises naturally: "In 1966, what can Negritude, the ideological underpinning of this festival, possibly mean?"

Does the Negro still exist? Are we still at a point where we have to racialize thought?

Senghor defines Negritude as "*the sum of the cultural values of the*

*world, as expressed in the life, institutions, and creative works of Black people
. . . a cornerstone in the edification of the civilization of the universal, which
will be the shared work of all the civilizations of the world—or will not be."*[6]

This definition is generous and imbued with naive humanism, but
it lacks objectivity. Negritude has never been more than a violent racial
reaction by the Negro-African world and the Negro diaspora against
the monstrous and inhumane project undertaken by the exploitative
white European capitals to strip away their culture and assimilate
them. Appropriating the monikers *dirty negroes* or *niggers*, for Africans,
or reclaiming their slave ancestors deported from Africa in the dirty
lower deck of slave ships, for Americans and Antilleans, such has been
the form of struggle undertaken by Blacks around the world against
depersonalization.

It's also revealing that the colonized African world has only attempted to assert itself culturally against the imperialist West and not
against all civilizations (Chinese or other).

But apart from this, what purpose can Negritude serve at a time
characterized first and foremost by decolonization and the achievement of national sovereignty for most African countries. Nothing, or
close to nothing. The problems of Blacks in Mozambique are radically
different from those of Blacks in Los Angeles, who themselves do not
have problems in common with the Senegalese and Kenyans, and all
this is true because the Negro no longer exists. The Negro has disappeared and the African has come into existence. The African, a product of unique socio-historical circumstances, must face up to the same
sorts of economic and cultural problems as the Cubans and Koreans.
We should not forget that *"questions of race are but a superstructure, a
mantle, an obscure ideological emanation concealing an economic reality."*[7]

To fail to recognize that promoting Negritude is nothing more
than looking at pieces of art in a museum and comparing sarcophagi
amounts to living outside of one's times and betraying the future of
Africa. It's with real economic and social emancipation—the condition
for a true revolution—that the two cultures, national culture and the
culture of the former occupier, can come together and truly enrich one
another. To parody the president-poet, universality is nothing more
than the reciprocal relativism of different cultures; only then will we
avoid all forms of hegemony.

AN INTRODUCTION TO POPULAR MOROCCAN POETRY

Ahmed Bouanani

Translated from the French by Robyn Creswell

> *He who is ignorant of poetry does not know the path of intelligence as it progresses to wisdom through the stages of science and art.*
>
> Song from the Sous[8]

Morocco's oral literary tradition is extraordinarily lively and unbroken. Handed down since time immemorial, it has been enriched by generation after generation and by its contacts with a great many civilizations. Yet so far this tradition has been the object of a very limited number of anthologies and scholarly studies, and those have, for the most part, focused on linguistics. The narratives in such collections, whose translations often leave much to be desired, fail to render the nuances, the storytellers' richness of idiom and image as well as the subtlety of allusion and the characteristically Moroccan flavor of these tales and popular legends.

Translations of popular songs (fragments of which are occasionally available in certain collections) are even worse than the translations of stories and legends, giving only a very vague, not to say false, idea of the true nature of popular poetry in Maghrebi dialects.

Such studies may be of interest for researchers, sociologists, folklorists, ethnographers, or linguists seeking the source of a particular ritual or word, but they cannot be used to analyze traditional oral literature. To judge the value of a poem or story properly, one has to consult the original text. This is no easy task. It would require an enormous effort to collect and categorize a decent sample of the stories and legends—as performed by professionals, who alone retain the secrets of traditional narration with its richness of images and idioms—as well as the popular songs, sayings, and proverbs that one may still find in different regions of the country. Once this encyclopedic task was complete, one can analyze the texts in the original dialects and thus identify characteristics of the popular genius that produced them.

Certain authorities have collected stories that were poorly told, incomplete, or bastardized and hastily concluded that Berbers have no imagination, or that their tales are simple and utterly lacking in lyricism.[9] It would be a waste of time to demonstrate the falsity of such arguments. A story is nothing but the way it is told. Because it is oral, the story is not a prisoner of any particular language; it is only the themes developed therein that do not change. Each storyteller has his own style, his own way of making the story come alive during a performance [*halqa*]. He employs his art to draw in and captivate the audience. To do this, improvisation is essential. The storyteller will sometimes change the name of one or more characters, suppress certain scenes and then reinvent them elsewhere according to the circumstances of the telling. To tell a story is not simply to relate it in the manner of previous tellers, but above all to enrich it with new elements. The storyteller is also a poet. No study of traditional oral literature can afford to ignore the storyteller's creative role.

One fact is certain: tradition is lost when it is not maintained, and the oral literary tradition, more than any other, is now disintegrating, not to say disappearing. Today, it is unusual to find professional storytellers who still know the secrets of traditional narration, or singers who still know the poems of the legendary Sidi Hammou, to whom most of the great songs of the Sous are attributed. Hardly anyone knows the names of our popular poets and certainly not their works. If it had not been for René Euloge, who gathered so many Tassaout songs, who would have heard of the poetess Mririda N'Aït Attik? Classical historians and biographers dismiss anything not composed in literary Arabic, casting into oblivion these "vulgar and illiterate poets," who nevertheless have expressed the deepest sentiments of our people.

Itinerant Singers

In the old days, itinerant singers such as the acrobats of Ouled Hmad or Moussa and his storytellers would crisscross the whole country. They were especially numerous in the Middle Atlas range and even more so in the Sous. Their orchestras were composed of four players: the *amghar* or *imdiazen*, chief of the troupe; the *bou ghanim* or flute player, dressed in a colorful ensemble; and two tambourinists in accompaniment. In the Sous itinerant singers occasionally traveled alone or with a child, but more often it was larger troupes that circulated among the towns and villages, improvising poetic songs in their own fashion or chanting the most famous poems of their chief.

These itinerant singers earned an important place in the struggle against colonial forces at the beginning of the century as well as under the protectorate. "Today," writes Basset, "it is these troupes, these orchestras in barbaric costume, always on the move from village to village, who spread the most extraordinary sounds among the rebellious regions and agitate for struggle against the French. They are admired and listened to. They are formidable agents of propaganda."[10]

Many songs tell of the French invasion, the struggles of the tribes, the extortions carried out by local chieftains and government inspectors. They are anonymous songs that each singer makes his own, using forthright and virile language:

> More houses destroyed than houses standing.
> More dirt than soap.
> More hunger than wheat
> and more shoes with holes than good shoes.

A poet of Bni Mtir puts it this way:

> I speak for those seated around me.
> If I said what I have to say to the spring, she would dry up with rage.
> If I said it to the tree, he would lose all his leaves.
> If I said it to the rock, he would shake from side to side.
> If I said it to the 75 shell, he would explode.
> If I told my story to the stones, I would make them weep.
> All of you, you who have lived what my words report,
> Listen to me!
> You have eaten the meat of bitter fruit and your children's lips are
> blistered!

These singers today are quiet. They do not circulate in the towns or the villages. Even in the Jama'a al-Fna square in Marrakech there are really only charlatans, monkey keepers, snake charmers, and storytellers [rawis] who do not know how to sing. In the towns one sometimes meets a solitary singer whom no one listens to anymore. On rare occasions—the twenty-seventh day of Ramadan, for example, or

Ashura—the itinerant singers do come out. But these troubadours are becoming scarcer and scarcer. Modern life pushes them back into the interior of the country, into small towns and marketplaces.

The Poets

The role of the poet in ancient Moroccan society was considerable. In the first place, he was the chronicler, "the historian" of his tribe. He did not sing merely of his own love affairs and travails but also and above all of the events lived by his tribe or which he experienced as a member of the tribe. During a joust between rival clans, he would be asked to take up the defense of his own. He was respected and venerated as a saint, and his word was heeded, for he was wise and knew the secret of speaking words that went straight to the heart.

> *The black cloud announces rain;*
> *The wasps' nest, summer;*
> *The cock's crow, dawn;*
> *Smoke over the fields, walnut wood burning;*
> *But death comes without warning.*

These are the words of Sidi Ba'addi from Togurt. All those who have been given the marvelous gift of poetry or of song are welcomed wherever they go. They are feared as much as they are loved.

But the poet is not merely a troubadour, a bard who performs at celebrations, glorifies his tribe, and sings the praises of great men or benefactors. He plays an especially important role when his tribe confronts an enemy. Ibn Khaldun points to this function among the Zenata when he writes: "The poet walks in front of the ranks and sings: his song stirs even the solid mountains and he sends in search of glorious death even those who had never dreamt of it."[11]

The poet's inspiration always has a divine source. Popular belief, nourished by mythology, superstitions, and stories of the marvelous, grants him supernatural powers.

In this country there are many sacred spots (caves, the tombs of saints) that would-be poets visit to receive consecration. For the Aït Baâmrane of Tiznit, this place is Ifri Nkad; for the Ihahanes, it is Lalla Takandout; near Marrakech are two celebrated *marabouts*, Sidi Jebbar and Moulay Brahim, recognized as patron saints by many poets and singers. The would-be poet performs a sacrifice then sleeps in the cave or sanctuary of the saint. If his sacrifice is accepted, on the third night he will see "the mother of the spirit" emerge from the cave where she lives and invite him in. There she will have him drink water from a fountain or milk from a sheep. He then meets an assembly of genies, who offer him couscous. The number of grains he eats will be the number of poems he composes.

The figure of the poet is surrounded by myths. Some believe he is in touch with natural forces, that he can appease them or set them against an enemy, that he speaks the language of animals, plants, and insects. For him the world contains no secrets. But popular belief also acknowledges that the poet must perfect his art through contact with the best practitioners. He apprentices himself to one of the great poets, accompanies him everywhere, and learns what he has to teach. After a long period of poetic initiation, the apprentice can speak for himself and give a new, personalized stamp to his songs.

The musical instruments used by poets vary by region. The most important are the following:

— the *rebab*, a type of single-stringed violin, inset with pearls and glass, whose horsehair string is set at an angle, while the bow is curved into a semicircle.

— the *bendir*, a hide stretched over a circle of wood (an instrument often used in dances).

— the *guenbri*, an instrument with three or four strings, used by most of the country's troubadours (*gnawa* singers use a different *guenbri* with a longer sound box and whose neck is hung with small charms that make an intricate sound).

In the Atlantic plains (Chaouia, Doukkala, Abda, Tadla), the most popular instrument is the *taréja*. Elsewhere it is the flute, the *darbuka*, the *tar*, the *tebel*, and the violin played with a bow.

In the Zagora region, for example, there is an instrument one finds nowhere else, the *deffe*, made of skin stretched over two sides of a wooden box, whose dimensions are much smaller than those of the *bendir*.

It is impossible within the confines of this essay to give a complete list of instruments—these deserve a separate study that would take full account of the variety and richness of Moroccan popular music.

Amarg

Amarg is the Berber word used to designate sung poetry in general (in the Middle Atlas it is *izlan*). *Amarg* also signifies love, grief, regret, and a performance in which such poems are sung.

Amarg comprises mostly short pieces, the inspirations of a moment, which last until the conditions that produced them have faded away. The pieces are improvised, whether during an important gathering of tribes or traditional ceremony (birth, baptism, circumcision, marriage, etc.), or during a literary joust—veritable tournaments of virtuosity between members of the same or rival tribes. In these jousts each poet attacks his opponent with verve and wit, and it would seem that female jousters are often the winners.

These sessions, combining song with dance, are known in Morocco as *ahwash* or *ahidous*. Whichever name is used, the thing itself is a collective and ritual dance accompanied by song, whose several configurations are determined by the *rayyis*.

The *rayyis* proposes a poetic theme or declaims a phrase, upon which the musical phrase embroiders itself. The rhythm grabs hold of it and imposes a form, a rigid structure that the dance makes plastic.

Each song is made of an isolated verse called a *tit*—a shock, an attack, a strike of the *bendir*—which the *rayyis* modulates and is subsequently taken up and repeated by all. Each verse is itself a poem. Here are a few examples:

A friend one does not see—seek him out, that's no shame.

Hope is more resolute than Syrian mules—one is never wearied by going to visit a friend.

Love that goes unsatisfied is unhappier than the season of rains.

I would gather a harvest of beauties that will bring home to me the workers on their mules.

You who believe you have friends and wealth—keep your wealth if you would keep your friends.

One open hand is worth more than many closed hands.

Friendship thrives in trust; she is lost through lies.

Lovers, may each one pursue what he loves.

People, shall we not sigh when we have grief?

Sometimes in the midst of such sessions the singer will make a declaration of love, or humorous allusions to the conduct of unfaithful women and arrogant men:

He whom God sets in a saddle should not ride too fast
And he should not goad into galloping those who straddle the earth, for fear
*   that God will unsaddle him and make him just as they are.*

These verses were addressed to a sheikh of the Ghoudjama tribe who held himself aloof from those who came to greet him because he was afraid they would dirty his *burnous*.

The celebration, begun just before nightfall, ends at dawn:

Master of ceremonies, grant us leave, by God,
The morning star is risen and it is dawn.

Alongside this form of poetry, characterized by the popular spirit of spontaneity and improvisation, there is another category of songs linked to an archaic mode of life that many tribes still uphold. These types of song are the following:

(a) Songs of the field, appealing for rain, celebrating the harvest or the change of seasons. These seasonal celebrations are most probably the remnants of the dances performed by the sons of Sumer and the shepherds of Homer. We should not forget that the dances of antiquity accompanied all religious and political festivals. They provided a living and concrete form for hallowed ideas.

(b) Songs whose rhythms serve as accompaniment to daily work: songs of wool spinners and carders; songs of henna sung by the women who decorate the young bride-to-be; songs of artisans, of millers, wet nurses, etc. The songs of millers no longer exist except among certain Atlas tribes, such as the Aït Bougmez, the Aït Atta of Tazzarine and the Mgouna (whose songs are called *herro*). Their survival is precarious. Grain mills have become increasingly rare, and these songs, unique in their genre, are at risk of becoming a vague memory if measures are not taken to preserve them in the near future.

(c) Songs of marriage, songs of mourning, etc.

(d) Nursery rhymes still sometimes recited by rural and urban children during their games or when it rains.

(e) War songs that rouse the cavalry and urge the troops toward battle, etc.

The songs of the Rif, which have the same inspiration as the songs of the Middle Atlas, are less primitive in form. The songs of Tangier, Fes, and Larache (like those of the Atlantic plains and eastern Morocco) are of an incontestable richness and depth. Primping songs, bathing songs, songs of the great pond, song of the geranium. There are humorous examples too, such as the song the women of Tangier sing about old men:

Beggars and vagabonds
seek out fancy meals;
pale and wrinkled old men
yearn for young girls;
The cat who has lost his teeth
likes a tender mouse
and the one with no teeth
likes the crackle of candy.

Songs composed by poet-bards typically treat an anecdote derived from legend. Its origin is invariably the Qur'an, the life of the prophet, or the lives of saints. The subjects of certain songs strangely recall classical myths, such as the poem by Sabi that tells the story of a young man whom God has permitted to visit his parents in hell so that he may save one of them. Neither husband nor wife wishes to leave without the other and so God frees both, and pardons their family. The poem shows clear affinities with that other Sous song, "Hamou Ounamir" (collected by Justinard), which recalls in turn the myth of Orpheus.

There are other poems—indeed, the majority of those from the Sous—attributed to a legendary poet, Sidi Hammou, one of the best-known minstrels. He was born in Aoulouz and died among the Iskrouzen, though his dates are not known (he is said to have lived in the sixteenth century). The patron saint of singers, Sidi Hammou did not leave any written works and there is probably no one today who can recite his songs. Some of his long poems have been collected in anthologies—though perhaps in a modified state, and it is not known for certain if they should in fact be attributed to Sidi Hammou. In any case it is extraordinary that no study (to our knowledge) has attempted to rescue from oblivion the colossal oeuvre of this great popular poet.

After a long absence Sidi Hammou decided to return to the woman who was the object of his first love. Traversing the Atlas range to reach Aoulouz, he sought to lighten the pains of the journey with fond memories, giving voice to his hopes and fears:

> *Ah, mother, have mercy on me—I've finally become a student! I walk with my chest out, notebooks in hand. But the song dissipates and my learning earns me no credit among ladies with rings at their ears.*
>
> *Should I return to Ouijjan, to Tikiouin, to Ighil Mallan, there where I saw those lovely gazelles at rest on their beds? A sight worth a hundred-weight of gold!*
>
> *When the caravan tires, it must rest. If the mill turns slowly, add some water to the stream. If friendship grows cold, let it be.*

The works of Sidi Hammou are infinitely full of proverbs. In this poem, in which he sings to his beloved Fadma Tagurramt, he often expresses himself through allusions and parables.

> *Does one bring water to the mountain's summit to let it flow to the plain?*
>
> *Weigh your words rather than your wealth.*
>
> *Do I ask the camel to be as noble as the horse?*
>
> *Will the rose-laurel give me sweetness?*
>
> *One does not look for a dry spot in the ocean.*
>
> *And I, shall I wait for words from a dead man?*

With his characteristic reticence, the poet leaves us at the end of the poem to suppose that all is well, that the course of his passion, formerly so troubled, will henceforth run to his full satisfaction. *Fadma, daughter of Muhammad, do you think among the drugs of Rome there is a remedy for lovers? Whatever it be, give it to me, and quickly.*[12]

One of Sidi Hammou's favorite themes in the poems attributed to him seems to be friendship.

> *May he that has no friend never say that he has lived*
> *For life is lived for friends.*

When the heart is broken what will heal it
If not the word of a friend, or his laugh?
Nothing crueler than a friend's tears.
The rose laurel is bitter — who has ever eaten it and found it sweet? —
I ate it for my friend and did not find it bitter.
May the rifle never be far from the bullet
Nor the painted eyes from antimony
Nor the heart far from its friends
Until they are welcomed beneath the ground.

The wisdom and beauty of these verses is incomparable, but as the song says:

The words of Sidi Hammou are so numerous they are like the sea — one never gets to the end of them.

In sum, popular Moroccan poetry is composed of:

— *Short songs* in praise of sentiments honored by the tribe: friendship, love, courage, etc. They are very like proverbs. The verses, often sung out in the course of a dance, are not linked together; only the theme unifies them.

— *Longer songs* composed by poet-bards. Most if not all of them are today transmitted anonymously. Who can tell us the names of these poets? Who will tell us the name of the one who said:

A spring gushed up from the tomb of Fadel.
A spring gushed up from the tomb of Attoush.
They met each other and circled the world.

And who will tell us the names of all those who cried out against the oppressor, who marched in front of the soldiers singing:

Men, all as one! For I see a river
And every place it flows
A road must cross it.

— Finally, *customary songs,* whose origins are lost in the night of time, the accompaniments of rites to which the peasant remains faithful.

THE MAGHREBI NOVEL AND NATIONAL CULTURE

Abdelkebir Khatibi

Translated from the French by Claudia Esposito

Since 1945 there has been a relatively important change in the form of the Maghrebi novel. This is not an isolated phenomenon: on a historical level it corresponds to the period of political maturity and armed struggle.

This is why it is necessary to explain this phenomenon and connect it to the sociopolitical conditions that preceded it. Furthermore, this literary genre allows for the definition of a number of problems related to national culture.

The novel is a Western aesthetic that has gone through its own evolution and, as it is incorporated into other cultures, prompts certain intellectual attitudes and adapts to new settings. What does this transformation mean for the countries of the Maghreb?

Born in the context of a feudal society and an aristocratic culture, the novel developed in parallel with the rise of the bourgeoisie at the beginning of the last century. In today's consumer societies, the novel has become a staple of everyday life.

Putting it this way is not simply a question of situating the novel historically, it is also a way of pointing out a theme that is characteristic of Western literature. As we know, Lucien Goldmann uncovered a strict homology between the economic structure of capitalism and the structure of novelistic imagination. This hypothesis needs to be considered in light of the evolution of formerly colonized societies.

In the Maghreb the growth of the novel from 1945 to 1962 corresponds to the period of struggle against the colonial system. It is clear, then, that the politicization of Maghrebi literature blurred questions that were specifically aesthetic. How can we interpret what remains of the cultural production of this period? What is the meaning and the scope of this phenomenon?

To be sure, in North Africa there existed—and still exists—a literature that is more specifically concerned with traditional forms of poetry (*al-qasida*), but as we know, Arab culture in the Maghreb was both petrified from the inside and assailed from the outside by colonization. Writers of French expression should be praised for integrating the novel as such into Maghrebi culture.

Some maintain that there is nothing Maghrebi about this literature, as it is written in a foreign language. Admittedly, all national literature must use a national language. Furthermore, this literature of French expression was the result of an exceptional situation. It was produced for metropolitan consumption and its audience was essentially French. It is therefore not surprising that Mohammed Dib was more widely read in some working-class French families than in Algeria. It is also not surprising that this literature almost died with the end of colonization.

Let us now consider the question of Maghrebi writers rather than that of Maghrebi literature. After the Second World War the first generation (Mouloud Feraoun, Mohammed Dib, Mouloud Mammeri, Ahmed Sefrioui, . . .) endeavored to describe local society and draw a rather accurate portrait of its various social strata; to say, in short, "here is who we are, here is how we live." This is why it was said that this literature was first and foremost a form of testimony of a certain era and a given situation. This was, to an extent, a beneficial description in that this literature already provided a sort of descriptive assessment of the colonial situation. But even in this capacity, it was overwhelmed by the events that were taking place in North Africa. For example, when Algerians took up arms to violently liberate themselves, novelists were dedicating themselves to the description of daily life in Kabyle villages and poets sang the angst of their torn personalities.

Condemned to follow a reality that is always changing, the writer is caught in a bind. If he wants to follow this reality in a consistent way he lapses into journalism. If he distances himself too much, he risks ending up with a disembodied literature. The Maghrebi writer is hounded by a "guilty conscience" at all times.

The situation became more complicated with the Algerian War. A number of writers (Malek Haddad, Assia Djebar, Mourad Bourboune, Henri Kréa, . . .) tried to write in service of the Revolution. In their own way, they exposed the Algerian problem to the world. Unfortunately this literature has largely run its course; it died with the war. Now that we are faced with great problems of nation-building, the question of literature must be asked plainly and frankly: in countries that are largely illiterate, that is to say where the written word has very little chance of transforming things, can we liberate a people using a language it does not understand?

Perhaps I am for the temporary death of literature and for the intellectual's commitment to the political struggle: he must make others aware of their fundamental problems, develop this awareness. As far as structures and ideology go, radical liberation is the very foundation of national culture.

But I am probably exaggerating in that I am taking my reasoning to its logical conclusion. The need to write is the result of a combination of feelings, attitudes, emotions, temptations, and dreams. To take up one of Sartre's expressions, can one legitimately forbid a poet to sing his sorrows and joys when children are dying of hunger?

In its own way, writing is a praxis, an action that has to play its role fully. What a writer must understand is that culture is not the will of solitary men, but the construction of a set of values and ideas in the interest of a greater liberation of man. The problem now is in the balance of power. Our culture is still primarily traditionalist or imitative. Our challenge lies in knowing how to debunk this tradition, how to demystify it, how to find new ways to appropriately express our reality and embody our deepest desires.

PART TWO

SOUFFLES 4–7–8 (1966–1967)

LESS THAN ONE YEAR INTO THE *SOUFFLES* ADVENTURE, the journal's editor-in-chief, Abdellatif Laâbi, articulated with renewed urgency the need for "cultural decolonization" in the postcolonial era, denouncing French cultural imperialism and Orientalist scholarship while calling on Maghrebi writers, artists, and intellectuals to forge new languages, forms, and genres that were not tributary to European cultural norms. This section, which spans the second year of the journal's existence, is bookended by Laâbi's two lengthy editorials on "national culture," a concept he borrowed from the Martinican theorist of colonialism Frantz Fanon to describe the need to resist persisting forms of foreign control over Morocco's economy, politics, and culture. The first article, published under the title "Realities and Dilemmas of National Culture," focuses on the question of language use, a topic hotly contested during the anticolonial struggle and in the aftermath of independence. Rejecting the view famously propounded by the Tunisian anticolonial theorist Albert Memmi and the Algerian writer Malek Haddad that post-independence Maghrebi literature would abandon the colonial tongue, French, in favor of the national language, Arabic, Laâbi urged Maghrebi writers to fashion their own literary voice in any language at their disposal. Laâbi's "In Defense of *The Simple Past*," a novel published in French by Driss Chraïbi at the height of the Moroccan struggle for independence, and Laâbi's extensive interview with the author as well as Memmi's "Self-Portrait" testify to the journal's commitment to Maghrebi literature in French at this time. Accordingly, the centerpiece of *Souffles* continued to be French-language poetry (in this section, Mostafa Nissabouri's "Manabboula," fig. 3).

Toni Maraini's essay on contemporary Moroccan painting, which closes this section, shows that the journal's cultural decolonization efforts extended to the visual arts as well. The painters she discusses, including her husband Mohamed Melehi, *Souffles'* artistic director until 1968 and the author of the abstract painting that adorns the cover of the first fourteen issues of the journal, and Mohamed Chebaa, who designed *Souffles'* trademark logo and subsequently replaced Melehi as artistic director (fig. 1), are among the most important contemporary Moroccan painters. Despite its meager operating budget, *Souffles* was a pioneer in disseminating the works of the Casablanca Group, as this collective was known, and other avant-garde artists, many of whom are featured in a double issue (7–8) devoted to contemporary Moroccan art (figs. 2, 4–9, 11–13, 18, 20).

If Laâbi defended a "decolonized" use of French in the first essay titled "Realities and Dilemmas of National Culture," he would ultimately align with his anticolonial elders Memmi and Haddad a few years later with the launching of *Souffles'* Arabic-language counterpart, *Anfas*. Laâbi's second "National Culture" essay, published less than a year after the first and, crucially, after the June 1967 Arab-Israeli war, is markedly more trenchant in its critique of European thought than the first, targeting not only Orientalist traditions but also what was then called the Third Worldist and anticolonial left. Laâbi's celebration of "atavism," "jihad," and "extremism"—by which he means the struggle against continued forms of cultural imperialism—vividly captures the journal's cultural decolonization project. It is not surprising that Laâbi begins his call to arms by citing Aimé Césaire's letter of resignation from the French Communist Party, in which Césaire accused the European left of placing anticolonial struggle second to class struggle. With this epigraph, Laâbi reactualizes the critique of European universalism bitingly delivered by one of the founders of Negritude at the height of the Algerian war, and deploys it for the postcolonial era, setting the tone for later issues of the journal.

REALITIES AND DILEMMAS OF NATIONAL CULTURE[1]

Abdellatif Laâbi

Translated from the French by Olivia C. Harrison and Teresa Villa-Ignacio

National Culture: Historical Fact and Necessity

At once a controversial concept, an all-encompassing demand, and the racialized superstructure of a narrowly defined nationalism, the idea of national culture has been modified and misunderstood in recent years by conflicting opinions and terminologies. Though Frantz Fanon's oeuvre should have clarified the notion of national culture once and for all, it was read only in a fragmentary manner. The aspects that were most often discussed were his analyses of the psycho-affective dimensions of colonialism and his contestation of the colonial system.

Fanon's insights have had no afterword. They were not completed or contested as they should have been, nor were they updated in the new context of independence and decolonization.

Fanon's oeuvre elicited astounded admiration and praise on the part of some (another thinker who has said it all) as well as the rancor of his complex-ridden detractors, those who could not "stomach" the consumption of a system that guaranteed them moral security and material privilege. In the meantime, spectacular changes have affected the economic, social, political, and cultural realities of Third World countries.

Whether real, partial, or skin-deep, decolonization has produced a stillborn new man reeling from political takeovers and his new responsibilities. Improvised micro-castes and micro-classes have sprung up in haste.

Amidst the chorus of fake liberations and "new" relationships with old hegemonies, ill-prepared intellectuals have given interviews (usually to foreign journalists, "specialists" in the Third World) and have written hasty articles. Everywhere the same old tune is heard: the obsession with definitions gives rise to set phrases, a confused jumble of all kinds of terminologies.

To limit ourselves to North Africa, with the exception of several lucid writings by Mostefa Lacheraf,[2] no one has been able clearly to define the problem of national culture or place it in the current context, in terms of the new balance of power. We confine ourselves to specialist opinions, sectarian polemics, religious convictions, or simply party directives. To each his own revolution.

At the same time, entire cultural groups, be they traditional or modern, are being bastardized and used to fuel a reckless scorched earth policy.

At the heart of such excesses, the concept of national culture will continue to generate serious misunderstandings if we do not immediately describe the context in which it was formulated.

This expression was first elaborated after World War II by Third World writers and thinkers as well as progressive Western intellectuals who undertook to research and analyze the human and cultural problems of African countries and others fighting colonization. "National culture" was part of a general terminology elaborated for these purposes, which we will call the "terminology of decolonization."

As we know, colonialism was the logical culmination of the development of European capitalism. Initially premised on territorial expansion and economic exploitation—its principal motivation—colonialism later felt the need to justify its oppressive policies by giving them humanitarian and cultural foundations.

In total command of a triumphant humanism, Enlightenment Europe, followed by a Europe awash in science and positivism, fell under the illusion that it possessed universal truths and values that could be applied to all peoples. Theoreticians and ideologues of European anthropocentrism went along with this logic, appealing to scientific rigor to acquire the rights of legitimacy.

Thus material exploitation, the exploitation of human activity, overlapped with cultural imperialism in a Manichean policy. After military supremacy and technology, Western science colonized us as well.

For this reason, it seems to me that *any process of cultural decolonization must begin by questioning the status of the humanities and social sciences in the colonial context.*

Let us start by looking at the specifically cultural changes this system triggered within colonized societies.

Fanon's legacy is particularly important here.

We know that cultural imperialism manifested itself in the colonizer's attempt to graft elements imported from his own culture onto the colonized—elements that were foreign to the mental habits and psyche of the latter. This violent graft aimed to erect an abyss between the individuality of the colonized and anything that could connect him to his own culture and memory. This policy, which was presented as a means of salvation, was not applied to the entire population, however. In creating modern schools, the colonizer aimed to form a small elite of subaltern natives. The vast majority of the population did not have access to the privilege of education. All that the colonizer offered them was a protective wing, saving them physically, as it were. As Fanon wrote, "the colonial mother protects the child from itself, from its ego, its physiology, its biology, and its ontological misfortune."[3]

The colonial school system is a perfect illustration of this depersonalizing policy. Albert Memmi has analyzed this aspect of the problem, showing how this school system instills a dangerous duality in the colonized child. In school he is confronted with an otherworldly absurdity, a universe perfectly calibrated to prepare the graft that will forever alter him. This education is conceived as an initiation, a foundation intended to give access to a world of wholesome values and ensure his liberation and self-mastery. The often brilliant graduate, the colonized intellectual, finds himself in the throes of disorientation, uprooted, split in half. He will also find himself at odds with his environment, his people, either in a state of shock or disgust before the traditional values that first shaped his personality.

This is the first historical dilemma. The transfer might have occurred, but instead of giving birth to a new species of conscious men who benefit from the mutual enrichment and exchanges of two cultures, as some would later be fond of saying, this transfer created cultural monsters, a category of men struck by aphasia and gripped by bad faith.

Despite these negative consequences, this phase of rupture and assimilation would later enable the colonized intellectual to become conscious of his paradoxical situation. Linguistic and cultural frustrations, as much as economic and social ones, allowed the colonized to become aware of an all-encompassing state of oppression that he needed to resist, both physically and mentally.

But it is only with the advent of national liberation movements that the colonized began explicitly to reclaim his own national culture.

Thus political and cultural struggles go hand in hand.

To resist dispossession the colonized followed a dual course of action. On the one hand, he tried to undermine the Western culture the school system had instilled in him. On the other, he threw himself into rediscovering his own culture. The colonized investigated and rehabilitated his cultural heritage. With the energy of rediscovery, he brandished it before the eyes of the oppressor as an object of pride.

This rediscovery is characterized by both demonstrative and explanatory dimensions.

The repossession of one's cultural destiny is governed by a harsh relation of acculturation. The colonized has not yet discovered his culture for his own sake at this stage. He displays it to convince the oppressor's camp. Culture is an object for exhibition. Fanon has discussed the infirmity of such a phase. And yet, he explains:

> Reclaiming the past triggers a change of fundamental importance in the colonized's psycho-affective equilibrium. It revalorizes national history and enables him to become conscious of his cultural alienation. But it is not specifically national. It follows the colonial thought-process, which consists in condemnation and alienation on a global, continental, and racial scale.
>
> The resulting racialization of thought is a consequence of Western Manichean structures, which have never stopped placing white culture in opposition to other non-cultures.[4]

While Fanon's theories accurately describe the coming-to-consciousness of the colonized, they cannot be indifferently applied to the Negro-African and Arab worlds. Indeed, with the exception of Algeria, where cultural assimilation was far-reaching, most Arab countries eschewed this relation of acculturation. When it approached the Arab world in the nineteenth century, classical colonialism met with a dynamic and organized ideological and cultural opposition, al-Nahda. The colonization of Negro-African countries, which occurred earlier, conflicted with forms of culture, which, while lively, were comparatively self-contained and not part of the modern world.

As for Morocco, where the traditional school system survived despite oppression, a double "intelligentsia" was formed. The first followed Fanon's model of perdition, frustration, and coming-to-consciousness. The second was trained in the free establishments where Arabic was still taught—albeit with old-fashioned methods—and at the University of Al-Karaouine, which would become one of the most ardent centers of Moroccan nationalism. From the outset this second intelligentsia confined itself to a vehement rejection of French culture.

The notion of cultural resistance took on an entirely different meaning for them. Because this group was already aware of the danger of depersonalization, it simply translated cultural resistance as absolute impermeability to the occupier's culture.

This group's attempt to rediscover the colonized culture did not have the same status as it had for the Negro-African. Moroccan Arab culture did not need to be on display to be present. It already existed.

Yet the Arab-Muslim world needed to counteract the continental and racial condemnation of the oppressor by rehabilitating Arab culture rather than the culture of this or that country within the community. In this sense the Arab-Muslim world followed a procedure similar to that of the Negro-African.

This can be explained by the fact that the Arab world has always constituted a unified cultural and spiritual entity. Its reclaiming of Arab culture in the context of colonization explains its profound attachment to a common heritage and cultural destiny.

Colonialism is what prompted the creation of narrowly defined nationalities. Its territorial dismemberment of human and cultural groups is artificial. It simply retraces the history of conquest by delimiting zones of political, economic, and strategic influence. Though it disturbed the traditional cultural circuits of the Arab world, this territorial isolation enabled a localized resistance, founded on the conditions and needs of each people, that enabled a coming-to-consciousness on a national scale.

The concept of national culture must be understood in this context, in relation to the historical situation of colonized countries.

The reclaiming of culture on a continental, racial, and then national scale, undertaken through the struggle for national independence, translates the historical efforts by the colonized to escape the mental and cultural alienation that were part and parcel of colonial policies and strategies.

National Literature and Language of Expression

Described during the colonial era as a tangible effect of depersonalization, as part of a conflict of hegemony and dependency, what has been called the "linguistic drama" of the colonized needs to be reformulated today according to another terminology, that of *postcolonial* decolonization.

In the particular context in which they were formulated, the lucid analyses of Albert Memmi and the somewhat more passionate conclusions of Malek Haddad constituted a sincere attempt to denounce the foundations and effects of colonial policy in the realm of culture. They were of tremendous importance at a time when the colonized intellectual needed to dismantle the structures and mental habits that the colonizers had tried to graft onto him, when decolonization was felt to be a wholly physical need premised on reworking, re-membering, and disarticulating the System's most hidden structures.

The rediscovery and reconquest of language certainly cannot be separated from the total reconquest of a personality that was alienated, not only through socioeconomic constraints, but also through the enterprise of cultural assimilation.

Studies focusing on colonized writers using a foreign language, and in particular literature produced by North Africans during the colonial period, have been less prophetic and convincing than they were thought to be.

These studies were no doubt instrumental in enabling the writer to become conscious of his paradoxical situation: he had to break with his deepest roots while limiting himself to a superficial dialogue with his oppressor. But they were also arbitrary in pronouncing the death sentence on a future literature when, in all honesty, it was impossible to foretell what it might look like or in what new conditions it might take shape, affirm itself, or transcend its first preoccupations. The situation in which this literature found itself would indeed have only constituted a problematic legacy, one it would have been entirely capable of reevaluating.

These judgments would have been less problematic if they had limited themselves to a provisional conclusion, explaining a cultural anomaly through the relation of acculturation tying North African literature of French expression to the "metropolitan" cultural sphere. The motives, philosophy of communication, and occasionally the exhibitionism of this literature made it legitimate to denounce its *culturally mendacious* approach. We have already shown that such an approach has become obsolete, that it no longer corresponds to our current preoccupations, which are shaped by different realities. But we have not invalidated the revolutionary effectiveness of this literature, however inadequate and limited it may seem today.

And yet the abusive dramatization of the issue, especially in Haddad's *Les zéros tournent en rond* [The zeroes go round in circles], and its macabre pessimism seemed to us to arise from a shortsighted vision of things. In addition, this dramatization was in danger of producing persistent misunderstandings of these burning questions, which turned into passionate debates fueled by diverse inhibitions, interests, and preconceptions. Indeed, this dramatization was an instant success since a more or less sectarian ink flowed from every horizon to track down, slander, and falsify the issues.

It would moreover be tiresome to retrace the chronology of the polemics surrounding the issue of "national literature and language of expression." Very few writers, intellectuals, critics, or even spectators were able to maintain their composure when analyzing and discussing this issue.

While the issue is somewhat resolved in the countries of Black Africa, it remains acutely polemical in the countries of the Maghreb.

The multiplicity of autochthonous dialects in each country of Black Africa as well as the lack of unified and transcribed vernacular languages have prompted writers to resign themselves to the use of foreign languages. In the Maghreb, where the language of culture has for centuries been Arabic, the issue is much more complex and its appraisal requires great prudence.

But above all we will have to leave aside simplistic or emotionally-motivated stances.

During the colonial period Maghrebi writers were accused of betraying their people by choosing to express themselves in the language of the oppressor, one that had been substituted for their own, which now suffered a devalued, if not clandestine, existence.

This is an arbitrary accusation. It does not take into account two essential factors that motivated this forced usage: almost all these writers were educated in French schools, and they had to submit to a unidirectional educational system that had been developed for another culture. Accordingly they expressed themselves in the only language they could wield with ease: French.

The rudiments of Arabic these writers picked up furtively could hardly allow them to achieve a fully formed mode of expression.

Furthermore, the fact that these writers wrote in French cannot in any way depreciate the witness they bear to our society and the revolutionary combat role they play within it. You do not betray your people by glorifying its struggle, whatever the means.

Let us also leave aside a simplistic stance adopted by Maghrebi writers of French expression themselves. For some the use of French was an invaluable personal triumph. It allowed them to express in a language of "clarity and flexibility" that which they could not have expressed by any other means. Writers easily condemn and slander an Arabic language they admit they haven't mastered. They say the Arabic language is fossilized and does not correspond to the demands of our time. Aristocratic and half-dead, it must undergo enormous mutations before becoming an efficient instrument of literary expression.

We can easily respond by showing them what Arabic writers have produced and what has been expressed in this language over the past twenty centuries. From the pre-Islamic Mu'allaqat to contemporary times, this literary movement has rarely been interrupted.

It is true that these writers know of Arabic literature only the rare texts gleaned from the skeletal anthologies of Orientalists, who readily admit that, as a result of translation, these texts have been stripped of their character and, we might add, authenticity.

Another rather widespread simplification asserts that language is nothing but a sort of neutral instrument, and that an author on the threshold of writing can choose from the repertory of international languages any written idiom whatsoever to express himself. This is certainly not the case. A language is not raw material. A people's language is a living reservoir that constantly testifies to its evolution, cultural transformations, and memory. It is the medium and organ of any culture. And it is certain that the destiny of the Arab people has long been interwoven with the evolution of Arabic, its language of expression.

Apart from these summary opinions, the central problems of acculturation have already been lucidly presented. At the beginning of his argument in *Portrait du colonisé*, for example, Albert Memmi rightly states that the linguistic dualism of the colonized cannot be

> assimilated to a simple diglossia. Possession of two languages is not merely a matter of having two tools, but actually means partici- pation in two psychical and cultural realms. Here, the two worlds symbolized and conveyed by the two tongues are in conflict; they are those of the colonizer and the colonized.[5]

Memmi goes on to explain that since the colonized's mother tongue is the one that is devalued, enjoying no dignity at the national or inter- national level, its restoration alone will allow the colonized to recover himself, to regain a lost continuity and history.

Malek Haddad concurs somewhat with these arguments when he pushes them toward more dramatic and sentimental conclusions and, I think, ultimately distorts them. For him the Maghrebi writer does not totally adhere to the French language:

> We write *the French language* rather than *in French*. We make our- selves understood. Words, our everyday materials, do not measure up to our feelings. There is only an approximate correspondence be- tween our Arab thoughts and our French vocabulary.[6]

There is for Haddad a distance between intimately lived language and its formulation in words that are far from being simple conventional graphic signs. Between the thought and the written sign that captures it, something escapes. "Whatever I do," he explains, "I am forced to denature my thought."[7]

Memmi and Haddad come to the same conclusion. For them, North African literature of French expression is condemned by this linguistic infirmity. If he does not wish to produce a work in bad faith, the writer of French expression must put down his pen.

Malek Haddad has gone to this extreme. For the moment he has stopped writing. Albert Memmi, who in spite of everything analyzed this issue as a sociologist and from an outsider's point of view since his mother tongue is not Arabic, continues to write in French.

We have already specified that these analyses were formulated within a framework of harsh acculturation, that they described psycho-social crises provoked by attempts at assimilation and depersonalization.

We have also indicated the need to reformulate both the obsolete aspects of the problem and the new elements that have intervened in the context of decolonization.

It is true that in the colonial context the linguistic frustration of the colonized went beyond the mere coexistence of two modes of expression. It undermined his psyche and depreciated his culture.

During this repressive phase, linguistic dualism was a drama that even many intellectuals of the independence era were not able to surmount, since the cultural structures mobilized by new pedagogies and improvised Arabization experiments did not effectively destabilize the foundations of the colonial status quo. Not only did the entire problem persist, but the new policies overhauling the teaching system also had catastrophic effects on the ability of adolescents to master any language. Even if he was frustrated with his mother tongue, the colonized adolescent still had at his disposal a medium of thought with which he could formulate his revolt and his ideas, and with which he could externalize his personality. After independence, the adolescent lost this imposed medium, but he has not yet reconquered the Arabic language. He is aphasic. His deepest thoughts and personality emerge only in sporadic and imprecise fragments. His linguistic infirmity does not stem from a relationship of conflict but from the methodological imprecision, the ad hoc negotiations of this stage of decolonization, or the stagnation in which most newly independent countries find themselves. This deepening drama will simply have acquired a new nature and new motives.

To return to the specific drama of the colonized, we can note that it has not always been experienced in the same way, and above all that it has not been confronted with the same kind of logic, the same force of lucidity. Some intellectuals and writers have lacked the force and will to push their arguments to their furthest ramifications in order to arrive at viable solutions.

This coming to consciousness has remained, for some, a painful fact that has led them to give in to a tragic caricature, a mourner's discourse lacking a reflexive energy that might break down the problem.

Once the mechanisms and motivations of this linguistic duel have been broken down, once this lucid assessment and actualization have occurred, the colonized intellectual will find the real terms with which to pursue his revolutionary struggle. This struggle must be conceived within a praxis whose terminology is not one of words or of writing.

The struggle for the establishment of national dignity, for the reconquest of alienated bodies and minds is the result of a coming to consciousness and the work of acts of internal recovery. The stumbling block of language can in no way compromise this recovery if it is truly authentic.

The reconquest of a national language is only one aspect of a total recovery whose inherent movement concerns the whole of one's personality: thought, flesh, perception, and also, certainly, language. The reforging of the colonized's personality is a more serious quest than one realizes. It was previously thought that, in order to recuperate and restructure oneself, it was enough to invoke one's land, to describe in minute detail the places and habits of one's compatriots, to condemn the colonial order with great verbal violence. This was an error of perspective and context.

All militant Algerian poems, for example, are declaimed in the name of the homeland. They are populated by a delirious toponymy. This need to name constitutes a kind of reaction against a painful loss, an uprooting by asphalt. There is in this order of perception only the insane physical appeal to a suspended personality, a labyrinth in which to engulf oneself in order to come out again, re-membered. It is a physical claim, not an organic one. A large part of this literature has remained, as we have already indicated, a literature of colonized subjects, in spite of its revolutionary character. The writer challenged realities that were not profoundly examined and sensed at an organic level. In expressing this physical revolution, the writer was not yet able to adhere totally to the reality of his people, to its intrinsic mentality, to its organizing mythology of the world. He had not succeeded in apprehending his own roots, in renewing contact with the sap of life, the popular matrix. This is the typical path of the colonized intellectual, who often lived in exile and, following a pattern we have seen many times before, sought inspiration in the cafés of Saint-Germain-des-Prés. Louis Aragon and Paul Éluard (to cite only writers of the finest quality) inventoried the topography of Algiers and the Aurès and, according to an obscure syntax of reflexes and nauseas, set about addressing the usual Parisian public, not the Algerian one.

Thus Haddad can speak to us of his "orphanage of readers."[8] Driss Chraïbi and Kateb Yacine also wrote in French. But they are not particularly bereft of readers. Simply put, the mythology that Kateb deploys in *Nedjma* and *Le cercle des représailles* [The circle of reprisals], for example, surpassed the framework of colonization by far. This mythology was an admirable agent of decolonization: it extended bridges between fragments of history segmented by colonialism in order to distance the oppressed from their memory, their body, and their living heritage.

In spite of everything, Kateb's oeuvre constitutes one of the first works of decolonization. Moreover, it has made itself a part of both national Algerian and universal literature. This is because his work covers the distances of human history and also because it retains, despite its "distancing" brilliance, an adherence to the concrete, to the historical event, a thickness of testimony entrenched in daily human combat.

I myself can affirm that one does not decolonize with words. Only a mental reforging, a rediscovery of our heritage, a questioning and reorganization of this heritage can allow us to take the reins of our personality and destiny as human beings. At that moment we will have entered upon our own path and initiated the effective, concrete stage of decolonization.

From the outset we must remain absolutely suspicious of the language in which we write, whether French, Arabic, or any other.

Moroccan literature written in Arabic is a good example. With rare exceptions, it perfectly illustrates a prototypically backward literature at the margins of historical upheavals. This is not by virtue of its language of expression. Arabic lends itself to all kinds of modulations and variations. But in Morocco it has not yet found writers capable of *executing* it, of using it idiosyncratically. These writers are subjected to a state of language in which they indulge in vain jouissance and unrealistic nostalgia. Reading their work, one has the impression that all of them write in the same way. The same stereotypes reappear in each text, whatever its quality.

Now, the truly great writer is one who makes a singular and irreplaceable use of language, who proposes and imposes a new language, marked with the seal of his creative universe The Moroccan writer must disarticulate his language, do violence to it, in order to extract all its possibilities. Yet he will only do so when he has acquired, through the difficult experiences described above, the organizing and exorcising faculty of creation.

All told, the question of linguistic dualism must be raised today in the broader context of decolonization, no longer as a colonial frustration but as a practice, as a conquest of disorganization. It is ultimately a problem of writing. And here we find the litmus test for talent, the ability to perceive a given human condition.

A writer who can attain the lofty strata where the germinating blood wrestles with itself can communicate his anguishes, his heartrendings, his flights in any language.

If none of these languages are available, he will express his vitality in the language of deaf-mutes.

Forthcoming issues:

— Culture and the public.

— Defense and safeguarding of our cultural heritage.

— Contesting the status of the humanities and social sciences in the colonial context.

— North African literature of French expression in question.

DRISS CHRAÏBI AND US (INTERVIEW)

Abdellatif Laâbi

Translated from the French by Safoi Babana-Hampton

1. Driss Chraïbi, you left Morocco in the midst of the colonial period and war. What in general were your preoccupations then? What was your position regarding your country's sociocultural and political problems?

My preoccupations at the time were not entirely conscious ones. I was an adolescent familiar only with two limited worlds: home (no friends, were the father's wishes) and school. But then I have always been inspired by four passions: the need for love; the thirst for lucid and direct knowledge; the passion for freedom, my own and that of others; and a desire to share their suffering. I was the offspring of a bourgeois family; I was one of the privileged few who could have access to secondary schooling. Do you remember those times? At any rate . . . When I came home from school, I would see people simply sitting around, kids left to themselves, people aimlessly waiting . . . I was like a little monkey, dressed in European style, my head filled with words and sentences. My own revolt goes back precisely to this period. It was suppressed for many years. I would say to myself: "How is it that we, Moroccans and Arabs, have let colonization prevail?" Yes, I would say to myself: "The farm laborers hired by my father to work his lands eat a meager piece of bread." I would hear my brothers complain: "We've had enough of eating tagine every day." The revolt brewing within me was directed against everything: the French protectorate, social injustice, political, cultural, and social stagnation. Then there was something else: my mother. Consider this: I was reading Lamartine, Hugo, and Musset. In that other world, in Western literature, women are lyricized, admired, elevated to the sublime. When I came home however, what I felt and saw before my eyes was another woman, my mother, who wept day and night because my father made her life so unbearable. I assure you that for thirty-three years she never left the house. I assure you that I, the child, was her only confidant, her only support. But what could I do for her? Law, tradition, and religion prevailed. On your knees, my brothers. These are experiences that leave a permanent mark. My emotions had been so deeply affected since childhood that at nineteen years old I still knew nothing about life. Not even the notion that there could be a difference between a man and a woman. Well, that's essentially it, Mr. Laâbi. I left in order to set myself free and grow away from a closed and ossified world. If the *only* problems were the French protectorate and colonialism, everything would have been simple. As a result, my past, our past, would have been simple. No, Monsieur Sartre, hell is not other people. It is also within us. I brutally said what had to be said about our past, and I regret nothing. But perhaps I should have only attacked the others and followed the pack, isn't that right?

2. *After your departure, you had to wait several years before publishing your first novel,* Le passé simple [The Simple Past]. *Why has this cry of revolt, which seemingly reflects your desire to bear witness and denounce what you saw, been contained for so long?*

Le passé simple was completed in 1953. I needed ten years to see my revolt through. As a rule I see things to the very end. I refuse all compromise. You will recall the end of this book: I left for Europe in search of new ideas, revolutions, eruptions . . . something, anything, that could help us get moving. In the 1930s and 1940s who was doing anything in Morocco? Eh? Aside from a few men who were conscious of the idea of the Nation? The bourgeoisie did nothing. The people were resigned to their fate. I contained my revolt for so long. Any doctor will tell you that there are individuals who react slowly. I am one of them. And then, over a period of ten years, I had accumulated a certain amount of life experiences.

3. *In the days following independence you were attacked for the denunciations and the choices you made in your first book. The chronology of your reactions appears to us today in retrospect a bit ambiguous. It was said at some point that you disavowed your novel. Whatever the case might be, in my view the problem of* Le passé simple *deserves to be elucidated clearly once and for all.*

This is how things happened regarding the attacks. A publisher consumes and makes money. He published my first novel in the middle of the Moroccan crisis. As a result it is the right-wing media that seized hold of it—the French right-wing press and the right-wing press in Morocco, led by Moroccans. Need I mention some names to you? I have known a beggar who overnight became someone capable of giving alms. Need I be more precise? Yes, I confess, I did go through a moment of weakness when I renounced *Le passé simple*. I couldn't bear the thought that people claimed that I was playing into the hands of colonizers. I should have held out, I should have had more courage. But allow me to ask you this: don't the problems raised by this book still exist in 1967? Remember that Senegalese peasant who went to see President Senghor and said, "Tell me, Mr. President, when is this independence going to be over?"

4. It has become customary when commenting on your second novel Les boucs [The Butts], *to discuss the conditions of North African workers in France, their abject uprootedness and the racism that they are often subjected to. Is this all there is to it?*

It seems to me that this book also expressed, if only in its disturbed writing style, a much larger drama, that of your whole generation and its exile. Do you agree?

I was a chemical engineer when I wrote *Les boucs*. I could have contented myself with my diploma and made a comfortable living for myself. But I turned my back on chemistry all of a sudden, and the bourgeois son that I was came down to join the North African workers. Did you know what Nanterre was like in the 1950s? I lived with them there, not as a witness but as one of them. I had to do it. I had to fast endless Ramadans . . .

Why did I do this? Well, let me tell you: during ten or eleven years of living in France, I had *seen. Understood.* Our souls were bleeding in the land of equality, liberty, and fraternity. I will go even further: I live in Aubervilliers. Do you know Aubervilliers, La Nouvelle-France Street? The "butts" still live there in 1967.

5. In L'âne [The donkey], *you still remain attached to a specific human and social realm, which is extended this time to the Arab-Muslim world. What particular situations and events within this world served as your points of departure for conceiving this book? In this respect, do you have what one might call "a political vision"?*

With *L'âne*, I had a dream. For many years. Perhaps I took my desires for realities. I was wrong. I saw the Arab and African worlds gain their independence. I heartily embraced it and welcomed it with all my heart. I said to myself, with utmost confidence: "At last, this world that suffered so much in its being will bring to the West true democracy, the spiritual values that it needs, religious and racial tolerance." Then these countries became independent. I stress that, for the most part, theirs was only a nominal independence. In *L'âne*, I predicted all this: fratricidal conflicts, the impossibility of forming a monolithic bloc, the lack of upward mobility here and elsewhere, military regimes, and a kind of police-style socialism. But let's consider what really matters to us, mainly literature and art in general. In this period of great choices, literature must also choose. It can either serve as an instrument of the tiny minority playing the role of Fate for the large majority, demanding above all else the latter's blind faith, or take the side of and entrust its fate to the large majority. It can carry men toward exhilaration, illusion, and miracles. It can increase ignorance or deepen knowledge. It can appeal to forces whose efficiency lies in their destructive powers, or to those that reveal themselves to be constructive. If I have any political vision at all, this must be it.

6. You personally told me that La foule *[The crowd], your fourth novel, was a farce. How do you explain this departure from your previous work? Or do you think there is some continuity?*

La foule is in continuity with my previous work. It is, if you will, a transposition of *L'âne* into the Western world. Instead of being a drama, the action is seen from the angle of the grotesque. I always need to demystify statues and heroes. I took a head of state and reduced him to barely one meter fifty. I put in his mouth the words of you know who. In a nutshell it's the story of a poor guy who reflects the anonymous crowd and has no real ambitions; he becomes a head of state. And what a head of state . . . think of Popeye. Here he sits in his presidential palace giving . . . recipes to his subjects. What I mean is that we never laugh enough in life. He clings to power, he is glued to his seat; it's impossible to make him resign . . . ; he has an entire crowd behind him, a crowd that sees itself in him.

7. It seems to me that your penultimate novel, Succession ouverte *[Heirs to the Past], is your latest encounter with Moroccan reality, a logical and delayed sequel to* Le passé simple. *This book sets up an inheritance, it constitutes a literary testament to the present reality as a source of testimony and creation. Am I right?*

No, no testament, especially not a literary one. Allow me to explain: It took me eleven years and six books to bridge the gap between my past and what I am now. I have accepted the image of the father, the image of the past (this took quite some time); the past was demystified, its shell and all received ideas stripped away. I have finally come to terms with it, and this brings me peace. But I had to wage a long struggle in order to know who I am, what I am, and to live my life accordingly. Now I have different concerns. My life has been split into two phases: nineteen years in Morocco and twenty-two years in Europe. During the latter phase I accumulated a great deal of experience, and it seems to me that I need to talk about it. So how is this a defection? Eh? Later on, I will return to Moroccan and Arab reality. Especially in books based on memories. My horizon has opened up, and I can't close it again.

8. In any case, Un ami viendra vous voir *[A friend is coming to see you], the novel you just published, is deliberately rooted in the specific problems of the society you currently live in.*

You have talked about the universal themes and concerns of this book. However, can one talk about universality when the conditions you describe pertain to a certain type of civilization, one that is grappling with the tyranny of consumerism and the alienation caused by technology and automation, the typical outcome of a long evolution that for the moment still only concerns this one civilization?

Who would see in the drama of happiness, love, and connection that the heroine of your novel experiences any echo of the condition of, for example, a Moroccan, Iraqi, or Indian woman?

Universality in this case runs the risk of simply becoming an invasive universalism of a narrow human condition.

How then should we interpret your book?

How surprising to hear your limited reading of *Un ami viendra vous voir.* You're free to do as you wish. After all, when a book is printed it no longer concerns me. But I have too much regard for you and your journal to let this opportunity for dialogue pass. It's true, consumer culture is specific to the West and America which are in search of their deepest values. But aren't all of us in the Third World headed toward this type of society at breakneck speed? In this book I presented the extreme example of a woman who enjoys all the conditions for happiness yet experiences a profound malaise. But tell me, isn't woman, wherever she happens to be, the last remaining colonized being on Earth? Especially in our society? Is there a real dialogue between man and woman? Wasn't woman always considered a mere function? Is she able to realize herself in any way other than through one or more romantic experiences? This is what's absurd, unnatural. Because man forgets too often that his companion is something else, above all a *human being*. She is the very source of life. Yet we compartmentalize her, placing her in the roles of housekeeper, wife, mother, and warrior's solace. There is something else, my friend Laâbi. In my book I pointedly denounce the sexual taboo. I emphasize that most women in the world—one in every two the experts would say—lack love because their education, parents, and this pseudo-freedom that men grant them hold them in bondage from the very start. I could clinically dissect an example for you. Oh yes, man does not know how to love, even physically. I can attest to this, having visited plenty of psychiatric clinics in a white coat. There with my own eyes I have seen humanity wallowing in the mire. Wasn't it *Souffles* that recently published these words (I'm quoting from memory), "We still live in a pre-human era"?

9. Up to now you have been the most controversial and most attacked Moroccan, and perhaps North African, writer. Your work gave rise to polemics that have profoundly affected you. Almost all of them deal with the following important points:

— *Your denunciations and choices in* Le passé simple, *as we just discussed.*

— *The problem of language.*

— *The problem of exile.*

Do you think you have already responded to all the questions that were raised?

Considering the objections and misunderstandings that never stop surfacing, can you redefine your position once again, point by point?

It's true, I was often attacked. I didn't respond most of the time. I don't know how to respond to insults. But I'm glad to have stirred up the public conscience. Aren't you doing more or less the same thing in your journal? Well? As to the problem of language and bilingualism, I refer you to the excellent study that appeared in the fourth issue of your journal.

10. Do you think that North African literature in French is in an inauthentic position vis-à-vis French literature? What place can it aspire to have within Arabic literature?

I have no idea. I can only speak for myself, and not in the name of my fellow writers.

11. Since the spread of nationalist movements in Africa, a subversive and intellectual movement has shaken the Continent as well as the Maghreb. The movement that accompanied political struggle took aim at cultural decolonization, the remaking of old structures as well as the redefinition of a specifically African heritage and context, first in the colonial and then the postcolonial context. How have you continued to position yourself in relation to this movement?

I was a kind of maverick, difficult to fit into a definite category.

12. How do you see the future of literature in the Maghreb? What are your expectations for young writers of the new generation?

They must wage a battle of ideas, of deeds, of pressing issues—and not of words or appearances. I'm certain that writers of the new generation will successfully take over and express themselves more—and better—than the old wave. But their writing will be addressed to a local public through national publishers. I hope they will call every kind of authority into question. We have obtained our independence, many years have passed, and now writers have the task of rebuilding. Tomorrow's literature will not be reserved for the elite, however. It must be far reaching. In the meantime, from Paris, I stand ready to offer help to any Moroccan writer.

IN DEFENSE OF *THE SIMPLE PAST*

Abdellatif Laâbi
Translated from the French by Edwige Tamalet Talbayev

It is well known that what has been called "North African literature of French expression" for the past ten years or so was a predominantly Algerian literary movement. With the exception of some isolated, minor works penned by Moroccans or Tunisians, the wave of publications that started around 1950 in France focused on works by Algerian writers. In the rest of the Maghreb two names in particular have encouraged critics to reach beyond Algeria and to adopt the now accepted phrase "Maghrebi literature of French expression": I am speaking of Albert Memmi in Tunisia and Driss Chraïbi in Morocco.

In those days Chraïbi was in fact a special case, an exception.

The Algerian literary movement had deep roots. It was the logical outcome of gradual linguistic and cultural developments. Furthermore, it emerged at a critical juncture of Algerian national history. It is no accident that these works were published right before the start of the liberation struggle. Works by Mouloud Feraoun, Mouloud Mammeri, Malek Ouary and especially Mohammed Dib assessed the sociological impact of the colonial order. They were paving the way for the works of combat literature that saw the light of day during the war.

This classic description of Algerian literature of the last two decades does not characterize the evolution of Moroccan or Tunisian literatures. Such a contrast can be explained by an early phase of political decolonization as well as specific linguistic and cultural realities. These two literatures were for the most part written in the national language.

If in those days Tunisian literature followed a course closer to that of eastern Arabic literatures, Moroccan literature written before independence—to limit ourselves to the twentieth century, which is the period in focus here[9]—did not possess the armature of a modern literature, such as that which emerged in Algeria. Even in the most critical moments of the national struggle, it remained scattered and surprisingly paradoxical.

Indeed one of these obvious paradoxes was that this literature expressed dissent and mediated nationalist and at times revolutionary content in deeply medieval and aristocratic forms.

It was addressed to a privileged, hyper-literate audience drawn from the national bourgeoisie and the intellectual aristocracy, the classes at the helm of the political struggle, and not the popular masses. Moreover, this literature, in which poetry was predominant, was not entirely centered on the national struggle: bacchic, hagiographic, and court poetry flourished and sometimes openly indulged in treason (poems dedicated to the residents and generals of the Protectorate and feudal chieftains such as El Glaoui, for example).

At the same time there was a dearth of essays that might have reflected and hastened the development of self-awareness and national ideology. Pamphlets, the daily press, or the instructions relayed by political parties could hardly fill that role.

Admittedly, such literature was meant for an audience of insiders. It was not marred by an exclusive relation with the colonizer's cultural arena. The outrage that it could have caused remained contained. Besides, it never reached the scope of a true national literature in the modern sense of the term. It remained the idle pursuit of an isolated caste, a sort of medieval fossil onto which a few ideas and testimonies relevant to our contemporary moment were grafted.

Such was still the situation when the first Algerian works saw the light of day.

Avowedly, in the case of Morocco, there were a few precedents—notably the publication of Ahmed Sefrioui's works.[10] But these works did not bring about any significant change. They described a lethargic daily life, wallowed in it, portrayed "emotional pangs" that delighted a foreign public fond of serene exoticism and orientalism. This petrified world thriving on anecdotes, on this so–called "picturesque description," was driven by various complexes and, most importantly, by the need for exercises in style: he was "a wizard of the French language" in the words of a very benevolent critic. A. Sefroui wanted nothing more than the consecration that such a badge of honor and merit afforded.

The wish that Pierre Loti formulated at the end of last century was fulfilled. The "Moghreb" has not changed.[11] It has remained dazed in its contemplative state, deaf to anything that might have disturbed its lethargy.

In 1954 Driss Chraïbi's *Le passé simple* appeared.

A threatening book, dazzling with rage, where for the first time the flaws, the inhibitions, and all the depravity contained by the barriers of tradition and respectful reformism *à la* Lyautey burst out. The Morocco of "enchantment," nostalgia, "secrecy," righteousness, etc. was clinically dissected and exposed by a young writer from the bourgeois class, which knew how to combine political struggle with the defense of sordid interests and privileges.

It is the solitary revolt of a hybrid adolescent, the product of the first crop of young educated Moroccans, taught in French schools and nourished by humanism from overseas, a humanism that succeeded in upsetting the static balance and traditional values of everyday life and provoked a deadly struggle between two generations living under the influence of different solar systems.

The bookish humanism that spurred this divorce was a liberation project. Its magnitude, logic, and persuasiveness could not but violate minds attached by necessity to a tradition woven of taboos, imperatives, vengeful exercises in authority, unwavering dogmas—all of them limits which stunted any attempt at self-affirmation. The hierarchical and compartmentalized nature of family and social life was revealed as a total anachronism, in its most grotesque aspects.

Le passé simple did not describe or seek to pinpoint the remote causes of such a situation. It was a physical cry rising from the depths of a submerged continent, a hand-to-hand combat with a world of adults and thaumaturgists rooted in ancient certainties, acting out the comedy of decency and piety, content with small acts of in vitro heroism of which their domesticated dependents would bear the brunt. Thus the sadistic authority of the father is revealed, the alienating constriction of the family unit, the social enslavement of women, the hypocrisy used at all levels of society as a measure of pomp and perfect excuse. D. Chraïbi engaged in a veritable carnage, slicing through a gallery of false situations and fetid masquerades.

The novel denounced its immediate surroundings, the relationships in which the author or hero was a significant party. A spatial crisis was under way. The adolescent, the hero of *Le passé simple*, was leaving Morocco in the hope of some salvation, of redemption, if only of his body, his skin.

Had he been any "sacrosanct" Rimbaud or other "fantastic" accursed-poet-in-revolt from anywhere else in the world, such an escape would have been forgiven. It would have been understood that certain temperaments sometimes need a vacuum or foreign space to put themselves back together and take stock of their pains and stigmata, of their hemorrhagic physiologies. Well, not Chraïbi. He was a Moroccan, "educated" what's more, and he had fled his country at the very moment of the struggle etc. . . . stabbed in the back . . . Betrayed . . . What's that? The colonial order, you say? Didn't he sufficiently explain the situation not to need to talk about it or denounce it before doing anything else?

Literature and revolution. Commitment. Historical realities.

Of course, one must either be Fanon, Nazim Hikmet, or nothing at all.

Or maybe one needs to start from the postulate that colonized peoples are fundamentally good and that in the battle of Good and Evil only the attacker is a scoundrel.

Chraïbi refused to play this game. Consciously or not. As an act of political maturity or by lack thereof. It is of little importance. He came to a diagnostic guided by his revolt, not pre-established economic or sociological schemes. Besides, revolt is not inexorably lucid or calculated. It can manifest itself as a need to break everything in sight, to vomit, or to rape passersby. Needless to say, such actions will be labeled anarchism. I will rather see them as the organic expression of discontent, the salutary trigger of dissenting violence.

Chraïbi was a trailblazer. His first book came out very early on, too early. Logically—and we will leave the pleasure of demonstrating this to a scholar of the year 2000—this work cannot be explained through a harmonious process of evolution. It came about almost by accident. And this is for the best. Driss Chraïbi will have had the privilege of prematurely rattling a structure whose rotten foundations were crumbling a little more each day without alarming in the least the minds drugged by various somas. He did not assess the sociological impact of the colonial order. However, he may have demonstrated the tangible causes that deepened and fed colonization. In this respect, he was in all likelihood the only Maghrebi and Arab writer who had the courage to present to a whole people their cowardice, who exposed their lethargy to them, the mechanisms of their hypocrisy, of the auto-colonization and the oppression that they exerted on one another—the feudal chieftain on his farm laborer, the father on his children, the husband on his object-wife, the libidinous master on his apprentice.

One must assuredly have a good sense of humor to accept such a debunking of pride, of the marathon of physical love, of the certainty of belonging to a good people, of believing in the right religion. In this respect Chraïbi had a deadpan sense of humor. He was a troublemaker at the very moment when all this intrinsic depravity was meant to be silenced so that only heroism would stand out and be deserving of future historiography (streets named after martyrs and secure positions for the survivors).

We must be honest with ourselves. We are too fond of epics, too prone to putting ourselves on pedestals. When wars come to an end, when great historical disruptions take a turn, the literature testifying to these events is sometimes laughable for its monolithic, pious nature.

The darker side of our history has remained in a state of inhibition in most of our writers. It feeds their guilty dreams. Chraïbi instilled flexibility. He started clearing the way, cleansing minds and bodies. At the same time, the specialists of Morocco's epics were writing out poems following the rhyme patterns that they had previously established.

Chraïbi did not simply perturb a petrified situation. With the publication of this book alone, he simultaneously gave Moroccan literature its first modern work. We use the term "modern" not to express an obsessive fear of modernity, but because this work was undoubtedly imbued with precious novelty in comparison with everything produced at the time. Chraïbi contested not only our writers' inhibited and contemplative attitude with regards to language and writing, but also the literary function that was still the prerogative of aristocrats and buffoons.

And so, what's next?

Thirteen years later, *Le passé simple* still beckons to us. Since then, Chraïbi has written other books, based on other experiences. Avowedly, this ever-evolving work presents us with problems. At times, our positions differ and we do not appreciate one or another characteristic of the work in the same way. Our generation has other preoccupations; it is faced with different realities than those the author of *The Simple Past* knew. But we are too aware of Chraïbi's contribution to let his work be unfairly criticized by professional polemicists who only counter this creative force with disorderly powerlessness.

e. m. nissaboury

manabboula

Pour que vous doutiez encore plus de nos origines
nous vous proposons des corps pour les usines-salut-de-l'humanité
sans ablutions
des corps tranquilles sur le sable les bureaux de placement
des corps tannés
    l'histoire tuberculeuse
      nous autres les chiens les perfides
nous autres au cerveau paléolithique les yeux bigles le foie
            [thermonucléaire
des corps avec des tablettes en bois où il est écrit que le sous-
            [développement
est notre maladie congénitale
       puis m'sieur
          puis madame
            puis merci

22   *sans oublier notre interminable procession de dents jaunes*
et les vappes
notre sang moitié sang moitié arbre
des corps nourris de sauterelles et de pisse de chamelle
nous ne sommes pas
      même épileptiques
         dans les grottes de vos Platon
ni dans les contes de Shahrazade
pas dans vos statistiques sur la culture des peuples les maladies
guérissables par bouchée de petite ruine
          pas
dans vos bilans vos rapports frénétiques sur les grandes et inhu-
maines certitudes
ni les médailles
ni les cités de jade contre
      nos refoulements
         nos stigmates purulents
nos matrices aboyant sous le vent

pas dans vos traités sur la biologie de l'homme pétrifié
bien que nous ayons
     nos guerres fratricides
        et que
         nous révions de
          [planètes

FIGURE 3. "Manabboula" (excerpt), poem by Mostafa Nissabouri. *Souffles* 5 (Rabat, 1967), p. 22. Reprinted with permission.

MANABBOULA

Mostafa Nissabouri

Translated from the French by Teresa Villa-Ignacio

So that you may doubt our origins even more
We offer you bodies for the salvation-of-humanity-factories
without ablutions
peaceful bodies on the sand placement offices
leathery bodies
              tubercular history
                          us dogs the perfidious ones
us of paleolithic brain squinty eyes thermonuclear liver
bodies with wooden tablets where it is written that underdevelopment
is our congenital disease
                and sir
                    and madam
                        and thank you

without forgetting our interminable procession of yellow teeth
and stupors
our blood half blood half tree
bodies nourished on locusts and camel piss
we are not
              even epileptic
                  in the caves of your Plato
or in Scheherazade's stories
not in your statistics on the culture of peoples diseases
curable with a mouthful of small ruins
                          not
in your balance sheets your frenetic reports on the great and inhuman
certainties
nor the medals
nor the cities of jade against
                    our repressions
                          our purulent stigmata
our matrices howling under the wind

not in your treatises on the biology of petrified men
even though we have

our fratricidal wars
                    and though
                              we dreamed of
                                        planets
of alleys of arcades of suns at the center of the earth (we are familiar
with mental alienation and speak of fallen sacked civilizations)
and though we accorded you
at the foot of fortifications and fortifications of heroin
tetanus
wars of the stomach and of the jackal
to satisfy your calculating mind regarding the Rome and Vietnam files
your necrophagous pilgrims' glasses upon the ramparts of Marrakech
our rumors of demented, caravan-swallowing crowds
our shantytowns sun on sun and djinns with matches
our brotherhood's strawmen—ah with oranges and rifles of rebellion
ah me madam arrange steal not I sir happy new year and good
health—
of all the little women with little green stars on their foreheads
the whole pernicious legend of our diaphragms
all the torments of blood in a vertigo of shanty-mosques and
slingshots
our bodies
            decked out
                      in tornadoes
                              to conjure your bodies in chunks
hibernation of a little neurosis of sand ourselves
without casbahs or idioms not Mediterranean-dementia not
                                             memorizing
rerooting memory
                this cave
                      this shit-hole
                              this death running through the alleys
feet and arms tattooed chewing gum toothbrushes
with a heap of phosphate factories a heap of books heaps of kings and
it never ceases to converse in
                              heaps of artificial dens for drinking a
magnificently deserved tea sesame twigs

and
    to your health motley
crowd that changes course but not enemies
                      and who will change all
the length of your rat traps
old unconditional murder that would have given us
                            for a revolver a
whole paradise of whims
heaped on our spines but then
                  heaps of medinas full of poppies
until it makes of our remains vestiges of incomparable cities
the bird
the bird
and the bird thieves

barbarian
        the bird like our pilgrimages from one tree to another until
the tree of violence that passes through our body
and your breasts mistresses of blood your breasts we don't love the
snickering city the leech city no longer its eras of nomadisms and the
nicknames of the sun
this fucked up sun that never stops turning we will
chase it with stones

us
    with kettledrums upon serpents' nests to fraternize
with blood
        recover memory in an orgasm of moons like those calm
camels who throw blood clots upon our chest
(bleed camel from your delirious neck)
we want
mugs of foaming blood
blood clots as big as fists accomplishing
voyages hailing the desert become fish
bleed more camel bleed bleed

cities for the roses
while the roses get the twilights of the Dadès Valley

we want in this blood
the eye
        the sword
in this blood petrifying the nape of the wind
assaulting its bosom and pursuing
the crowd up to your windpipe artery
bleed camel more more

we will give you again
the bearded conspiracies of our sex
to complete your catalog of superstitions
                                        cut-off
disarticulated
                hands
streets severed head where we have pressed
all possible humanities against our terrorist breasts
streets
        ringing with the cries of heifers flogged with writing

Photo R. Huber

FIGURE 4. Untitled painting by Mohamed Hamidi. *Souffles* 5 (Rabat, 1967), p. 28. Reprinted with permission.

SELF-PORTRAIT

Albert Memmi
Translated from the French by Lia Brozgal

I was born in Tunis, in North Africa, and before the age of twenty I had hardly traveled further than sixty miles from my hometown. And because the city was divided into neighborhoods that were hostile to and suspicious of one another, I avoided wandering too far outside my own quarter. Each group, then, lived on its own terms, steeped in its own traditions, prejudices, fears, and hatreds: Arabs, Jews, French, Italians, Maltese, Greeks, Russians, . . . but I already recounted all of this in my first novel, *La statue de sel* [*The Pillar of Salt*].

Still, it may be that my second novel, *Agar* [*Strangers*], holds the key to unlocking my current existence. Two months after leaving Tunis and my neighborhood—which today seems to me like a simple dream of a past life—I married a blonde girl with blue eyes, a Catholic from eastern France, the France that looks so much like Germany. Another strange dream, one that I could never even have conceived of . . . I told this story in *Agar*: the difficulties of a mixed marriage, the clash of two cultures within the couple, and the ensuing heartbreak that led to madness and catastrophe. But in truth was this story at the root of what was to follow or was it a kind of foreshadowing?

My entire life from then on was altered, reconfigured, confronted by this event. I was forced to ask myself who I was, who I had been up until that point, and what I needed to become in order to be able to live in this new world that opened up before me. How to reconcile, within myself, East and West? A past that reached so deeply into the heart of Africa and the rational, clear study of philosophy and social sciences that I had undertaken in order to resemble the image of the Western professor that I have apparently become?

Thus, because I wanted to understand why mixed marriages failed so often, and so terribly, I undertook another book (for me, the only way to survive is to write). In *Portrait du colonisé* [Portrait of the Colonized] I believed I had uncovered—beyond what I sought concerning mixed marriages and myself—the drama of colonization and its effect on both partners within the colony: the colonizer and the colonized.[12] How their entire lives, their roles and their behavior, found themselves determined by this fundamental relationship that bound them to one another in an inexorable duo.

At the same time I had just caught a glimpse of an infinitely larger and more terrifying phenomenon: the dynamics of dominance that shapes relationships between so many human beings. It occurred to me that the same mechanisms that had helped me to understand the life of the colonized could also help me to understand the condition of the Jew. For I was Jewish as well, and even after the end of World War II, after colonization and the social upheaval, I remained separate, a minority, a frequently attacked object of suspicion. So it became necessary to undertake an inventory of my life as a Jew, and this account became *Portrait d'un Juif* [*Portrait of a Jew*], an essay that either irritated or touched so many readers because in it I revealed my unhappiness as a Jew, the Jew's constant unease, and the continued threat of others.

In *La libération du Juif* [*The Liberation of the Jew*], which has just been published by Gallimard, I continue telling the story of this journey, while at the same time attempting to catalogue the various paths to liberation—both the blind alleys and the open roads—that are available to the oppressed. I begin first with the Jew, and then extend my analysis to all kinds of oppressed people found in the contemporary moment: the Colonized, Black Americans, Women, etc. . . . . It is my belief that today the oppressed are more similar than they are different and that any man or woman who wants to be free must undertake the same struggles. Perhaps in the end I might one day sketch a general portrait of "the oppressed."

Meanwhile, and to sum up, I continue to take stock of my life. Yet, from the dreamlike happiness of my early years and the games played in the Tarfoune Impasse in Tunis—a long, deserted passage that circled back on itself twice before ending up in an abyss of silence and shadow—to the abstract life of capital cities, and through war, work camps, and decolonization, the road is too long, too chaotic: the hero no longer recognizes himself. I spend my time trying to fill the gap, to mend these multiple rifts, to sign, at the very least, a ceasefire with myself as I wait for an impossible peace.

FIGURE 5. Untitled painting by Jilali Gharbaoui. *Souffles* 6 (Rabat, 1967), p. 28. Reprinted with permission.

REALITIES AND DILEMMAS OF NATIONAL CULTURE II

Abdellatif Laâbi

Translated from the French by Safoi Babana-Hampton

> *We want our societies to rise to a higher degree of development, but on their own, by means of internal growth, interior necessity, and organic progress, without anything exterior coming to warp, alter, or compromise this growth. . . . No doctrine is worthwhile unless rethought by us, rethought for us, converted to us. . . . There is a veritable Copernican revolution to be imposed here, so ingrained in Europe (from the extreme right to the extreme left) is the habit of doing for us, arranging for us, thinking for us—in short, the habit of challenging our possession of this right to initiative, . . . which is at the end of the day the right to personality.*
>
> Aimé Césaire (Letter to Maurice Thorez)[13]

The Current Phase of Cultural Decolonization

It was incumbent upon the Third World to define itself.

The man of culture has finally grasped that no matter how objective and sympathetic the attitude of the foreign Third World expert appeared to be with regard to our sociocultural problems, the meaning of some of our circumstances would always elude him. The Third World man of culture can no longer content himself with simply watching his society, his history, his culture, and even his decolonization efforts being treated like guinea pigs in a scientific experiment. Rather he is determined to circumscribe, in accordance with his own worldview and in new terms (which now need to be urgently developed), the autopsy of colonization, the import of Ibn Khaldun's work or the spirit of popular poetry.

After all, the anxieties engendered by the colonial phenomenon are widely shared.

The European intelligentsia never wrote so abundantly on the Jewish question before the genocides perpetrated by the Nazis during the recent war. It has never been so relentlessly intent on dissecting the colonial corpse since the declaration of the System's bankruptcy.[14] The Third World man of culture cannot remain eternally trapped in the logic of these self-examinations.

On the one hand, he should unfailingly honor all invitations to call things into question and approach them with a renewed vision. On the other hand he cannot be content with unconditional admiration of a self-critique whose most ulterior motives he must seek to uncover.

The anticolonial critique undertaken by European intellectuals often rests on inauthentic logic.

We can no longer put our faith in half-measures.

What are they trying to prove to us? That the Western world simply woke up to total justice and cultural and civilizational relativism? That a dissenting West is constantly denouncing an oppressive West?

It is as if Europe were seeking to cushion its downfall with lifesavers while the loss of its civilizational luster is in full swing. At least with colonial authors we know where we stand. The scientific exploration of our bodies and of our cultural heritage had rational and openly expressed goals. The colonial author does not bog himself down with niceties and glances in our direction. He offers us up on a leaden platter to the direct experts of "pacification," to future metropolitan recruits. In this sense it is quite clear to us that he doesn't give a damn about our nightmares.

Today's European intellectual faces a more arduous task. After the dismantling of old colonial frameworks and the widespread dismissal of its politics of oppression and assimilation, he must confront a new set of dynamics and another approach.

He can no longer bar our access to his preoccupations. He is moreover aware that we have become serious interlocutors, thanks to our heightened self-consciousness and to our revolutionary struggle. We have taken our seat at the international ceremonial banquet that is the United Nations. Everything seems to indicate that our voice carries as much weight as his. He is also aware that we are informed critics.

Despite these facts, the logic of his analysis remains essentially directed to the European public whom he wants to win over to his quixotic cause as a just man and decolonizer.

From our ruins, from our babbling beginnings and our backbreaking momentum, he takes off, reassured in his endeavors by systems of thought, methodologies, and the correct terms, in order to offer us up on a platter in his turn, purified, rehabilitated, civilized perhaps once and for all, martyrs of a West that, in our compassion or our anger, we consider sullen, generous, or miserly.

It is necessary therefore to ascertain the motivations of all anticolonial works written in Europe over the past twenty years.

Are these works a simple feature of the European intellectual trends that we know to be numerous and fluctuating? Are they an outcome of the critical effort carried out from within upon the social, cultural, and human problems that Europe has been debating as a result of the past two wars? Or are they motivated by a traditional need to maintain the "propriety" of Western civilization? For isn't Europe also seeking to overcome guilt and bad conscience by a process of thorough purification?

We risk substituting the image of an open and progressive West, defender of the oppressed, for the image of a closed West, progenitor of imperialism and cultural monolithism.

A true sense of solidarity can only emerge at the level of oppression and of lived experience. It would be illusory to believe that intellectuals of the developed world, of officially recorded history, of triumphant values can share the vision and consciousness of intellectuals of the underdeveloped world, of coups d'état, illiteracy, and absent values. Furthermore, they cannot possibly share the same thought processes and human psyches.

In today's standardized world, where the technical power of the West imposes the uniformity of its sociocultural products, there is a frequent tendency to reduce *atavism* to irrational remnants of primitiveness, if not of latent racism.

Yet this atavism exists. I believe in its liberating force. Europe is distrustful of atavism only because it allowed millions of human beings to perish in its name, resulting in a feeling of immense guilt that Europe is valiantly flaunting today.

But the atavism in the name of which Nazism caused human beings to perish is a simple pretense: a set of biophysical calculations.

The kind of atavism to which we are claiming a right does not partake of this racist reductionism. It is rather an organic consciousness of cultural experiences, a descent into the history of the body and of memory.

Besides, the West's distrust of the body is not new, from Christian precepts discrediting the human organism to the extremely mechanized intellectualism of contemporary philosophies. Civilizations of the Number defend only a vague sense of embodiment referred to as "interiority."

Commercial culture in Europe suffers from sterility and castration. It eloquently testifies to its loss of the body.

If the rest of us are acutely aware of our bodies, if we sense the need to recover it in all its dimensions and correspondences, it is because colonization was a veritable *cannibalistic phenomenon,* a graft that sought the annihilation of the other and the assimilation of his body to the larger and supposedly universal body.

The atavistic sentiment is a supreme sign of authenticity and rootedness. Should the thread that links us to this atavism be broken, we would wallow in the mire of anonymity and automatism. We would align ourselves like electronic apes with the alien ways of living and thinking that exert their magnetic pull on us.

The loss of atavistic consciousness has already engendered the dehumanization of a host of Third World intellectuals and sometimes even entire social classes.[15]

These facts might seem antagonistic both to the Westerner who is generously preaching equality and universality and the Third World intellectual who aspires, following the lead of internationalist ideologies, to the equality and universalism that he considers to be a salutary gain and an acquisition of existential dignity.

We are no longer duped by such aspirations.

In the face of the current situation of appalling inequalities that exist between the developed world and the other, granting or demanding universalism can only lead to cultural, sociological, and mental assimilation of the powerless by the more powerful.

Today assimilation, which was enforced through violence during the colonial period, occurs, slowly but surely, through erosion.

Recently offered up to Latinization by one of its early advocates, African culture is ill prepared for this dialogue. The two cultural traditions cannot dialogue. Dialogue takes place on equal terms and starts from equal blank slates. The barter cannot take place when on one side values are systematic and benefit from historical continuity and an age-old prestige that protects them from any distortion, while on the other side (African culture), values are still in an embryonic state, rarely assumed by their stake-holders, and frequently drawn up and selected by actors of the opposing camp.

In this case exchange is nothing but a hoax. It is a demagogic exchange of prestige, a premature exchange that disrupts the course of development of one civilization without bringing any genuine benefit to the other.

A discordant amalgam. Not a dialogue.

On one side, centuries of growth and advancement, crises, rebirths, and on the other, barely a few decades of taking stock of things, cries of pain, the grueling work of clearing things out.

One must be very careful not to believe, at this stage of analysis, that we are opposing an older generation to a younger one, or the assurance of maturity to the chaos of vitality.

The Third World has the monumental task of bringing forth a universal contribution. But the West too must continue to question itself, not for us but for itself, according to its own social and cultural frames of reference.

The bankruptcy of many Western values is proclaimed almost everywhere in Europe, by the left and the right alike, and the West cannot meet us today or tomorrow with rotten eggs. For our vitality has become very demanding. In any case, we don't need to do for others the same work of self-examination that we are undertaking for ourselves.

The West cannot stay in the race and can no longer be of any use to us if it continues to beckon us with the plaintive echo of its inertia.

If the West truly desires to contribute to the birth of a new humanity, it must carry out its own internal cleansing, propose new ideas, abandon its own despair, its old absurd stories and destruction of the world in order to experience a fresh start and regain a new vigor.

For now the West hasn't gone beyond the recognition of its failures and guilt, chaotically protesting against the socioeconomic apparatus causing its alienation.

But this moment of self-analysis continues to expand, becoming a cycle of new beginnings where vast amounts of energy are wasted, sometimes reflecting a certain disinterest that pushes the Western man to seek elsewhere new sources of replenishment and action.

It is often at this precise moment that we encounter him.

We are sometimes compelled to turn down this extended hand. We cannot accept light-heartedly abdications of responsibility, wherever they come from.

We do not always have the strength to tell the West: Leave us in peace, this is our own business, we are now equals, there are things that you cannot understand.

Often we cannot help but let the West think for us. If there is surplus in the West, we suffer from deficiencies in the areas of research and creativity.

And all the Western intellectual has to do is take our place.

And take our place he does. Nothing appears unnatural to him in the process.

Imagine what would happen if tomorrow a futurist army of Third World experts threw itself on the history, culture, literature, and all the human sciences of the West in order to reassess and reorganize them. It's unthinkable. Such gratuitous utopias are simply unimaginable. Yet the reverse did happen and has continued to happen for over a century and a half, and nothing seems more natural in the world of equality and universalism.

Some will think this is a discourse of Jihad. The "open-minded" ideologues of our countries will add that these words are bitter expressions of powerlessness and reverse chauvinism.

No matter. The vast majority of formerly colonized populations have not yet regained a sense of self, existential self-sovereignty, or access to speech. Most intellectuals (the spokespersons of these populations) who claim to be decolonized continue to struggle unknowingly within extremely subtle structures of alienation.

For in the name of an abstract humanism, injected in heavy doses by the culture of the former oppressor, these intellectuals have rarely followed through with their reasoning and their re-evaluations.

The effluvia of humanism, the so-called sacred values of Art-Beauty-Wisdom-Reason-Self, and all the bibles handed down from Socrates-Aristotle to Marx-Lenin-Sartre, are so many lessons and indoctrinations. This has endowed the fiercest Third World representatives with flashes of gentleness in the eyes, a fervent tone of voice, the human virtues of tenderness and sensitivity, an avant-garde progressivism, all qualities that are highly valued in former metropolises where one is struck with wonder in the face of so much resemblance and verve.

However, authenticity is a state of perpetual vigilance within the psyche and the body. In sum it is an extremism!

For a Third World intellectual, extremism means that one should not let go of the thread in the middle of the labyrinth; it means that one must not prematurely compromise. It is an uprooting of contingencies and easy friendships, a permanent anxiety of being, of being whole with no artificial limbs or spare parts.

Universalism, then, is a hornet's nest, not only for major intellectual or ideological trends, but also for personal interiority, for the lush forests of human feelings.

The way we apprehend death, love, war, or the cosmos are so many signs of our authenticity or alienation.

The extremism we have in mind is at the antipodes of fanaticism.

If the Third World decides to choose for itself, to define itself on its own terms, to rebel against a politics of assimilation or to be wary of interventionism, this does not necessarily mean that it condemns the West entirely in order to strip it of the monopoly of thought, creation, and action.

In the long run the Third World will certainly need to relearn the West, to re-approach it not through psychological complexes or caustic critiques, but rather with the serenity of knowledge turned into a need for dialogue.

The West is still for many of us a complex concept, if not an opaque one.

The forced marriage that we entered into failed with the brutality of any divorce. We are realizing that despite all this mental and cultural coexistence we have neither given nor received anything definitive.

If the West wishes today to learn about us all over again, it is not up to us to refuse it. But the West is equipped for that. Furthermore, such a learning experience is wholesome for its moral wellbeing.

The time is not yet ripe for us to engage in a similar enterprise.

In our circuitous return to the world, we have discovered that some phases are more urgent than others. The unconditional reappropriation of our cultural destiny is, at this stage, an infinitely more urgent and vital decision than any nuanced redefinition of the West.

Those of our intellectuals who are encouraged by the Western trial of colonialism and its sequels, who are "understood" and welcomed there with open arms, should not rush to thank the West at the expense of their lucidity and of what remains most urgent for them: the quest for their own identity. Often denigrating structures of alienation specific to the colonial period, these intellectuals soon fall into other traps.

For almost all the critical and analytical tumult taking place over there keeps us in an invisible role. The Third World intellectual who finds himself in this situation is unable to attain a stage of full responsibility. As a speaker, critic, or dissident, he most often undergoes the significant ceremony of "introductions." Publishers, opportunists, and progressives are entangled against their will in a production-consumption system controlled by capital. There is a market for culture. Generous ideas do not put bread on the table, and so the Third World intellectual is always "introduced." Whether his work is addressed or not to the European public, the presenter (who vouches for him through his name) always succeeds in demonstrating that Europe is not wholly absent from it. What we finally end up with, in the areas of publication and distribution, is an economic and moral integration of the work.

But an even more dangerous consequence (which follows from the first two integrations) is the work's cultural integration.

Thus, if colonization produced decolonizers in Europe, it also produced a state of mind among a class of intellectuals who are increasingly out of step with European cultural realities. This group is acutely aware of Europe's cultural breathlessness and ardently turns to any form of vitality coming from the outside.

Through friendship, encouragements, and support, this class of intellectuals at times directs the work of the Third World intellectual, pushes him toward various literary and artistic temptations (strongly shaped by an underlying exoticism) which appeal first and foremost to its own needs and obsessions.[16]

The Third World intellectual can no longer accept such a state of affairs. It represents a diversion from the normal course of things, a communicational dependence he can only accept at the detriment of his creative authenticity.

And yet he must be aware of this situation in order to free himself and grasp the urgency of an action in its proper context. A total revolutionary act that must thwart pathological slogans and borrowed formulas and which, by disrupting the obstacles of dependency and the multiple forms of exploitation under way, will allow the Third World man of culture to finally fulfill his responsibilities.

National culture is neither a negation nor a will to closure. *A will, a necessity, and a condition of being,* it cannot be reached through the back door.

It is an arduous journey that Third World men of culture must take on. An epic of the body and of memory involving a measure of risk.

ahmed cherkaoui
n'est plus

Depuis jeudi 17 août 1967, Ahmed CHERKAOUI n'est plus. Sa disparition, survenue au moment où il s'apprêtait à vivre définitivement au Maroc, a eu un effet de profonde consternation sur tous ceux qui avaient eu l'occasion de le connaître lui ou son œuvre.

L'homme et le peintre, tout au long d'une vie courte certes mais combien intense cependant, ont su donner, l'un à son pays, l'autre à la peinture, le meilleur d'eux mêmes. Esprit à la fois tendre et violent, généreux à coup sûr, cœur ardent et tenace, CHERKAOUI a milité activement pour la création d'un musée d'Art Moderne en même temps qu'il a assigné à son œuvre la tâche difficile et magistrale d'inscrire la peinture marocaine dans le sens de l'Universel.

Abdelhamid DZIRI

FIGURE 6. Abdelhamid Dziri, "Ahmed Cherkaoui is no longer with us," homage to Ahmed Cherkaoui, with painting by Cherkaoui. *Souffles* 6 (Rabat, 1967), p. 48. Reprinted with permission.

MOROCCAN PAINTING TODAY

Toni Maraini

Translated from the French by Addie Leak

Thanks to the aesthetic experiments and choices of a few artists, some of whom have taken these choices to the limit, Moroccan painting has begun to be liberated from the "absurd" cultural factors that characterized it in the past. Although those factors continue to shape official art as well as the work of marginal painters, they have been self-consciously eliminated from the works discussed in this issue.

In the past few years a new situation has arisen that is defining the role of the avant-garde in the history of Moroccan painting.

It is not my intention here, nor is it within my capabilities, to outline a history of painting in Morocco. Here and abroad this history too often is summarized in overly generalized rhetorical studies when what is really needed is a rigorous, sustained analysis.

Our primary goal is to isolate the main characteristics of the Moroccan avant-garde. However, with the help of the materials assembled in this issue (chronology, biographies, etc.), the reader can develop an idea—general, but as clear and documented as possible—of the path that Moroccan painting has followed.

We know that avant-garde cultural action is only possible if we can destroy the provincial superstructure based on egotism, opportunism, intellectual laziness, and artistic conventionalism. Then it becomes possible for artists to set forth on a creative adventure that is free, open, proud, and without inhibitions. The painters that we present here have, more or less completely and more or less recently, developed an awareness of this superstructure and have left it behind.

Two basic issues arose as painters sought to promote modern art through their works and ideas: that of the "avant-garde" (the present in relation to the future and the demands of contemporary life) and that of tradition (the present in relation to the past and the traditional values of the visual arts). In questioning themselves on these issues, or in being brutally confronted by them, they had to make choices. Each of these artists did so according to their experience and degree of engagement; for some, they were both urgent and painful.

It is in the rational balance between these two forms of coming to consciousness that the most important work is to be found.

These painters have chosen different aesthetic paths and visual forms of expression. Although the figurative—in its open and graphic aspect—interests some of them, most of these artists pursue the non-representational and abstract.

Theirs is an unfinished language in terms of material usefulness (its purpose is not to commemorate a battle or glorify a landscape), but—as has been the case in popular aesthetics—it speaks to the inner sensibility of the viewer. The artist's use of a deliberate "sign system" suggests a particular interpretation, yet without constraining the viewer's free participation in the work. Such freedom always disconcerts academic audiences—whose imagination has atrophied as a result of scholastic explanations—because it shakes them up and asks them to participate actively in the painter's creative process.

Non-representative language is traditionally predominant in Morocco, and when we consider the context, this is more for its immanent and collective qualities than for its contingent and descriptive ones. It is by way of this biological heritage that some of the painters in this issue are able to grasp in direct and intense ways the artistic problems that have forced their way into the field of inquiry today, without going through the cultural battles European artists had to wage against centuries of academic dogmatism.

Each of these painters has a unique technique and style.

Gharbaoui's work largely focuses on movement and nervous brushstrokes. With chromatic disorder and an automated vitality, he creates a neutral space and an active, expressive material. *Bennani* is interested in space insofar as it can contain movement and balance forms. Controlled by that structure, forms subdivide into solid juxtaposed masses. In *Hamidi*'s work the chromatic construction opens up the canvas to different dimensions. Just as he chooses superposed horizontal elements as his focal points, he establishes a balance with the complementary vibrations of his colors. A more formal relationship between visual and mental realities can be seen in *Seffaj*'s work, but that search carries him towards an original analysis of forms and materials cut asymmetrically in a graphic order. The paintings of *Melehi, Ataallah,* and the last period of *Chebaa* are constructed in geometric spaces by means of signs, signals, well-defined forms, and optical colors. Carefully choosing only the elements that interest them, they compose and superimpose them in a balanced and intelligent order. Through the vibration of colors and spaces, they sometimes achieve dimensions that project them off the canvas. Coming from a more "physical" emotion, *Belkahia* manages, in his last work, to isolate forms, organic and surreal entities, which he organizes on a monochromatic metal background.

Parallel to these experiments, some of these painters have investigated the invariables of tradition as it relates to the present, analyzing, inventorying, and detecting its different aspects and values.

Melehi, Chebaa, and Belkahia, and the pedagogical and cultural initiatives taken by l'École des Beaux Arts in Casablanca have provided a solid base for these investigations.

In analyzing the world of forms surrounding them, these artists discovered an entire tradition that had been forgotten and neglected: popular rural and urban art, its visual laws, its stylistic patterns, and its psychological significance.

It is often through a discovery like this one—in conjunction with cultural demands and the search for an authentic source—that the artistic experience of a country is enriched (consider, for example, the cases of Russia in the 1920s, Mexico, and Japan).

What was discovered in Morocco was the artistic production that accompanied, and still accompanies, the daily visual life of the population. In the past, foreign studies have taken into consideration some aspects of this visual life, but the ambiguous, rigid character of these studies harmed rather than contributed to a better understanding of the subject. Thus, poorly understood, little known, and only superficially appreciated, this artistic production was catalogued alongside folkloric curiosities, relegated to the scholar's warehouse. It was also directed towards a commercial and speculative productivity that finally landed it in the impasse of touristic artisanry (here, see the particular role played by the Service des Arts Indigènes, with its official "stamping stations," its "artisanal reeducation," etc., activities now continued by the Services de l'Artisanat.)[17]

This popular artistic production is at once mobile (various individual pieces) and monumental (architecture and architectural "ornamentation"). Function guides the production process: the aesthetic elements are organically coordinated according to their intended use, aim, and materials. It is based on canons that have been "rationally" determined by time, experience, and the continuous collectivization of individual inventions, yet, at the same time, these canons are always open to modification, interpretation, and new and irrational interference. These works are generally created in nonfigurative or abstract language that is often also "iconic" or stylized. It is a rich, warm language, visually quite varied. Linked to the ancient Mediterranean, Saharan, and African traditions, it developed in keeping with the fundamental "Gestalt" and "iconographic" laws.[18]

While on a superficial level this art is considered "decorative" in an academic terminology and tradition that assign decoration the secondary role of "embellishment" (see the Larousse dictionary), it is in fact as meaningful and expressive as any other art form. The only difference is that the visual means (geometric, abstract, or figurative) and succession of ideographic "signs" that it employs to draft its pictographic composition are, by their universal, primary, and symbolic nature, too radically distanced from the visual means to which official and urban art has often had access in order to allow for a more open, unconditioned appreciation of art. However, the sensitive observer should be able to detect the creative factor at every level of human artistic production.

Indeed, it is no accident that in Morocco this "discovery" was first made by painters. But for them it wasn't about recopying traditional popular art or about formally, mechanically drawing inspiration from it. Their reciprocal relationship goes deeper. In this art they locate a spirit and collective invariables and draw from them an interiorized visual strength.

In the end the different aspects of popular art offer material for analysis that is of utmost importance. This is why the traditional, preindustrial, harmonious aspect and—in some ways equally urgent and imperative, its degeneration into touristic artisanry and its transition into urban pseudo-modernization—draws the attention of artists. This transition—made worse by the rapid introduction of speculative sub-sub-par Western products, as well as by the creator's lack of modern aesthetic preparation when he mechanically "makes" ugly, half-utilitarian, half-decorative objects without being able to express himself either traditionally or personally—threatens to remain a long and hybrid process, giving way only to sterile, grotesque production.

Painters must intervene to suggest an appropriate and healthy aesthetic, either in terms of the quotidian technological object (industrial design) or in terms of the means of collective communication (graphic art, advertisement, calligraphy, photography, etc.).

Their work, then, is not only at the level of individual creation but falls into the framework of collective visual education.

For some time now the artists of l'École in Casablanca have been constructively committed to this path.[19]

*

Toni Maraini was born in Tokyo in 1941, grew up in Sicily, and studied art history in Rome, Florence, at the University of London, and at Smith College (USA). She wrote her dissertation on contemporary art and was granted her doctorate in 1964; she is currently preparing a publication on popular world art.

When I moved to Morocco, my encounter with art was very important to me. But when I tried to better situate, historically and culturally, what I saw in the visual realm (especially in terms of applied and popular art)—not because I wanted to become a specialist, but for the sake of my own curiosity and intellectual need—I realized that, in terms of "general culture," this art existed in a void, a psychological hole. Almost all the studies I consulted failed to satisfy me.

I am interested in certain issues in visual perception and the contemporary aesthetic and social experience. I have thus chosen to undertake a study of popular world art, the function of collective and nonacademic rural and urban art, its social role, its benefits for psychological equilibrium, and in some cases, its disappearance and reappearance in the context of collective urban and technological art. This study will be the subject of a larger work.

FIGURE 7. Untitled painting by Mohamed Ataallah. *Souffles* 7–8 (Rabat, 1967), p. 82. Reprinted with permission.

FIGURE 8. Two untitled paintings by Mohamed Chebaa. *Souffles* 7–8 (Rabat, 1967), p. 84. Reprinted with permission.

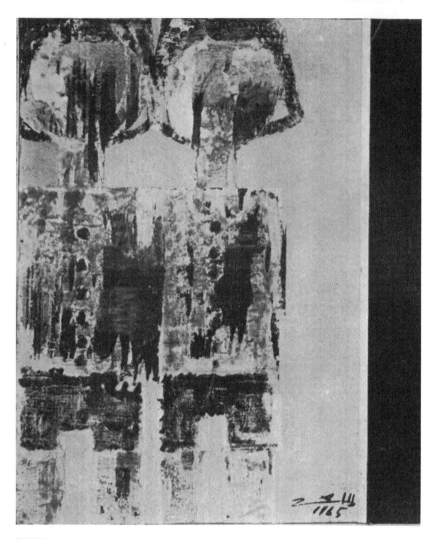

FIGURE 9. Untitled painting by Saad Ben Seffaj. *Souffles* 7–8 (Rabat, 1967), p. 85. Reprinted with permission.

PART THREE

SOUFFLES 9–13–14 (1968–1969)

BEGINNING WITH THE NINTH ISSUE, *Souffles* widened its horizons to the postcolonial tricontinent, including expressions of solidarity with Palestinians after the 1967 Israeli-Arab war, coverage from the January 1968 Cultural Congress in Havana, and reports from China and Vietnam. In its ninth issue *Souffles* published a dossier of documents from the Havana congress, from which we have included a public talk given by the Haitian writer René Depestre, entitled "The Winding Course of Negritude." Depestre lambasts François Duvalier and the Haitian black bourgeoisie for coopting Negritude as a marker of difference and exploiting the history of racial conflict in Haiti in order to perpetuate ever-widening class distinctions. In contrast, invoking Aimé Césaire as the Black Orpheus (a title originally bestowed on the Martinican poet by Sartre), Depestre praises revolutionary Cuba for embracing Césaire's strategic valuation of blackness as a step toward the social integration of the races. Comparably irate, Bernard Jakobiak's "Camus the Colonizer in Denial" offers a prescient postcolonial reading of *The Plague*, Camus's best-known novel. Jakobiak censures Camus for misrepresenting the Maghreb's colonized populations to the vast metropolitan audience that had canonized him as one of France's most acclaimed contemporary writers.

These issues of *Souffles* also showcase Maghrebi literature in both French and Arabic, staging a dialogue between two corpuses that had been confined to separate spheres owing to colonial-era divisions between the French and Arabic languages. In his energetic essay "Generation Drive" the prolific Arabic-language author and critic Mohammed Berrada outlines the challenges and responsibilities of the up-and-coming generation of Arabophone Maghrebi writers. Remarking that these young writers are fortunate to be able to draw their inspiration from past and present revolutionary writers of the Arab East as well as Europe, he insists that they must be wary of creating a "hybrid" literature unmoored from national concerns and calls upon them first and foremost to write an activist literature. While Berrada echoes some of the concerns expressed by Laâbi in his prose contributions to the first few issues, he emphasizes that an avant-garde response to Arabic literary tradition could and must serve as a powerful motivation for contemporary Maghrebi writers of Arabic expression.

We have included two texts that appeared in Arabic in *Souffles*, which, in different ways, criticize the Moroccan sociopolitical status quo. Mohamed Zafzaf's "Afternoon, with the Sun" delivers, in mesmerizing monotone, a hyperrealist attention to the internal and external events that befall a young man one afternoon as he suffers from the boredom of underemployment and the anxiety of an uncertain future. Ahmed al-Madini's "A Beginning but No End" interpellates the reader in the second person as witness and propagator of an all-consuming fire that at once allegorizes rage and advances revolution.

The texts written in French range in tone from furious to jocular to fantastical, and experiment with the politicization of all modes of literature. Tahar Ben Jelloun's first published poem, "Dawn of Tombstones," puts into question the political role of poetry in the context of repressive state violence. In the preface to his collected poems, Ben Jelloun recounts how his participation, along with his fellow college students in Rabat, in the protests that led to the violent state repressions of March 23, 1965, resulted in their forced conscription into the Moroccan army. He traces his origins as a poet to this eighteen-month period of thinly "disguised incarceration," during which time he secretly wrote this poem and others in the bathroom of the barracks.[1] Extending a colloquial metaphor for young men who can find no skilled employment—"the shoeshine boys"—he fantasmatically portrays how his generation's aspirations for collective social prosperity have been crushed by political and economic repression. Denouncing the exploitation of Moroccan space and culture as a tourist haven for American soldiers returning home from Vietnam, Ben Jelloun critiques global networks of neocolonialism by which his country, by serving as a vacation destination for the soldiers employed in a neo-imperial military campaign in another part of the world, remains shackled to the interests of the military-industrial complex. (Vitriol against Orientalist tourism also dominates his "Planet of the Apes.") In these contexts the speaker accuses Orpheus, the personification of poetic tradition, of silence, ignorance, and indifference in the face of his suffering people. Calling him back to the "city"—an invocation of the Greek polis that exemplifies the ideal of a democratic, participatory society—he instructs Orpheus to bury the dead and lead the reckoning of the country's losses through violent forays into independence. The double invocation of Orpheus in this issue indicates that *Souffles* contributors continued to envision poetic creation at the center of the sociopolitical transformations they so proactively sought.

GROTTE

Mostafa Nissabouri

Translated from the French by Guy Bennett

The bird had opened a number of doors as well as windows, the room had become a sort of fortress whose walls were only partially visible; the rest was shrouded in nitrogen. He believed the doors were open so that the extravagant paraphernalia he used to activate what-I-told-him could be brought in.

We called him the fowl because he only had one leg and because he looked like a cross between a falcon and Ali Baba. Fowl? I don't get it. At any rate his missing leg had been cut off by a black genie who had flung him into the Egyptian desert; having more than one trick in his bag, the fowl managed to turn the genie into an ass and rode him all the way back to Chaouia, where he changed him into a pebble: What became of the genie turned ass?

a pebble, a pebble.

Plus he could stir up a whole cemetery to dig you out some old talisman (like those two sheep jawbones tied with string around a piece of fabric used for the menses of a peasant girl now working as a barmaid in the sirocco, for example) or conjure their movement beneath, or quite simply besiege your brain with Akkadian and Sumerian temples, proceed to the resurrection of Nineveh or the famous Bilqis, Yemeni queen and gazelle. He wields both shadow and mythological symbols with equal dexterity to reveal treasures to you (he mated with an octopus) in the midst of ruins or even in a no-man's land son of the radiant collapse of Writing and of the bark that filled Us with smoke. Too late for machines, too much, the love of the woman Split open from navel to spinal column, he hunts reptiles, wolfs them down; he is in a position to ward off all calamities.

So much for the sirocco. Regarding your fondness, said he, for destroyed cities, it's a question of epidermis and biological organization. But the fowl hadn't immediately grasped the importance of the epic I was clamorously demanding of him. He grabbed a scapula and threw it through one of the doors that surrounded us. But I was born under the third moon of peregrinations and would need suitcases. Take the elevator. I don't know how to use an elevator or a monkey wrench or even a radio set, it is truly depraved for me. Call on your great intuition; put humanity in one hand (your left), your heart in the other hand, next knead them into a dough good for stunning jackals, then you enter. I enter. I leave the fowl behind and I enter. He wrapped himself in trees and opened the hatches of his memory.

I don't know how to enter a fortress? Maybe there is and there is. Maybe a woman in a kif-filled landscape saying here's your dinner. Maybe I don't know how to do the twist? I've seen people doing the twist with delight beyond compare, full of handbills and trolleys, or even with truly picturesque ease since we could see their heads rocking and nodding at will. Let's not mention the whole body, especially not the hips, but I don't know how to do the twist. The *guedra* maybe. Besides the *guedra*'s easy; all you have to do is spread your hands and fingers, make like a camel, it's a desert thing even if it's oddly modern. I want to make love and fight! aren't the arabesques spellbinding? each motif has a touch of soul but can I take it further, go beyond? Useless leap say the astrologers as I report this entirely human side of the disorientation that I'm afraid to make longer as. Very much agree with myself, that's the main thing. Let me make it even longer. The mutations. I'll take humanity in my two hands I calculate suicidal distances and tell myself Love the brothers they are victims of the bee's dappled dreams and Western incomprehension. As for me, I never knew, I have only ever seen turbans and eyes with a long-repressed pain. In other words:

I leave the fowl and reconsider my compass. I haven't yet gone through the door, the fortress is still there. The fowl spoke of ships. Speak my brother. There would be ever so many doors, but all would apparently be made of illusions; verily, they wouldn't exist, only a princess is exempt from this abstraction because of her breasts, her bulbous breasts. I shall go through it. My only condition is an irrational bird.

There is something terrifying in the family tree, especially when there's a bunch of walls talking left and right. A slaughter. And there are camels that go unmentioned, can you imagine? Not one photo in the paper (I've seen some bearing a pouch filled with hydrogen and coagulated blood in their mouths going glug in this venous balloon big as two fists).

I shall enter no door, the fowl is purely legendary, I go out. I leave the scapula, princess, and fortress. The miracle is not at all the fact of being accepted with one's head, oblong, farcical, surgical; both comic and tragic; for a gravity worthy of the gods of Jama'a al-Fna; not to mention that irritating nostalgia the words of love that throw you from one end of yourself to the other. The miracle would consist of a resistance permit that you camouflage to deceive your incivility, your scorn for age-old traditions; your invariably unreasonable calculation your sexual Middle Ages; your lack of rigor and luck; your meaningless universality, your circulatory upheaval, your conspiracy-filled Sundays. To you I shall only dictate (said the fowl) the voice of reason. They wrap you up in a *gandoura*, they decorate you in the name of the multifarious fraternity, your hands are full of silhouettes, the fortress the princess and the rest. Such is our miracle comrades, false, unfortunate, wrecked by tears. With a resistance permit you can get clogs and hardtack. Yet let us glorify ourselves with our voices, they are irresistible, we shall call stars the Mothers of fornication, the oh how high I could have been had there not been roses and more roses in the night. How high we could have been, comrades. It is the secret of a tiny princess we must unveil. For the glory. We keep silent. The fowl has returned.

With a volcano he has returned. Says so much the better if Arabs have no clue about metaphysics and sits down. I, sir, am very well versed in metaphysics. He says that's all right that's great.

Then addressing the volcano O volcano he devours it and sets fire to the fortress which collapses. All that remains are the blackened doors where astonished we shall sing the decadence of peoples, tenderly, worthy, heroic O volcano you hide in the roses and roses are hard, so called roses that depart this life O volcano burn the room and Nineveh and Bilqis: to muck up the complexity of history, get the f*** out, elsewhere, toward the shanty towns to get armed, elsewhere, what I said to the fowl, the big laugh.

THE WINDING COURSE OF NEGRITUDE

René Depestre

Translated from the French by Laura Reeck

If one is interested in following the winding course of Negritude Haiti is the best country in the world to consider at present because, as Aimé Césaire said, "Negritude rose for the first time" in Haiti and because Negritude is now the ideology sustaining the most hideous tyranny in contemporary history.[2] In light of the collective horrors Haitians have experienced, critical examination of Negritude can have profound meaning for oppressed blacks around the world. We know that every ideology, in its representation of reality and the objectives it pursues, tends to give imaginary value to a particular social class's aspirations. Marx called this process of deforming reality "mystification." In Haiti, when studying the role of Negritude in our national history, pseudo-sociologists like François Duvalier have always scrutinized the concept in isolation instead of analyzing it within the context of the history of class relations. In separating the question of race from the economic development and social history of Haiti, and in giving it an absolute and mythical dimension, they have reduced Haitian history to a series of chaotic ethnic conflicts between mulattos and blacks, who from the time of our independence became the reigning oligarchy of the country. On a broader level this is also what happens when one separates racist dogma from the evolution of colonial societies: the history of colonized peoples becomes a series of conflicts between "Blacks" and "Whites." In the case of Haiti, the question of race, far from being a determining factor in the development of Haitian society, has only led to *mystification*, which in the consciousness of two competing aristocracies has served to hide the real stakes and motivations of class struggle.

And yet this question of race is a very important *social reality* in Haiti. We know that Marx, while denying spiritual dogmas a pivotal place in the historical process of a given society, retains them as a *social reality*, so while they cannot change the general course of history, they can modify its shape, pace, and circumstances. In its function as a social reality, racial ideology has influenced the unfolding of our national history and, at certain moments of acute crisis, modified the pace and circumstances of class struggle in our country. Since 1946, Haitian society has been in a general state of crisis, primarily because of U.S. economic domination, and the color question once again occupies center stage on the political and ideological fronts and again veils the reality of class struggle. Since 1946 people of the black petite bourgeoisie, like Duvalier, have been allied with landholding blacks and "compradore" mulattos. Together they control political power, use the notion of "Negritude" demagogically, and have attempted to make the black masses believe that they hold power and that the "Duvalier revolution" is a resounding victory for Negritude. For the past ten years the atrocious acts associated with the Duvalier regime have completely destroyed the falsified image of this myth in the minds of our people. The horrible Duvalier dictatorship has led Haitians to question the ideas they have long had of themselves. In their eyes Haiti is no longer fixed as that mythical figure imprinted in school on the consciousness of every Haitian: *Haiti, first Black Republic in modern history, homeland and myth to black men, cradle and "paradise" of Negritude!* As a result of their intense suffering, Haitians have realized that power, whether in the hands of blacks, whites, mulattos, or indigenous groups in a semicolonial system, is always a brutal force that dehumanizes people and their social and cultural history. For the past ten years as never before Haitians have seen what blacks and mulattos like them are capable of when they defend tooth and nail the interests of a small, privileged minority and a totalizing imperialism. Haitians now realize that the exaltation of any given race is a pointless absurdity that always masks violent attacks on the oneness of humankind. Haitians see blacks and mulattos, tyrants, criminals with no shame, obscurantists, Nazis, *tontons-macoutes*, because they do not have any *particular essence*; they are bourgeois through and through. And in the era of the terrorist dictatorship of capital, they may be guilty of crimes as heinous as those committed by Hitler in the concentration camps or those perpetrated today by Yankee Pentagon officials in North and South Vietnam. Of course Duvalier's tyranny provides a monstrous caricature of Negritude, and so one must not throw out the baby with the bloody bathwater and conclude that this concept was destined to lead to an assault on the human condition. As a doctrine, *socialism* aims to liberate man, but *national-socialism* was a means of exterminating man. It all depends upon how a dominant class uses an ideology to hide base and selfish ends. Today black bourgeoisies wield their power through neocolonial intrigues and violence in Africa and the Americas, and they have too hastily seized the concept of Negritude as their ideological weapon. They have done so because they know that at one point in history—in the works of such black writers as Jean Price-Mars, W. E. B. Du Bois, Aimé Césaire, Jacques Roumain, Langston Hughes, Claude MacKay, Nicolás Guillen, J. S. Alexis, Cheikh Anta Diop, Frantz Fanon, etc.—this concept expressed very forcefully the double alienation of oppressed blacks. And so, this concept of Negritude belonged to an isolated moment in the history of decolonization, when the brutalized and humiliated black man offered his *affective rebuttal* to the white colonizer's thorough disdain. Just as the white colonizer turned his privileged position in the systems of slavery and colonization into an *epidermization* of his supposed biological superiority, the black man, in his oppressed, pariah condition—of being alienated in one's own skin—was led along a completely different path to *epidermize* his lamentable historical situation. In this way, at its best Negritude was a cultural movement through which black African and American intellectuals seized upon the worth and originality of Negro-African cultures as well as the aesthetic value of the black race and the ability of its peoples to enter into the history that was forcibly denied to them in the colonial adventure. In its most legitimate expression, for instance in the poetry of Césaire, Negritude inspired *the realization that the black proletarian is doubly alienated: in the first instance he is alienated like the white proletarian insofar as he provides a labor force traded on the capitalist market; in the second he is alienated because of his black skin, in his epidermic singularity*. Negritude was thus the new consciousness of this double alienation and of the historical imperative to move beyond it through revolutionary praxis.

One must not forget that, as a result of racist dogma, the great majority of Whites believed that the black man's eternal crime (in addition to being of the proletariat) was his *skin color*. This despicable ideological mystification is still leveraged against Blacks in the United States, South Africa, Rhodesia, etc. The epidermic singularity of blacks or mulattos, instead of being one of the objectively random phenomena at work in the history of humankind, became an *evil essence* in the consciousness of all the slavers of the world, *the sign of the absolute evil of the black man as a social being*, the sign and the stigmata of an unassailable inferiority. Metaphysical and aesthetic meaning were given to the skin color of both blacks and whites. And, as if issued by divine right, it was irrevocably decided that only the black man is colored, whereas the "White" basks in the light. As Sartre has said, "the whiteness of his skin was another look, condensed light," and it was thus the white man's historical destiny to enlighten the rest of humankind with the lumines-cent virtues of his white skin.[3] The desire to *objectify the black man as a commodity* found its rationale and pretext in the long colonial process of epidermizing the historical situation of black peoples. Negritude, in literature and art as well as in ethnology and history, was in its be-ginnings *a legitimate form of revolt* against the detestable manifestations of racial ideology in the world. By force, fire, and blood, colonization opened up the floodgates of universal history to the bloody *white-black binary* in order to hide and justify capitalist exploitation. Negritude postulated the need to move beyond this binary, not through a new mystification, but rather through collective revolutionary praxis. Un-fortunately more often than not Negritude is used as a myth that obfus-cates *the existence of the black bourgeoisie*, who, in Haiti as in numerous African countries, formed a dominant class. And just like any class that oppresses another, the black bourgeoisie relies on ideological mystifica-tion to hide the real nature of social relations. Today, for both black and white mystifiers, Negritude implies the absurd idea that the black man is endowed with a particular "human nature," equipped with an es-sence that belongs to him alone. And so he is called upon, according to writers like Janheinz Jahn, to give to Europe and the West in general "more soul"—of which the West is apparently in great need. For the Senegalese president, the poet Léopold Sédar Senghor, *"emotion is black like reason is Greek."*[4] In this way all class contradictions are abstracted, and the black bourgeoisies from Africa and the Americas can, in all confidence and with the good blessings of neocolonialism, freely take advantage of black workers in the name of a shared spirituality. That is what we find in the writings of the Belgian essayist Lilyan Kesteloot, who wanted to show *"Negritude as being-in-itself"*—the permanent and eternal state of a singular essence. Like other European "specialists" working on Negritude, Lilyan Kesteloot locks the Negro man in black-ness and the white man in whiteness. She writes, "Understood in this sense, 'black soul' belongs to all time and has not been 'surpassed,' as maintained by Sartre and others whom he influenced. No more than

Slavic soul, Arab soul, or French *esprit* have been surpassed."[5] According to this elementary and impudent logic, "Negritude," far from articulating a revolution leading to dis-alienation and the total decolonization of Africa and the two black Americas, cannot hide the fact that it serves as one of the pillars supporting tricks, traps, and hypocritical neocolonialist actions. *Abstracted from the historical context of the revolution in the Third World, and separated arbitrarily from the immediate needs of the global tricontinental struggle* of underdeveloped people against imperialism and neocolonialism, Negritude has given rise to an unacceptable "black Zionism." It has become a way of *leading black peoples away from their duty to make revolution.*

BLACK ORPHEUS IN THE REVOLUTION

Twenty years ago, when the *concept of Negritude* was defined by the great Martinican poet Aimé Césaire in his unforgettable *Cahier d'un retour au pays natal* [*Notebook of a Return to the Native Land*] and by Jean-Paul Sartre in his famous essay "Orphée noir" ["Black Orpheus"], wherever one turned one's gaze, one could see this Black Orpheus taking the wind out of the white bourgeoisie's sails. At that time in Africa "Black Orpheus" was not President of the Republic and did not drive around in a luxury Mercedes-Benz; he did not buy shares in the mines of the Upper Katanga; he did not align himself, over the dead body of Patrice Lumumba, with the most adventuresome speculators in international finance in order to obtain profitable shares. In the past twenty years the waters of the Congo have passed under many bridges, and it is not merely with Aimé Césaire's poetic lyricism that Negritude has flowed into the sea. Césaire's Negritude was expectant patience. It was the necessary irruption of the rebellious consciousness of the oppressed Negro. It was an opening onto the specific requirements for a national liberation movement. Twenty years ago Sartre asked the following question: *"What will happen then if he allows himself to be defined by only his objective condition?"*[6] Our response to Jean-Paul Sartre: look at Cuba and you will find the answer. Notice how Negritude has integrated the socialist revolution, and how it transcends itself through a historical process of dis-alienation through which whites, blacks, and mulattos are less and less opposed with every passing day and through which *the dramatic outcome of their destinies resolves itself in the same obvious human truth: revolution.* Not Negritude but rather *this very real process of decolonization* is alone capable of mobilizing all the energies of underdeveloped people on the three continents. *Black Orpheus cannot find his lost Eurydice except through revolution,* and in the revolution, which alone can, with the creative force of the people, annihilate all the hells that humanity has constructed for itself. The new Black Orpheus will be revolutionary or will not be.

PALMA

Mohammed Ismaïl Abdoun

Translated from the French by Jennifer Moxley

> 'Tis the times' plague when madmen lead the blind.
>
> Shakespeare, *King Lear* (4.1.46)

. . . here I am at the end of my secular sleep. I let out a snort and its thrust pulls up from the dwarf palm tree all of my old sap.

I'm here. It's chilly. I am here and it is chilly. My long thin fingers stiffen. It's chilly. I am here. I am here and I don't even know if she will show up. It's chilly. It's chilly. It's chilly.

I waited for her. It rained. She showed up. She showed up lost inside her hair. She was picking at her teeth with a wire brush—tooth pick, mirror, and comb—It was raining. We drank coffee; smoked; we eyed each other guardedly. Then we ate a tuna salad with tomatoes and some scrambled eggs. Drank coffee; smoked; eyed each other guardedly.

It rained all night. All night long she told me her life story in a voice sometimes monotone sometimes fiery, hoping to *change* me she said. By dawn the rain had stopped. She left brought low by my inability to promise an eternity to her. She left lost inside her hair and tears worrying her cheeks with her wire brush.

Truthfully I knew well what she wanted, what had driven her to speak to me in this way. Women fear frogs. She feared Palma, but above all she was jealous. I tried my best to explain to her that it was absurd but she didn't want to hear any of it. I want you all to myself she said. I tried in vain to make her understand that in this place everyone is for himself alone and God is for no one . . .

In the morning when the rain had stopped she left in a rage threatening to return with the police, to sue me for having betrayed her . . . She left. I am here. It is chilly. She showed up for real. Her chilly fingertips let me know. I am in a graveyard of absence.

Eventually I too went out. The rain had stopped but it was foggy. An empty shell of a day. A chamomile day. A deworming day.

A one-way day. A day wrapped in barbed, rusted, electric wires. A half-blind day. A pus-filled day. A bald pimp of a day dressed up in a Napoleon hat. A swimming upstream day. An indecent day.

The streets were steep and slippery. People gathered together in groups on the corners. Anyone who lost his footing was dead. It was necessary for people to walk in small groups and cling to each other in order to keep from slipping.

When the rain stopped the silence of long days of bad weather was replaced by a tremendous brouhaha. Impossible to distinguish a clear utterance. People *talked just to talk*. They waded through an uncertain language.

I left my garret. All I had with me was an ash-gray piece of lichen, a pair of moth-eaten socks, black glasses, and an old transistor radio.

In the streets the people grouped face to face. They went spontaneously towards each other as if old friends. Those on their own didn't last long; after an astounding glide they crashed, dead, onto the ground. They were quickly removed so as to not block circulation. Though some groups were more audacious than others. They succeeded in freeing their arms—which were long—to keep their balance, and with their hands cupped in front of their mouths they shouted jackal-like cries through the opaque air and then waited, serious and satisfied, for the returning echo of their voices—which plunged others into ecstasy and fright by turns—. Afterwards they noisily applauded and embraced each other. Unable to applaud, the others let out great incomprehensible and lacerating cries.

As for me I knew the score. These acrobats were pranksters. Some of them, well hidden, stooped down to catch hold of their feet while they launched their cries and jiggled about.

I went out to join the group festivities. But really I was running away. I was afraid that she might return with the police. Here the price you pay for indifference to love is permanent incarceration.

I shaved the walls walking sideways like a crab. I was careful not to lift my feet, which would have been fatal. I gripped onto the wall's rough surfaces and integrated myself quickly into a group when it passed close by to me. I made rapid progress to my great astonishment and to the surprise also of some groups, who, envious of my equilibrium, tried to give me chase. But because they were so numerous they became lost in disorderly gesticulations and dreadful curses as they watched me move away from them. In the end I have no idea how long this went on nor how I found myself under the full sun amidst the palm trees in the area near where Palma lived.

I turned on the transistor. At the sound of the music Palma leaped out of the water. It was our signal. She croaked with joy. Bright and always cheerful she understood why I was fleeing. What's more she wanted to come with me. Personally I didn't want to weigh myself down, no matter with what, but in the face of so much insistence I gave in. After all she was the sole creature who understood me. She jumped into my outstretched hand and into a red scarf—pilfered from I don't know who as I walked through the streets of the city—; this is how, when a kid, I captured frogs so that I might sell them to Spaniards who love to eat their legs . . .

And we were off—in the meantime, as a precaution, I unburdened myself of my socks and especially of my glasses, just in case someone had given out my profile; one never knows, I thought.

Vapors of hot air danced on the caramelized asphalt.

We took off, Palma in the left pocket of my shirt right over my heart, and me, walking, whistling, and amusing myself at the sight of the indents left in the melting hot asphalt by my shoes . . . No, I wasn't wearing any shoes . . . The warm soft tar tickled the soles of my feet.

Perhaps I was wearing shoes . . .

But it's a detail without great importance because the asphalt is MY MEMORY.

I was walking therefore on-in-my memory, with Palma in my shirt pocket and the transistor turned on full blast.

I wanted to listen to the news one last time. It was the news hour. National anthem. Freedom of movement is once again possible. From now on we can move about without the risk of a deadly slip. The mail service has been reinstated and the stores have reopened. It's a day of celebration but also a day of mourning because the number of dead and wounded is considerable. A man's voice alternates with a woman's. They do their best to sound aggrieved while reading off the list of victims.

On it I recognized many of my own. There will be a rally at noon in the square in front of the large mosque. There will be an hour of silence to mark the memory of those martyred by these bad times. The evening will be devoted to festivities of all sorts. National anthem.

Memory is cowardly when it comes to evoking the dead.
In this way the newly disappeared are added to my graveyard.
Speak not of ancestors. I've never known what is meant by that word.
It began with my father. At my first birth cry he vanished. His voice was lost in a deadly fog. Many others followed. All I had left was my old blind grandmother whom I drove every Friday, acting as her eyes, to the graveyard—a windswept and sun-beaten graveyard. A miserable graveyard, tired from birth. An undemarcated graveyard, the kind that crops up just any old place. A graveyard barely above ground level. A graveyard to put brakes on your death drive—I was the transitory and itinerant bitterness in the murky ocean of her past. She made the places where I stepped come alive. I guided her through her memory. I was Ariadne's thread in the labyrinth of her darkness. One day she lost what was left of her vision. My eyes took a long time to accustom themselves to the light.

And then I met this woman. I want you all to myself she said. But I was busy counting my graves. And it was a disaster. I didn't know I didn't manage to hold onto her.

I got off the highway. I placed the scarf on top of my head, the lichen on top of the scarf and on top of the lichen Palma.

I walked for a long time. I sold the transistor at a flea market while passing through a small town before getting off the highway. With the money I drank a nice cold beer and bought a pack of American cigarettes. A way to celebrate my leaving, if you will.

I walked under the oppressive heat on the paths of my memory with Palma on my head while smoking Lucky Strikes.

I left the town and the highway without a single regret. I walked under the sun down a dusty incline. I wanted to get as far away as possible. Every departure is a flight. I walked and I told my life story to Palma. I wanted to settle the score with my memories. Tell her my life from A to Z. When the sun had reached its zenith Palma began to complain. She was suffering from the heat. She emitted a hoarse plaint. But I wanted to tell her my life story. My childhood beneath laurel and pomegranate trees . . . elementary school . . . my first hates and loves . . . I wanted to tell her about all my tragedies, to describe in detail the life of all of those who had died on me. But she just kept complaining and interrupting me at the most interesting and pathetic moments in my story. Her plaint continued. I explained to her that this act was essential to me, that I was determined to tell her my life's story, to unburden myself once and for all. In vain. I ended up nursing a genuine hatred for her. And in my anger I decided to make her pay very dearly for her lack of understanding. I devised a secret plan to rid myself of her.

And so I set her free. I made a little hammock out of the scarf and lichen, which I then attached to the end of a stick. I put the stick over my shoulder like travelers of old and continued on my way.

At sunset we were following the bed of a dry wadi. A sandstorm that threatened to become violent began to blow. I stopped.

I took Palma out of the scarf. I stared at her for a long time, reluctant to lose her. I tightened my grip. I wanted to strangle her . . . I tightened . . . she croaked with joy because she took this as a sign of friendship. I squeezed tighter. I looked at her. She battled back and I saw in her eyes that she understood my murderous plans. I saw it in her eyes . . . she wasn't angry with me . . . but seemed to be warning me about something. Her bulging eyes spoke.

This is what will happen to you:

When all has come to pass there will be no more water for your ablutions. You will brandish your sex at the sun and from your blistering sperm sons who will never recognize their father will be born. Children of silence.

When all has come to pass you will ask yourself where you left behind the one—yourself—that followed you more closely and faithfully than your shadow.

Only the sirocco will remember you.

When all has come to pass you will look even more deeply into your solitude.

You will be no more eternal than a language of death.

You will count your fingers your eyes your limbs.

You will experience your voice your gaze from inside and outside of yourself.

You will not overlook your nails they will have their say.

When all has come to pass you will reclaim the right to silence without having ever spoken.

At the tick of your heart you'll have nothing left but to follow the wind.

But perhaps you will prefer to cash in your skin—thoroughly tanned—thoroughly wrinkled—or mortgage your blood.

You will leave with only the rhythm of your rotten nerves.

You will not mark sundials nor ever count hours by the sand pouring through an hourglass.

When all has come to pass you will cut all moorings. You'll be an iceberg.

Sometimes you'll drop anchor in a nightmare.

You will not walk barefoot in the water for fear of drowning your chimeras.

Finally when you will have exhausted everything
    When you have nothing more to lose
    When you have only one trick left in your bag
    You will gamble your life in the confines of uncertainty . . .

I squeezed even tighter to silence her. But I didn't have the heart to finish the job. I closed my eyes and threw her away from me with all my force and then I turned and ran. After all she alone had tried to understand me . . .

I wanted to tell her my life story. She was complaining. I wanted to unburden myself once and for all. She kept on complaining. I tightened my grip around her twitching body. Her protruding eyes bulged even more. She croaked with happiness but I wanted to suffocate her. I wrapped her up in the scarf. I closed my eyes and I threw her far away from me and then I turned and ran.

I followed my path alone with my lichen. It had grown over the only stone at my father's house built all of bronze so hot in summer and so cold in winter right next to the highway under the brilliant sun of an eternal July. The lichen upholstered almost all of the pale gray stone with its spiderlike convolutions. Desiccated brain withered over its history.

But Palma's scent kept following me. You will leave with only the rhythm of your rotten nerves. Sometimes you'll drop anchor in a nightmare. It was the lichen that retained her presence. In time I would chuck it as well.

That's over. It's dark. The sandstorm blows more violently. So I am alone? Really alone?

My nerves
my heart
my neurons
         deranged
WHAT SHOULD I DO?
where is the center
where is the why of interrogation
must one retreat, fingernails digging into palms
renounce one's skin
remain deaf to the blood's rhythm
attempt a senseless crucifixion
expose oneself to all infernos
trace once and for all a cross
—a real one—over oneself perhaps to be reborn
from one's own ashes
an absurd death
or what's more
must one like a stray fish allow oneself to be caught in a net
of dead words
amen to all loopholes
I hate those who know where they are going
as for me an epithet can make me change my path.

A quiver in my scalp warns me of the next disaster.

It is dark. The wind redoubles its force. At the tick of your heart you'll have nothing left but to follow the wind. I will not sleep, I will not sleep anymore. My flight stops here. I'll retrace my steps. I'll go back there. Back there everything is to be done over. I don't know . . . redo the geometry of the streets, right the sun to predict all eclipses, create a committee for the defense of stray dogs, write a constitution for the birds. In the end everything is to be done over. I'll retrace my steps. En route I'll mobilize an entire wildlife fraternity. I will teach them the true language. The language of the raid. We will seed a single word into their hearts and minds. The word *essential*. A wildlife fraternity. The grasshoppers, the mites, the rats . . . There's nothing like it to put a tottering country back on its feet. Not to forget the blacksmith ferriers, their role is crucial. The maladroit acrobats—among others—will be entrusted to them. For some they will be able to rearrange the neurons—in sum to shoe their brains—; for others they will ensure better agility in the toes; and for others still they will strengthen the joints. I don't know, everything is to be done over.

I will turn back filled with a clear and cold violence and already I burst out laughing at the thought of their expression upon seeing me show up with my wildlife.

I will not sleep anymore. Insomnia a terrain of light alone can help me to defeat the obstacle of monsters. Just enough time to take stock, just enough time to walk back over the burning silica to the source of my nutritious prehistory before being born again *completely new*, and I will turn back. Just enough time to put the topography of my *future memory* right . . .

UNTITLED

Mostafa Nissabouri
Translated from the French by Guy Bennett

There is one city that conjures the eye, from which the eye cannot defend itself, were it endowed with the greatest of powers.
A city whose devouring is palpable, since we have been gradually reduced to a collection of bones that break up, turn frail, are scattered to the wind. Am I a city rebuilt bone by bone or am I an extinguished city? Or resurrecting fortresses not depicted in school books (kasbahs, foliage, from cave dwelling to small, low-roofed houses their windows askance) to revive the instincts of the deeply enamored ogress-moon and trigger the entire series of hideaways, shelters, cold and hot spells, ensure the eye works properly beginning with reappearances, perfectly detectable traps used to capture blood for some, landslides for others, the jinn.

Grottos open for my ribs' crawling
as if I were as if the city and grotto in me
were separated into computers each with its own way of calculating
pursuing its own adventure of furrowing destruction and dream
and machines that outstrip time
time in our head buried in a shirt of old cancers of paradise
since you can't cheat fate
since it's a question of eye something alive something tragic in our eye
since Sesame the grotto Sesame the city my entire town crumbled as
by electric reverberations and my prayer to the fowl the grand master
buried in Baghdad
the discord of my vapor my lymph bottles bearing the power of
ubiquity
sipped
by the vampire
neither geographer nor geometer had an explanation for the disaster
that threw me
into kif
          nor these ruin-girdled legends that
                                        I alone will be left
and I
     I shall be devoured by a monster

and who will knock up the moons?
who close the book?

It's no big deal I say if nearly every day I am forced to swallow the plate of couscous on which death has been laid out all plantlike and if the street is of anxiety. I telescope. I adjust the dreams that shot out my brain in vast but nearly invisible bands—waves—according to them, and my liver, according to me.

It's no big deal if all I can manage to grasp of the void are its symptomatic shocks and if, once localized, my deliria prove perceptible in the guise of fleeting stains—blood puddles. It's no big deal if my anachronism is unlike the electron, the electron and my anachronism forming that scandal of competing compromise whereby I maintain that transistors capture sirens' voices, black and white sirens, to capture the night, the night and every characteristic of the moon. And your teeth have little cracks that open Tanit-torpor lips in my imagination. And in this clairvoyance an old killer who is time and in my dream patterns abruptly reform, enrobed in sand, luxurious, a crowd full of territories where for myself I measure the city the street and me without managing to deal the decisive blow that would put an end to all Tanit-quivering and hurl this dream the city reflects back to me having never shot out as many heads as many fingers as many doors and as many electric poles as many numbers and caravan legacies nor been as convoluted nor as impossibly unattainable due to the placement of houses bordering it low-roofed as far as the gorge and due also to the electric lights that give it a desert air which reminds me that nostalgia is a virtue of the lunar crescent nostalgia crumbles, I was crumbled at having remembered, crumbled too my companions who stop to better sing the nearby relocation of housing debris affirming that Tanit it's about a lost love a consuming passion Sesame as night which calms which comes without my moving without waking a profound moon hardly recognizable in what it has created to spark an appearance of immobile time. I had a moon turned to spongy mass, half-purulent half-vagrant, gluing half-smashed *douars* from which I could extract nothing more than a book of calamitous descendants. I had a moon that paralyzed me could not chase it away even pressing my thumbs from my temples to the middle of my forehead to create a red dot between my eyes, and even if it's about the sun, which topples body after body in each articulation in the slightest cell its stench. Which strikes. Which must be chased toward the trees, toward the dunes, and which bears old grudges.

I have stayed behind to probe this slow
                                        infernal
                                                swelling

my voice
            muddy
                    stuck to death's hoof
                                        my brain
with the dimensions of a battlefield where Sayf ibn Dhi-Yazan might have dug up hundreds of golden scorpions. I, anemic. I and the rest in books the western galactic will come and detect to assure me of my Middle Ages, my resurrection, the beauty of my religion, my youth my primitivism my virility my pitiful sex organ, that it is a question of time, that man must be declared free, that Berber, that he Barbarian, that I Jew Hindu fatalist fanatical and Arab, that he Phaeton, that after all we are not so unlike one another except that he correct, his dog, his wife, his disciple who has not been able to obtain his passport, Carla, novel for two, kif, tea, I-rave-I-write-trembling-under-the-weight-of-raving, and Brahim whose life he knows better than anyone better than me Sicily Essaouira before the small photogenic Ayrabs dumb-founded as by some young folly listen up I'm a Roman prophet await-ing the revolution action first action for the galaxy and the moon in me then the moon where I am my entreaties he more Muslim than me the prophet in Rome
with his electronic calculators in the midst of the futurist desert
with a city with only two gates
pyramids totems
people in love with the same cow as me
in this city I know my official number
I too
lived in futurist deserts
I too conquered most of my satrapies
how many sirocco days I can gulp down I the Minotaur
how nonviolent I can be
how many fantasies circulating in my blood I have

tombless cadavers facing the city
                              to be destroyed
and of which all that remains will be another city that we shall call

Palmyra

the grotto

five men the sixth a dog and I the Minotaur
and I the Minotaur again the grotto six men and the seventh a dog and
I the Minotaur and the grotto again six dogs six men and the grotto
again a dog with no men and the dog appears
with the effigy of its absence
the grotto especially to populate with surreal visions where other cow
heads can be tracked down laughing in streets piled up open to the
very walls of the age-old lair of the sleeper with the cow the bronze
town lacking passports ropes machines wadis but with caravans
                                                            laughing
I the Minotaur and Tanit again the animal done to a turn in my
irregular daze of bookish insomnia
and Tanit again her embryotomies her drafty thighs
and my night apprehending the moon were it
only to photocopy it were it
only to reconnoiter my brain of sea foam only
my night my anachronism my double kif belt round my waist

I contemplate the structures

GENERATION DRIVE

Mohammed Berrada

Translated by from the Arabic by Maya Boutaghou and Hoda El Shakry

Each generation has its truth, . . . a *Zeitgeist* that tempts the artist above anyone else. It emerges from the changes that occur from time to time, forces that break monotony and renew values and concepts.

For every generation to question its truth is naturally a serious matter. Indeed, the greatest misfortune is for people to live with their comprehension paralyzed and their emotions dulled, having lost the courage that guides them to question and innovate, and the drive to extricate themselves from resignation and imitation.

There is no single voice that represents an entire generation; rather, there is a diversity of voices. Their melodies distinguish themselves to the extent of conflicting and clashing with one another. In fact innovative changes will only be accepted by the segment of the population that benefits from them. The dominant classes in particular would like to maintain the status quo for fear of losing their privileged position. This is a natural state of affairs because it characterizes the essence of historical dialecticism. The value of a generation is determined by its ability to understand and express its individual "truth" or historical trajectory as well as its ability to mobilize social powers to respond objectively to unfolding changes.

With respect to artists, there is another dimension that complicates the choice and the expression of their social views, or their stance on social and humanitarian developments. By this I mean documented art history with respect to the development of art forms, innovative compositions, and the aesthetics of a given era. It is true that art history derives its framework and features from History. In the end, however, art history demands diversity and individuality and calls upon artists not to ignore History but rather to take it into consideration when they create or innovate.

Now where do young Maghrebis writing in Arabic stand in the midst of these reflections? Many factors have created the air our young writers breathe. I do not pretend to probe them in depth but rather to point out the most prominent points. I think that the influence of the intellectual movement of the Arab East on our national movement can in no way be denied. One of the consequences of this interaction is that before independence Maghrebi writers knew the poems of Mahmoud Sami al-Baroudi, Ahmed Shawqi, and Hafez Ibrahim by heart. They were urged to weave according to these patterns in order to reinforce political, social, and religious concerns that shaped the national movement of that time. The same holds true for our plays and short stories (under the influence of Youssef Wahbi, Mahmud Taymur, Jurji Zaydan . . .).

Now is not the time to debate and reevaluate this phenomenon. I am however interested in investigating whether this literary influence of the Arab East continues to exert itself on our young writers.

I have absolutely no doubt that it does and it is an influence that sometimes borders on imitation. However, contemporary Maghrebi literature no longer derives its forms solely from the East; it is also in the process of building ties with the West. It has diversified its cultural influences and intellectual palate. This is how we have on the one hand the imprint of Naguib Mahfouz, Youssef Idriss, Badr Shakir al-Sayyab, Salah Abdel Sabour, Abd al-Wahhab al-Bayati, Mustafa Mahmud, etc., . . . and on the other, echoes of the philosophies of Jean-Paul Sartre, Albert Camus, Karl Marx, Maxim Gorki, Eugène Ionesco . . .

Is this to be expected? Possibly.

What is not normal, however, is for this situation to persist endlessly: the East imitates the West, while we imitate the East. Meanwhile, the West "discovers" our folklore and spirituality, while we are attracted to their reflection but leave behind the originals [*asala*]. And what is the result? A "hybrid" literature [*adab khalit*] that has lost its national grounding and historical authenticity.

In reality it can be said that the political and social philosophies of the past ten years or so emerged from the necessary task of searching for national origins. After political independence, it was natural for this new generation to sense the vast vacuum surrounding them, as well as the deep sediment resulting from the meeting of two cultures, and the confrontation of two epistemologies and ethics. It is impossible to return to precolonial times; yet it is futile and unproductive to continue acquiring the customs and traditions of the West just as we accumulate machines and technological tools. Where then is this "safe road" that can guide us without leading us astray?

Without a doubt the first step is to change and establish material foundations as a necessary precondition for all attempts to eliminate underdevelopment. What we fear, however, and what frightens many people is that these changes will be limited to the infrastructure without affecting the surface, allowing intermingling, confusion, accumulation, and "modernization" to continue without comprehension or assimilation.

Insofar as literature is a form of expression that transcends collective and individual realities, it must act to eliminate, through its own means and norms, signs of underdevelopment and stagnation. We must also open the door to popular forces in order to expose them, through literature, to the experience of the contemporary world.

In the Maghreb we too have witnessed heated controversies with respect to defining the role of literature in an underdeveloped society, the terms for actualizing cultural authenticity as well as the justifications for and dimensions of political commitment among artists (particularly between 1962 and 1965). We are faced with the task of examining the value of our literary production. Is the reason for its stagnation the absence of publication venues? Or are the reasons deeper than this? Do they reside rather in the content and forms made available to artists in this transitional period, ridden with both anxiety and productivity?

The goal is not innovation for the sake of newness, or to reach an avant-garde aesthetics by the easiest means (such as adapting foreign and Western artistic forms). The problem at hand is to see literature, and the arts in general, become one of the tools that will form the society that we aspire to become. Societal innovation is fundamentally a response to biological, psychological, and human needs. The dream of creation has been behind every leap forward and innovation. Every time a generation fulfills its dreams and potential, the air is full of youthful energy, overflowing with dreams and secrets capable of transforming the unreal into reality.

It appears that the end of the period of "fermentation" and its effects on Arabic literature have given rise to ideal conditions for a reexamination of the forms and content of our creative gifts. It is natural not to want to build in a void. Indeed, all experiences are foremost our heritage, worthy of study and attention. We must strive both to acquire mastery of Western concepts and conserve the foundations of our past and of our elites. The obstacles before us do not limit the realm of possibilities in this domain. But often obstacles emerge from within ourselves, and we must make choices with an equal measure of courage, perseverance, and defiance.

What is the value of the Arabic writings published in the journal *Souffles*?

It is difficult for me to judge them, because their authors are in a critical period of their development and formation. In addition, artistic achievement differs from one writer to another. These then are indicators showing the path rather than signposts determining their direction. What attracts our attention in the writings of these young Maghrebi writers is that, despite their diverse voices and forms, they agree on one point: things are not for the best. This is an advantage in my opinion because our new literature is borne out of embracing the problems of the people. It is as if these young voices reply with the tongue of Ahmad Mejjati:

"When will generation drive drum to its own beat?"

AFTERNOON, WITH THE SUN

Mohamed Zafzaf

Translated from the Arabic by Ghenwa Hayek

He was finally rid of the nausea that had dogged him since the morning. He looked at his shoes, then at the whitewashed noonday walls, then at the climbing plants that stretched all the way to the rooftops (the nausea came and went in short bursts, emanating from a secret source outside his control that he couldn't, wouldn't, identify) and he saw the trickle of cars that had broken off, then the gray, vacant street. At the end of the road were high white buildings and bodies scattered like seeds (a few meters away, two streets down, stands a shorter building that doesn't swallow clouds . . . in a room of that building he lies down each evening and looks at the scattered seeds: people overly preoccupied with themselves, loving themselves through their love of others). His vision (which he had always thought of as piercing) was now unusual (of course—from his gaze from the third floor of that building, all bodies appeared to be skewers, the heads attached like leather bobbles. The people now were like puppets, no, like skewers, and he began to suck down hungrily on a cigarette, awash with a white joy because his anxiety had dissipated, slowly at first, then suddenly . . . The most important thing to him now—the fever had weakened his body—was to sit in a café (the cafés were usually empty at this time) and drink his coffee, feeling his solitude, giving himself over to the solid world (the walls, the chairs, the cup of coffee, the unlit cigarette, then, afterwards, to the smoke, and the unsettled objects in his imagination). He felt the fever take over his body, he shook his shoulders and despite the absolute weight, the imagined and virtual weight, despite the suffocation, there was a lightness in his veins, in his feelings, in his body and in his head (this heaviness was their doom, and others felt it, even those wearing light summer clothes) because he had gotten rid of everything that had weakened him as he released the pressure of the air in his lungs. A few moments before, he had not been able to finish reading the poem he had begun, he couldn't focus his mind on the shadows and images, he reread the stanzas and didn't understand. He tried to eat something (it was noon), fever, then he tried to relax but he couldn't read and he couldn't relax or lie down, from his window on the third floor that opened out onto an ethereal cave a wind blew in, a suffocating, heavy wind, and his body could not bear it, his fingers were so tense he could kill himself (the wind was still the same way, but the anxiety had melted and left behind the idea of suicide, a path to bohemian joy). He looked at his wristwatch; it was two in the afternoon and around his wristwatch his thick hair was drenched in sweat (in spite of the sweat, he felt that the breeze was enjoyable, and the temperature tolerable). And now he was three buildings away from the street where his building was. The plants climbed up the walls of the short homes, squatting like little islands in the middle of the ocean, and he crossed the street easily because there were few cars. At the café he ordered a coffee (at night, he would ask his sister, who lived with him, to make him coffee, maybe she was now drinking tea instead of coffee, or maybe she was looking out of the third floor window onto the skewers sunk into the pavement; this coffee was different from the nighttime coffee his sister prepared for him. At least, that's how it smelled to him as he brought the Japanese coffee cup to his nose). He smiled to the girl he knew, coldly. But he did not pay attention to her, and began to tap his fingers on the marble tabletop. The cup shook, and car after car drove by. The girl was a ways away now, uneasy, she was his sister's friend and he had tried to flirt with her once, unsuccessfully, but she still tried to maintain their friendship and smiled and said hello, albeit from a distance (five years ago, when he was still a law student, he had tried several times to convince the girl of his dreams of his love, but she remained unconvinced. She ran away from him and he told his sister this. She said: Maybe she's married. He said: I know that she's not married). However, after that, he had won the hearts of several girls despite his failure at university, and this, the problem of love at any level, was no longer a problem for him. His failure to win over the girl that had passed by a few moments ago was insignificant (he had also told his sister of this failure, and she had laughed, then showed him a letter that had arrived from London for him, which she had forgotten for a couple of days in her desk drawer where he never looked). He sipped his coffee. His fever meant nothing to him, and neither did the girl who had passed by a few moments ago, his sister's friend. He would begin work at two thirty. He had only that long to get to his office. He had not eaten lunch, and was not thinking of having anything, not even one bite. He was content with his cup of coffee, but as he walked to his office, he would have to walk down the street he had just come from, the same way that the girl he'd smiled at had gone. He would undoubtedly find that the squat homes were still in place, that the plants still climbed up the walls, and that nothing had changed. He wouldn't eat anything. The coffee was coursing through his veins. In the evening when he felt hungry he would have some toast and jam, and he would drink the coffee his sister made him, smelling it with all his senses, when the evening was still warm. Just as the nights before. Now he feels everything clearly. He's in a peculiar psychological state. Other states don't exist for him. They concern others but not him. His own case, his special case, which he felt and lived, was the one that concerned him. And that was all that mattered.

CAMUS THE COLONIZER IN DENIAL

Bernard Jakobiak

Translated from the French by Lucy R. McNair

All Moroccans studying for the baccalaureate spend a trimester in French class reading Albert Camus's *The Plague*. And yet there is no single text or author that so fully reflects the good and very "humanist" intentions of the would-be professor of the Third World.

"Camus Camus Camus . . . ," purrs the haloed modern secular saint-professor, O, so pleasantly surprised to see how fully he devotes himself, giving his dear students everything that makes him who he is. . . . O sweet mirror, fraternal father, reflecting you . . . and how he sits upon that flying carpet, *The Plague*, transported effortlessly to the heights of a literature with a reputation three or four centuries old and a heap of Nobel laureates . . .

And because this whole story drones on, because the French university has a heap of money to extend its ravages across Morocco under the guise of universality, among other things its discretely pessimistic castrating idealism, which is essentially anointing and allied to the powers that be, I reread that dear old Camus, whom I had long forgotten for, let's be frank, he faded quickly, he's totally dead, and there's only the French university, that pyramid seriously shaken by May '68, that still worships him: a regal mummy. Thus I read him after scaling a seriously significant wall of praises . . . and there he was! The one we were waiting for after the traumas of World War II! . . . but enough with the barriers erected by classical tradition, the permitted encouraged applauded escapes, disguises, O panel of seated luminaries with their finesse galore and their delivering of its titles coats of arms! . . . I have seen Camus and *The Plague*'s deeper motivation, where the trickster tricked succeeds in proving to himself that noble self-image he sought and that would earn him literary glory.

"albert camus and the myth of prometheus"   "albert camus or the nostalgia of eden" albert camus or literature's metamorphosis

    apparition of Albert Camus
          1947
"The Plague: an ethics of happiness"
"The Plague: a philosophy an optimism a humanism"

                                  just in time
just   when the French stopped liking their own image
because they had been occupied   by the new superior man
the latest Promethean model   the Nazi

                        apparition of Albert Camus
then assumption of Albert Camus and all of his readers, saved by
him, "the just" "the rebel" we rediscovered the handsome face of the
honest man, the gentleman, European progress
we climbed anew the heights of "his" thought, clear and universal for
centuries on end
we rediscovered . . . we reclaimed . . . despite Guernica bombarded
despite London Hamburg bombarded despite Berlin Warsaw razed
Hiroshima Nagasaki pulverized
the stature of European man restored his coat of arms his flame
and yet it didn't stop

                         1947   massacres in Madagascar
1947   massacres in Tizi Ouzou . . . etc.
the workers at the Renault factory nor the Russians nor the Chinese
nor the soldiers in Indochina and later in Algeria nor their victims
nor the Arabs nor Aimé Césaire, nor Frantz Fanon discovering and
uprooting
old white humanism's vanity
nor those in favor of French Algeria nor those against French Algeria
could understand the Nobel laureate Albert Camus

                                      1957
"homage to Albert Camus" Le Figaro Littéraire
"homage to Albert Camus" Les Nouvelles littéraires
"homage to Albert Camus" La Nouvelle revue française
"homage to Albert Camus" "Simoun" Oran

"albert camus or desperate Honesty
albert camus and the philosophy of Happiness

albert camus and the Invention of Justice
albert camus or the Rebel Soul"

assumption of Albert Camus

Enough

because Albert Camus pure product of the Ultra-French University of
Algiers believes he is telling the truth, believes he has made a discovery
when he is only repeating lessons learned, only lying! He doesn't write,
he is written. Blind and meek, he enters into the system baptized by
others: Truth. He believes he is saving himself: eternal illusion. It will
only amplify into a full-fledged philosophy: the Absurd.

Consider *The Plague*: first step in the flight towards illusion and first
sign of success. The lie here is obvious and the distortions for the good
cause legion: a work of the tricked trickster, seeking to trick himself,
and succeeding. That is what *The Plague* is, though it was read quite
differently in 1947. For those who do not suffer from a feeling of well-
anchored guilt, carefully concealed, it is first of all an illegible work,
an insipid moral lecture, full of endless speeches that pedantically end
with the most well-worn precepts of the petite bourgeoisie: effort, te-
dium, happy medium, sensible rationality, powerlessness in the face of
pestilences, domestic happiness, friendship reduced to an intellectual
handshake, sporadic pleasure in the "warrior's repose," right up to the
part-time passions judged preferable to any sort of heroism.

It is false that Oran in the 1940s struck one first "for its ordinari-
ness" and was "merely a large French port on the Algerian coast."[7]
For any French person disembarking from mainland France, it is foremost a colonial city where the visitor is assaulted by miserable crowds
harshly rebuffed by the local Europeans. It is false that the inhabitants
"work hard, but solely with the object of getting rich"[8] because this
ignores the quite visible existence of beggars, shoe shiners, porters,
dockworkers, the unemployed, and overworked housemaids. It is
false that "our frank-spoken, amiable, and industrious citizens have
always inspired a reasonable esteem in visitors"[9] when in fact they
have been disturbed, to the point of wanting to flee, by the way the
"natives" are spoken to, bullied and humiliated in every possible public place, outraged by the reasons that are constantly invoked: "You

don't know them! . . . you'll see . . . they're all the same . . . lazy cruel lying thieves . . . you'll see!"

But Albert Camus eliminates what bothers him, minutely erases all trace of the colonized in this colonized Arab city. Albert Camus wants us to believe that Oran is a French city and that he is French without anything particular about him except that he was born in a harsh climate, a place without trees or the flutter of wings. And it is with the sole aim of convincing us that he becomes more classical than the most nationalist follower of Charles Maurras, a true right-winger, so utterly classical he replaces the novel—where in France since Balzac a real historical society has been the protagonist—by the "chronicle," a genre he invents by removing from the novel anything that does not obey the aesthetic rules of seventeenth-century tragedy. Although these rules may have been rejected and banished since the Pre-Romantics, they are the only ones that can justify his cover up. The so-called passage from the particular to the general and the pseudo-realism allowing him, in effect, to retain of Oran only the non-colonial Europeans—who do not exist—a few very French place names and a climate that apparently renders suffering, illness, agony, and death more unbearable than elsewhere—a fact that would have to be demonstrated since the Algerian consumptives in Lorraine must certainly see no consolation in the existence of the fog, rain, and cold.

But that is not enough. Avoiding the mention of Arabs, he could have allowed us to get to know the Europeans of Algeria. But no. They are announced. Then they are replaced by French people or rather by the French intellectual exactly as the French bourgeoisie conceives and wants him. Basically, in the whole book the people obsessed solely with earning lots of money disappear. To the contrary, from the first few pages the only protagonists lack all ambition and interest except for Cottard, who is more and more isolated and whose role is progressively reduced to that of a scapegoat. And while idealists like Camus are excluded from colonial Algeria, as he himself found out after his journalistic expeditions in Kabylia, in his mythical Oran, amputated of all its concrete and particular reality, they remain and even play an essential role. This invention of the efficient Just has the advantage of legitimizing a compromise that is in fact a form of complicity: in a meeting with a journalist, Doctor Rieux, presented to us as a true, modern man, refuses to speak about the Arabs because he does not have the right to tell the full truth about them. Camus's choice in writing *The Plague* is the same. But he forgets to admit that if he accepts this silence, if, moved by justice, he refuses to reveal the scandal of colonization and the colonial world, it is because he does not want to be excluded from it, because he is a part of it, because it is his true country, because he is a colonizer opposed to certain injustices no doubt but allied in reality to a system he refuses to put in question. Thus all the effort of the book consists in proving that one can still arrive at a humanity washed of all particular stain and thus of colonialism. But this will require yet more self-delusion and lies.

Thus it is false that a doctor in Algeria, even a worker's son—which is by the way an absurdly improbable case given how rare it is—would be so destitute that his very ill wife would find the train's sleeping car too expensive for the family. It is false that a person with a law degree would be a simple town hall clerk when in the colonies all Europeans hold positions above their educational qualifications, unless their political ideas are viewed as dangerous, a case the author omits to mention although it is his own. It is false that a European town hall clerk in Algeria would have need of his doctor's charity. Yet this systematic pauperization of the two principal heroes of the book helps to eliminate the scandal of 1940s Algeria where what shocks us every day is the misery of the masses. The Just are not only efficient; in this way, they also manage to avoid benefiting from social injustice and, as in tragedy where one neither eats nor drinks, the reader is able to ignore an economy created for the self-enrichment of the few and of the métropole.

But in order to invent this new aristocracy of the disembodied and eloquent Just, subtly substituting for colonial humanity, one had to stay vague. The only way to claim to be a realist while being in a completely mythological realm, in a complete fantasy was through form. Under cover of objectivity, focusing on what supposedly was happening in the streets, the sick rooms, the hospitals, and the brains of men, it was possible to refuse an analysis of motivations.

This evasion is the very subject and deeper motivation of the book and of its title, *The Plague*. Camus's art consists in persuading us that the plague is no longer the terrifying epidemic from centuries past, but rather the allegory of all that we have to undergo as mortal men.

The invention made on the basis of two concrete realities, the epidemic plague and the drama lived by Camus, this purely intellectual myth of *The Plague*, allows the reassuring confusion between natural cataclysms, earthquakes volcanic eruptions floods avalanches . . . etc. . . . or death, and the massacres or injustices inflicted by man.

> Everybody knows that pestilences have a way of recurring in the world; yet somehow we find it hard to believe in ones that crash down on our heads from a blue sky. There have been as many plagues as wars in history. . . .

The trick is played. While appearing to speak of other things, we gradually assimilate war and plague and then, in the same manner, Algerian Europeans and everyone else, which allows us a few lines further on to affirm logically, if not naively, that "our townsfolk were like everybody else."[10]

The trick is well played. We go from plague to pestilence, which is vast and vague; we include plague and war in these pestilences and then give them, without any justification at all, the characteristic of an epidemic: "a pestilence isn't a thing made to man's measure."[11] Since the inexplicable invasion of the city by dying rats announcing a plague has just been minutely described as an unavoidable stroke of fate, we've been prepared to agree quite naturally that historical phenomena like revolutions, revolts, repression, wars, occupation, and colonization have no human cause, so no one man is more responsible than another, the fault of each being only to have ignored the "absurd" existence of catastrophes or death.

An entire book is nevertheless needed to raise us, after this initial sleight of hand, to a different level altogether. An entire oeuvre is necessary, as well as the invention of the principles of an individual morality, that is to say a philosophy, opposed in all things to the quite logical theology of nineteenth century bourgeois Christianity: the absurd as opposed to salvation; the void of death as opposed to eternity; empathy for pain and the use of medicine as opposed to contempt for the body and science; altruism as opposed to charity; the refusal of sin—while remaining in the same powerlessness in the name of our mortal condition—as opposed to the acceptance of human powerlessness as the fruit of sin, etc., etc. One could thus present as a discovery such precepts as: "The thing was to do your job as it should be done."[12] And the bourgeois can continue to do business in all tranquility, whether they hail from Oran or Paris.

Albert Camus the ethical stand-in
"God is dead" but nothing changes
Hands off Albert Camus! but may each person attend to the
victims   stay in his place   the French in Algeria   the Arabs in
inexistence   the "watchdog" Albert Camus

But it is hard to know the man Albert Camus. He fled from himself too much. He wanted to be Algerian without being a colonizer. Classicism permitted him to muffle this impossibility, to project a new orthodoxy onto all men, his obsessive sense of guilt and redemption. The French who admired him after the Second World War no doubt had their own reasons to forget the causes of their existential malaise after the fascist wildfire, the "death camps," the occupation; he could not liberate them any more than he could liberate himself. They invited us to take up the sad and tedious task of signing petitions against torture or shrapnel bombs, they privileged art, novels, films, theater, where all spontaneity, all joy, all vitality, that crazy thrill of creativity, had been banished under the pretext of being anachronistic. And Camus is important for having largely contributed to establishing the exclusivity of this impasse.

Camus is thus a precursor and as such he presents meaningful cracks. The system is not yet quite perfected. Indeed, abandoning the traditional novel, he does not go so far as to eliminate characters, to say "I" or "he" . . . and through this he reveals himself. The invention of Cottard is the crack through which all that he wants to keep silent speaks.

Cottard is nothing less than the projection of a sense of guilt, namely Camus's. Cottard is Camus in Paris among leftist intellectuals, his peers, condemning him through their radical opposition to colonization—he could have met Ho Chi Minh or at least read those analyses of the colonial situation in Indochina. Cottard is Camus judged guilty of having considered Algeria his country, in his view unjustly accused, but incapable of defending himself, even in his own eyes and thus delivered to the rancor and nothing but the rancor of isolation. Cottard:

wanting everywhere to make friends able to testify that he is not a "bad man"—this is Camus writing *The Plague*. Cottard: hounded and finding solace in the appearance of the epidemic for it offers him a community of destiny with people hounded like him—this is Camus discovering a link between his malaise and that of occupied Frenchmen, pursued like them by a sense of guilt and forcing him to rediscover his attachment to his native land. Cottard is so much Camus that when the subject of discussion is Arabs he flees, confused, feeling accused.

> Grand had personally witnessed an odd scene that took place at the tobacconists. An animated conversation was in progress and the woman behind the counter started airing her views about a murder case that had created some stir in Algiers. A young commercial employee had killed an Arab on the beach.
>
> I always say, the woman began, if they clapped all that scum in jail, decent folks could breathe more freely.
>
> She was too much startled by Cottard's reaction—he dashed out of the shop without a word of excuse—to continue. Grand and the woman gazed after him, dumbfounded.[13]

In this passage Cottard is Camus—complicit, shameful, and fleeing. But the conscious Camus, by employing a kind of vagueness, exculpates himself. In truth while any tobacconist in Oran would have condemned the Arabs for this incident, it seems that here, although some doubt persists, she accuses the riffraff, including, one assumes, Cottard, yet certainly not Camus, the honest student of philosophy. But if this "scum" is a reference to Arabs, which would have been obvious for a woman from Oran in the 1940s, Camus the accomplice becomes Camus the progressive. The meaning of this passage changes. The famous Latin concision may be less intransigent here, the avowal remains partial. Camus is haunted by the discovery, disconcerting for him, of "the stranger." Writing this novel he discovered himself as he gradually created the stranger, he brought to light what he had always carried within. The stranger, much more than Rieux, who becomes a mere spokesperson, is in fact Camus. Yet this stranger, indifferent to everything, has killed an Arab. Camus, even if he tried to hide it from himself, must have felt certain that this murder, in some way, belonged to him. He must have had at least for an instant the shame of discovering that his fundamental obsession was that of all his compatriots: "an Algeria for ourselves, an Algeria without the colonized." This is precisely what the application of the laws and ethics of classicism allowed him to perform in the first pages of the book: to erase, in the mind of course, all traces of the Arab. For "the country would be magnificent without these people" the colonists confide to the visitor.

Cottard in these few lines is Camus, ashamed of such complicity and trembling for fear it will be discovered. The "chronicle" genre allows him to avoid looking into this troubling fact, and rather expel it. In this genre, where what is conscious alone matters, Cottard can naturally keep his secret locked up and Camus can push him further and further away from the lucid Just among whom he intends to place himself and us as well, by making him a dealer, a profiteer, even a pitiable though dangerous madman. One might even think, given the fact that he is the only one who is not an intellectual, that this poor man is quite simply a victim of his lack of education.

"The Plague"

                              or the hypocritical devices of classical aesthetics
"The Plague"
    the art of erasing, eliminating, choosing, generalizing in order to exonerate oneself, to sublimate one's drama, to escape by giving an ideal austere bloodless self-image to Western intellectual humanity
"The Plague"

                indulgence
                incense
                        for the bourgeois academic mind

                                        "The Plague"
                                        enough!

DAWN OF TOMBSTONES

Tahar Ben Jelloun

Translated from the French by Teresa Villa-Ignacio

I

certainly hope is not a coffee one sips upon a summer evening
it is not a wink at history
nor is it a palace on an intimate horizon
hope is more than a foundational idea

You cannot even speak of hope. You do not know what hope is.

It is yours, the city located between destitution and splendor, between
pride and diffuse light
yours the city of crystal and colors, city of plastic, thefts, and whores,
city that sells itself to ludicrous Yankees, city of shantytowns and easy
joy
yours forgetting and tranquility, sweet obliviousness, yours the ivory
sky and the silver stars,
yours the unchanging mornings, the days that run together, the
useless footsteps.

You know, the hours of your life have fallen into a rut and in your
skull lies a decomposing carcass.
You carry the contagious disease of horizontal insouciance.
You live in a fishbowl of invisible walls.
Like a gumball, you cling to your skin you cling to your blood and
you fall asleep with your mouth open.
You are opaque in your golden mediocrity, you like to smell your
stench.
Like a plant, like a plant you vegetate, useless in your inconsequence
you shirk responsibility.
Ceaselessly you shirk responsibility, you flee, you cut yourself off
from the world, you turn away, you hide your face behind a rigged
prism, for you know the sight of you is wretched, wretched and dull.
When a comrade shakes you up, you lose yourself in bittersweet
confusion. The event shoots through you in all your transparency, in
all your absence.

You are absent.
When will you get involved?
When will you realize that suffering is communal, that under the
Tourism Ministry's Mediterranean sun there is dignity to be regained.

A man disappeared this morning.

They tell me that poetry can do nothing
the words curling up in a shroud of blood
words coagulating in raised fists
and man, this man who no longer returns
a body
that they have dissolved in sulfuric acid
a body
that they have soaked in quicklime
What will
the erosive wind say
What will
the saber say to the slit throat
When
we will have to remember this man
This man disappeared in the clarity of morning
Would he have been a prophet of liberation?

Forbidden things between your freed fingers
through your oath to bring justice to the child
who pulls on
dried up breasts
on this day when I've drunk in your eyes the suffering of my brothers
and the event no longer bears a date. It was inside you. In you
through this man who stretches his hand out, the palm shriveled up
oh futile villainy
why
again
ask your lord and not vomit hatred snigger burn down blaspheme
and depart naked in your right-angled truth
you who no longer have anything
you live under the heavens waiting for a piece of land

you who must be hidden from the eyes of foreigners
you are not to be displayed, negative merchandise
for a negated folklore
no you are not to be displayed
you might scare off the yanks who walk beneath our sun to bury
Vietnam's ghosts
yes
go
rejoin your fellow creatures even if they no longer want you and learn
to stop stretching out your hand
stretch out your hand only to riddle time with your poverty
execute those who each day annul you
denounce those who undress you at every turning point who drink
your blood in double gulps
go behind the City Walls
go

I was ranking my blind steps in the street and imagined you

How to remain silent
not everything was disappearing in your eyes
not even the cries of that wife giving birth on dirty sheets in the
absence of her man
nor those neighborhood kids scratching the earth and who cannot
play as children, collecting cigarette butts, clinging to a foreigner's
coattails.

The sky might have fallen
everyone seemed to be born for serfdom
and yet under that incandescent fire
there was an awakening
but who would dig the first tomb on the public square?
All lives assemble there every night
drunk from digging the Pit
the symbolic Pit
the real Pit
just before dawn
the Pit that would be covered over with moss while the day broke
upon other wounds

Who
will line the Pit
this man who carves the stones
that other a late bloomer
this family that cries over a departed father somewhere beyond the
City Walls?
the thirteen hundred shoeshine boys
of my neighborhood?
The shoeshine boys, you know them, don't you?
yes
of my skin
you are thirteen hundred
to come out from under the tombstones to run to
the inexpressible
leaking your steely tears

Thirteen hundred pairs of hands
carved out of the pedestal to come
measured on a future pedestal
kneaded into an anachronistic mass
to swallow double doses of suffering
to bend over boots of enduring grime
that are more like boots than earth and cement

Thirteen hundred jawbones to stone to death your hybrid mornings to
undress you and soak your tongues in mud

Thirteen hundred children
pale gestures and voices
to slap you
to shoot at you
their eyes come to rest on your shoulders
like thistle
and, you who flee
shutting your door, closing off your memory

Thirteen hundred questions to ask
while their lungs spew blood in yellow spittle

Made in the gravel of hatred and the gas lamp

in the shadow of the bulldozer and error
you remain
thirteen hundred figures decimated, outlines of children
shattering blank space
dragging out bellies hollowed by hunger and suspended rags
However
time has gnawed on your lips like pus
your thirty-two thousand teeth

Thirteen hundred rapes clear as ordinary assassinations

Unbeknownst to the sun of whom you are the children
—as the West says—
you stretch your bodies out in harm's way and they march on your
chests

Yes I know the shoeshine boys
lexicon of spiraling misery
bruised hope

They invade my nights
My peaceful slumber
of my skin
they have become part of my skin

yes I will become a shoeshine boy
I will partake
of your emaciated slumber
but if you don't want me?
if you chase me away
where will I go with my recovered memory?

II

You know, Orpheus, in our country corruption is indispensible: from
the worker exported to the Western mines, they demand some five
hundred dirhams for a passport, a hiring fee of over a thousand, and a
few hundred as a retainer.
No, you didn't know.
Your memory, cloaked in deafness, still falters.

It falters while crime whimpers in the crumbled streets
No, Orpheus, you can no longer modulate your hymn to love
the winds have spoken to you of bitter freedom
existence without an oracle
Come back now
come back to your nubile earth
come back to City Walls overflowing with blood
come back to see the shepherds in the city
cast-iron faces
unveiled women in the streets scattering from balls of fire
children of all the streets in madness and disorder
crawl back on your belly to howl with the widows of Mars
come back, Orpheus
the path is bitter

dirty servitudes and their sloppy tasks
like the pillory's nails and hatred
it's your task to bury the cadavers in your belly
dead
bread littering the cemetery.
Shattered rock.
stones outraged in the shadow of ordinary amnesia
come back to trace your steps through the incandescent tar carve the
tombstones of robust flesh
pick up the mourning clothes embellished by the quilt of the others
come back to shell the rosary of sprayed bullets
blow away the bloody nights of fire
of the African Prometheus

No, Orpheus
no more biting the dust
nor shaking
hands decanting poisons
no more trembling at the shadow
of he
who performs his ablutions in lepers' piss
prays at the mouth of sewer drains
draws his fables from the abyss of his fellows

remember
there are no ambivalent shadows
when
from afar
the rumor already rumbling
announcing
Mars
No, you can't remember that Tuesday
when the sun didn't set
when tombstones were no longer tombstones
when a man bit the cross of a rifle before gutting the brazier of flesh
and steel
when his death was initialed by all the raised fists
No, no curfew for the sun
No, it didn't set, are you listening to me, Orpheus
its rays
pierced the mortuary processions
its clarity ran through the streams
of the clandestine burials
the moon was silent—it withdrew—
the cemeteries stirred
the children didn't cry
the widows were not in mourning
the sun danced in their eyes
while others imprinted the first stain of blood

They dug up the streets
with pick-axes dug into the rock of the City Walls
gaping entrails
but the City Walls melted under the children's gaze
again became gemstone earth and sand
on the plain, they drank from the darkened stream all the liquid grief
of those long days of hatred when ageless suffering reigned cracked
lips
bleeding mouths
nails plucked in the whitening chill of cement grottos
yes
cellophane barely moistened

no longer lets the air through
hands buried in the wall
feet shackled in absence and silence
no way out

And the rest of you
your eyes are ravaged by the rust of shame
you've soaked your hands in rage and stifled cries
your voluble hands
crush flames to pieces

What will remain?
nothing but the bristling mirror
nothing but the howling plains
nothing but the searing whips
facing this unending mirage

No, Orpheus
the sun did not set tonight

AN INTERVIEW WITH JEAN-MARIE SERREAU

Noured Ayouch

Translated from the French by Edwige Tamalet Talbayev

Why Jean-Marie Serreau and not Jean-Louis Barrault or Jean Vilar or anyone else? Serreau was the first in France to put on plays by Kateb Yacine, Aimé Césaire, René Depestre and many other poets from the so-called Third World, and to bring them to the public's attention. He staged Kateb's "Le cadavre encerclé" [The encircled cadaver] at a time when l'Organisation de l'Armée Secrète and the French government did not "spare" the free men who were struggling with the Algerians for their independence.

In the second part of this interview, without ambiguity or circumlocution, J.-M. Serreau discusses May '68 and those who exploited it.

At a time when the figure of the artist is being put on trial, at a time when the supreme master-sovereign-director is being contested and dragged through the mud for being an Old Sorbonne boss-professor, at a time when we are looking for men uninterested in financial gain, rid of bourgeois prejudice and dedicated to their task and to their political convictions, it would not be an exaggeration to put forward J.-M. Serreau's name as an example of this kind of man. The actors and technicians working with him know him well enough to talk about him. He has never been known to raise his voice. But he's adjusted spotlights with lighting engineers, he's helped to build and install theater sets. He listens to all suggestions and takes them into account before coming to a final decision. His authority stems from this camaraderie with others, this intransigence in his work, his integrity in all circumstances and with everyone. Paradoxically, he never takes himself too seriously.

Noured Ayouch: Together with a company made up of actors from different backgrounds, you have dedicated yourself to Third World theater. Why? What inspired that choice?

Jean-Marie Serreau: Because theater is only interesting if it relates to history—the history of a country, or world history. I think that Kateb and Césaire bear a direct relation to our history.

N.A.: Did you first come into contact with this kind of theater through an author that you met or as the result of a certain orientation at a specific historical juncture?

J.-M. S.: Of course like everyone else I have always been concerned with a theater that would be both poetic and political, that would bear a relation to our contemporary history. And so from there, meeting Kateb and then Césaire, starting with Depestre seemed only natural. I also put on Korean plays during the Korean War, which was one of the reasons for this concern. I don't think that it was particularly original. I was lucky to meet people like Kateb and Césaire who are true poets and who wanted to make political theater.

N.A.: In Kateb and Césaire, poetry is a form of struggle because both draw from their African heritage. The ritual dimension of their plays comes across as authentically popular, and their stagecraft makes obvious their desire to highlight dances, songs, myths . . .

J.-M. S.: Civilizations cross-pollinate, and artistic heritages, whatever their origin, are meant to be disseminated. I think that there are periods when civilizations evolve; they are periods of hybridity. Look at the influence that some American authors have today because we are living in symbiosis with all things American. Kateb's influence was very enriching.

N.A.: Very enriching for whom? For Europe?

J.-M. S.: For Europe, certainly. There is nothing more enriching than a language bringing something in from another language.

N.A.: I attended a conference at the Odéon Theater where you spoke. You raised an important issue when you said that Western theatrical forms were a bit worn out, that they were in a rut and that you needed to find new strength in Third World theater.

J.-M. S.: I think that traditional forms of theater in the West, in Paris in any case, no longer meet the demands of modern society and that the public needs a theater that connects it to the problems of the world as a whole. It needs to let go of its old nationalism. I believe this is true for the entire world, including formerly colonized countries. There is nothing more terrible than self-enclosed nationalisms. We are suffering from Europeocentrism and, insofar as writers like Kateb and Césaire inhabit a language and have experienced colonialism, their situation is exemplary in that they both contest that language and enrich it. Besides, it is likely that many writers who will come after them will not write in French. This isn't important; there will be translations. As far as I am concerned, what is important is the exemplary situation of a writer attuned to his work, inhabiting a language.

N.A.: Don't you think that it is a slightly Western view?

J.-M. S.: I can hardly have a different one. I try to go beyond it but it certainly is a Western view. I am a Westerner; I am not hiding it. What do you mean by that?

N.A.: These authors, this company, these people are targeting a French— and European—public; this richness and this theatrical energy which should primarily be targeting African peoples—from Algeria, Haiti—are reaching an audience that is not deprived of theater, and the ones cheated most in this matter are their countries of origin.

J.-M. S.: I absolutely agree. But I do not think that it is our fault that Césaire hasn't been performed in Africa by African governments. The word *cheated* isn't fair. Are you saying that because I stage these plays in Paris I keep them from being performed in Africa?

N.A.: I would say that it tempts our writers of French expression and our actors to revel in their prolonged exile in Paris.

J.-M. S.: Then African actors must be told to go back home and make African theater with Césaire. Of course they must do that. Algerians must stage Kateb, Moroccans must translate Kateb into Arabic and stage him and perform all of his plays. It isn't up to me to do so. I am not keeping them from doing it. Far from it. But I work in my own language. I cannot do things differently. I am not able to perform in Arabic and it would not be my job to do so. That being said, I would be ready to direct a play in Arabic if necessary.

N.A.: Has anyone ever asked you to do so?

J.-M. S.: The Egyptians invited me to work with them. And I will. But I would like you to elaborate on your idea. So you are saying, you have a company in Paris, an African one targeting Europeans. Well, why not? Besides, it isn't only meant for Europeans. We also performed in Africa.

N.A.: During your last tour, you went to perform in Eastern Europe and you stopped by Tunis and Algiers. But these countries do suffer from a lack of theater-men, producers, actors, texts . . .

J.-M. S.: But how am I to blame with regards to Tunisia or African countries if I stage Césaire?

N.A.: I am not accusing you. It's a point that I would like you to clarify.

J.-M. S.: In our company, there are a number of fellows, especially from Côte d'Ivoire, who hold important positions in their countries. There are Algerians that certainly will one day.

N.A.: So in some cases these people come from African countries just to train with you before going back home?

J.-M. S.: Certainly. There are eleven nationalities in our company and I don't feel like anybody's father. I'll go straight to the point. I feel free to stage the plays that I like in relation to contemporary world history. And to stage those plays, I use the actors who I think are most qualified. It so happens that the relations between France and the Third World are still relevant. Besides, decolonization concerns the ex-colonizers as much as the ex-colonized. We must fight just as much to produce our plays in France as in Africa. That's how we know that we are probably dealing with free men, the real kind; I am referring to Kateb and Césaire. Depestre too. And it is true that we must fight on both fronts. It's not that easy.

N.A.: You are speaking of fighting on two fronts whereas I am speaking of fighting on one. Your fight isn't theirs.

J.-M. S.: My fight is that of the political poet attuned to history. My history is also yours because there are no separate histories. I deplore and regret that authors such as Kateb and Césaire should so rarely be staged in their own countries. This is due to the fact that these countries suffer from a kind of Parisianism. It is true that in Dakar I have met people with all the flaws I abhor in Paris and I have seen the same thing in

North Africa. But again, my fight isn't mine alone. The fight for freedom isn't exclusive to anybody and when a writer has something to say in relation to his people's freedom, it is of interest to all peoples, even those of colonizing countries.

N.A.: I am thinking of the era of French colonization. In those days, you put on a play by Kateb Yacine — La femme sauvage ou le cadavre encerclé [The wild woman or the encircled cadaver][14] — *during the very troubled period of bombings and intimidation.*

J.-M. S.: On that topic I also put on *The Exception and the Rule*, which is similarly a story of class struggle that could never be performed anywhere in Africa except at the Algerian National Theater. It is exemplary of the type of play that should be shown to Africans as well as Europeans.

N.A.: But earlier I was speaking of Kateb Yacine and I was thinking that staging him during the French occupation was just another way for theatermen like you to participate in the Algerians' struggle. In that case, you were indeed fighting on two fronts.

J.-M. S.: We were participating in the Algerians' struggle from our little corner of the world, as much as we could. That's true. We performed for three thousand people, six hundred of whom attended on opening night. It was a way of expressing our solidarity as artists with the struggling Algerian people. Things are more complicated with Kateb because he writes in French and in the days following Algeria's independence, the Algerians' first concern was to reclaim their Arab character, and that also meant Arabization.

N.A.: Don't you think that Third World theater must engage in denunciation first, then in provocation, and finally in protest?

J.-M. S.: Certainly it must be a theater that helps the world to change, so it must ultimately spur spectators to question what they have always perceived as the norm. In Europe it is salutary for theater to call into question the pope's authority on temporal matters. Likewise, in Africa this kind of question must be posed in a useful, beneficial manner. I can only think about this through an analogy. Every man is in each man. Real theater must be three hundred percent political—as politics is what helps man change the world—and poetic—as the poet is there to call into question all that is considered to be self-evident or sacred. He does away with the dead letters of all writing, that is to say, all that is accepted as being impervious to change.

N.A.: You were speaking of Brecht and you mentioned The Exception and the Rule. *It is true that Brecht addresses issues of fascism, war, and exploitation, but don't you think that he will not move the African people as much as a Kateb or a Césaire could, since their theater is closer to the African sensibility?*

J.-M. S.: Certainly, especially since Brecht was influenced by a form of Chinese wisdom. Brecht belongs to the European social movement. I do believe that he is less close to an African sensibility than Kateb or Césaire. But I am not positive either—Brecht is a classic. We must approach him with the same freedom he showed when he dealt with the classics. This somewhat contradicts a certain tendency in Brecht criticism to try to boil Brecht down to overly systematic formulas. But the reality, the poetic fertility of Brecht escape these constraints. Brecht embodies a systematic questioning of received ideas. For Brecht, the issue is knowing how the poet can have an effect on the public as a Marxist? How does the fact of being a Marxist spur him to write in such and such a manner? Each poet encounters these same problems but in different historical conditions, at different times. It is Brecht's general attitude that matters.

N.A.: One day Brecht met Kateb Yacine through you. They expressed different points of view with enormous sympathy on both sides . . .

J.-M. S.: Yes, that was when Brecht was enjoying universal glory. Kateb was not very well known; it was at the beginning of the Algerian war. Brecht had come across Kateb's work through an oral translation apparently quite removed from Kateb's thinking, at least with regards to form. They debated the word *tragedy* at length. For Brecht, there is no tragedy today—if we take tragedy to be the expression of an ineluctable fate, the *fatum*—for there is always a scientific solution to every supposedly unsolvable problem. Kateb was not familiar with Brecht's theoretical work. He was exclusively focused on his own work, on Algeria's problems. He would say, "I too am a Marxist and we are in the midst of a war of liberation. But in the short term it is true that for some men tragedy exists." He was playing on both meanings of the word *tragedy*, the ancient meaning and the one we give to it today. Besides, Brecht did not really grasp North Africa's problems except maybe through the general framework of class struggle: obviously, Kateb was much more attentive to the issue, which was his own history.

N.A.: Looking back on the events that happened last May and June, what was theater's contribution? Everybody spoke of street theater, happenings, provocation, improvisation, unrest, but in truth there were no significant theatrical performances. What caused this failure? Whereas in China theater played a great role in the cultural revolution — Mao's wife wrote a resounding revolutionary opera.

J.-M. S.: There was no need for theater because theater was every-where. There was theater at the Sorbonne, at the barricades. In a certain way, this prerevolutionary situation was dramatized in the extreme. I am not too familiar with Chinese theater; in France, there is no tradi-tion of spontaneously expressing a revolutionary state through theater. There may be one in China.

N.A.: In Vietnam for example there are operas dealing with imperialism and war with the aim of raising awareness and sensitizing the Vietnamese people. Earlier, I was speaking about theater's failure to partake of the event.

J.-M. S.: An actor on a barricade doesn't feel like mimicking what is happening at the barricade next to him.

N.A.: And yet the actors, the directors did not take to the streets. It wasn't ac-tors who occupied the Odéon Theater, the 347 Theater, but students who walked into these places reserved for a certain elite and turned them into a forum.

J.-M. S.: That's quite natural.

N.A.: That may be so, but it was rather awkward. The so-called revolution-ary actors were not doing anything. In general they are not politicized and they are only looking to get parts.

J.-M. S.: Do you mean that the profession as a whole didn't par-ticipate much? That's possible. Were they less revolutionary than stu-dents? That may be so. But that can be said of all professions. It is true that for centuries the Vietnamese people have, in their struggle, shown a will, strength, and constancy that have been exemplary for all peo-ples. But using that as a basis to judge French actors as a profession doesn't make sense to me.

N.A.: I was really deploring the lack of political activism in the profession. In the old days the artist was a creator who lived in a vacuum, and last May's events have shattered that form of creation.

J.-M. S.: It is true that it forced people to reflect on their purpose in life. Does our work play any role in changing the world or are we here simply to give the refined Parisian elite pleasure?

N.A.: It's this notion of the artist that I would like you to develop. Nowadays, the artist is more akin to the worker, the collective. He tries not to be alone anymore. The people have partaken in a collective creation with artists. Everybody has had a chance to give their two cents. Up to now in theater the actors would come, perform, and leave again. The spectators envisioned it as a sacred object, a tableau . . .

J.-M. S.: Those are all the forms of the traditional theater ceremony in its managerial and architectural dimensions, which no longer correspond or strongly relate to the aspirations of a modern society (technically developed and socialist). In May the Odéon Theater, as a symbol, was one of the monuments of a civilization undergoing fundamental mutations. The government is facing the impossible task of making the Odéon run again. No coordinator wants to prostitute himself by taking over from Barrault, who was sacked by a regime displaying a certain liberalism, but which has thrown off its mask and shown its true colors when it laid off a theater director who had publicly disagreed with the authorities.

N.A.: In May we saw an interesting form of theater emerge: some agitators gathered a previously indifferent audience around an orator. This form of theater is known in North Africa as al-halqa: *a storyteller successfully piques people's curiosity, and the rest follows easily. Isn't that a sort of theater of provocation? From there, can't we move on to blowing up sacred theaters and taking to the streets?*

J.-M. S.: I agree of course. We must find the right form.

N.A.: In Avignon, The Living Theater disrupted the festival by wanting to perform on the street. The protesters who supported The Living Theater wanted to remove theater from its sacred performance space and to give it its true meaning by taking it to the street, where it is accessible to all.

J.-M. S.: I am fundamentally sympathetic to The Living Theater, I admire them very much, but I cannot ignore the fact that every time something was happening in the street, television crews happened to be there filming Julian Beck. Things may not have been as innocent as we thought they were. The protesters were very shrewd to use The Living Theater. But The Living Theater also used the protests. It's more subtle. What I saw in Avignon seemed artificial from all perspectives. The commercial nature of The Living Theater's protest was never denied, not even by The Living Theater itself. That's the American way.

N.A.: *In America some companies perform in the street. Why isn't this the case in France?*

J.-M. S.: The Bread and Puppet Theater. They are remarkable. They create a truly popular celebration by piquing the curiosity of an interactive audience in all the neighborhoods where they perform. In the countries of the so-called Third World, this kind of theater could be very significant and far-reaching for the masses who can't afford tickets for performances usually reserved for a privileged elite. This doesn't happen in France because no French artist has tried it yet.

N.A.: *Would you like to talk about the Maisons de la Culture now? Have they really formed a new audience who had never previously had access to theater?*

J.-M. S.: The policy behind the Maisons de la Culture envisioned the construction of an ever-growing number of centers. We would have needed to have ten of them after five years and a hundred after ten years. The economic conditions don't seem to allow for it. We will have to find additional solutions. For example, building new spaces or developing an amateur theater. We will need to substitute the notion of the tour to that of a fixed performance space. In the meantime, department stores such as the Galeries Lafayette, Printemps, and BHV, together with other workplaces, may well be ideal locations to make theater. What we need is a political system that would include theatrical performances, film screenings, and exhibits that would fit in the worker's schedule. What Vilar did fifteen years ago in factories in the suburbs, when he took his touring company to meet an audience that didn't know a thing about theater, still remains the best approach to this day.

N.A.: I would like you to tell me more about the importance of technical elements in your shows such as the role of images, projections, sound effects . . .

J.-M. S.: Sound effects more than anything else. We also use projections but, when we can't we try to do without. We live in a world of images, of signals that spectators perceive through advertisement and which affect their mental configurations. This can modify the actors' play. When we go to the theater, we bring with us the traditional structure of society and especially our direct perspective on the event. We perceive something that is delivered to us just like an image would be shown to a prince. Nowadays the spectator demands two or three viewpoints at a time. The public for whom we perform perceives the world through many signals—through TV, the radio, weekly magazines—it's more demanding. This is a cognitive process that doesn't lead to Italianate theater. We can no longer envision theater in the same way. And a political theater which draws on current events is better served by sound effects and visual techniques.

PLANET OF THE APES

Tahar Ben Jelloun

Translated from the French by Anna Moschovakis

Go quickly! It's a country that's ripe for the taking
It is there for your pleasure
Ah! What a beautiful country Morocco is!
Ouarzazate! Ah, these benevolent storks tucking their bills in the crook
of their wings.
Leave your office, your wife and your children
Come quickly, surround yourself with barbed wire in the ghettos where guts
lie drying in the sun
Come hang your testicles from the ramparts of the Zagora
Go retrieve them from Red Marrakech

> let your memories hibernate
> and bring back new neuroses

Point your finger toward the sky
Snatch some sun from our underdevelopment
Your impotence will be multiplied in decapitated memories

> And your inky night will deploy its fortification walls
> against sewer streams

Beware of ARABS
> *they are rotten thieves*
> *they can rip out your brains*
> *scorch them and serve them to you on tablets of mute earth*

(Listen, instead, to another voice):
The Club of my Med is your salvation
French ambiance guaranteed, *required, reimbursed*
Climb up on the dromedaries

> *your vertigo will be in the image of your gyrating hunger;*
> *your mouth will open to apostolate the Fall and tears*

In the morning, drink a little Arab blood: just enough to decaffeinate your
racism;

To your friends offer your tattooed memory

> *a postcard of beatitude in aluminum*
> *dim resonance of your skull-cemetery;*

And then go ahead, take an Arab

> *he is Natural, a bit savage*

>> *but so virile . . .*

Sex in shreds of deracinated flesh
will remain
> *Hanging from the thread of your shameful memory*
You will no longer be able to chase him from your fantasies
He'll ejaculate humiliation and rape right in your face
Wounded
>> *you'll collapse* beneath tame trees
>> *you'll see the stars dissolve in your facile dreams*
>> *a fever will come and you'll spit up blood*
>> *all over your good intentions*
>> *the bastards are going to crucify you dead*
>> *in the shadow* of the marvelous sun of the Club *of my Med*

abdellatif laâbi

mobilisation-tract

bonne année camarades
c'est le moment des bilans
                    on ne demande pas de statistiques
de nouvelles victoires s'inscrivent au calendrier des peuples
10ᵉ anniversaire révolution cubaine
cessation bombardements sur viet-nam nord
4ᵉ année déclenchement lutte populaire armée palestine
en angola 9
            au mozambique 5
sans oublier l'érosion violente du colosse américain
par la négraille debout
                    la gâchette froide
de nouvelles défaites tombent au livre noir des gorilles
écrasement insurrection petites antilles
apartheid crématoire du Continent
barricades guerilla urbaine sur cadavre occidental
combien de massacres
                    en frontières sûres au nom liberté peuples

27

A GENOUX LES DAMNES DE LA TERRE

bonne année camarades
la lutte continue
cette grande humanité a dit assez
mosché dayan inspecte
                    à l'ombre des mirages
                              shalom napalm
les cosmonautes ont vu à l'œil nu la face cachée de la lune
le dollar connait des hauts et des bas
la livre sterling éternellement menacée
                        de gaulle multiplie ses frasques
                        et se retire grand seigneur

FIGURE 10. "Mobilisation-Tract" (excerpt), poem by Abdellatif Laâbi. *Souffles* 13–14 (Rabat, 1969), p. 27. Reprinted with permission.

MOBILIZATION-TRACT

Abdellatif Laâbi

Translated from the French by Olivia C. Harrison

happy new year comrades
it's time to draw up the balance sheet
                              we're not asking for statistics
new victories are etched onto the calendar of the people
10th anniversary cuban revolution
bombardments on northern vietnam cease
4th year onset popular armed palestinian struggle
in angola 9
          in mozambique 5
not to mention the violent erosion of the american colossus
by the rising nigger scum[15]
                         the trigger cold
new defeats are recorded in the black book of strongmen
crushing insurrection lesser antilles
apartheid crematorium of the Continent
barricades urban guerilla on western cadaver
how many massacres
                    in secure borders in name liberty people

ON YOUR KNEES WRETCHED OF THE EARTH
happy new year comrades
the struggle goes on
this great humanity has said enough
moshe dayan inspects
                    in the shadow of mirages
                                   shalom napalm
the cosmonauts have seen the hidden face of the moon with their bare
    eyes
the dollar is seesawing
the sterling pound eternally threatened
                              de gaulle keeps making mischief
                              and then nobly retires
these days media corporations make huge profits
arabs buy more and more oum kalthoum records

the c.i.a checks its books again
computers drool surpluses
the legendary bull changes horns
great and small panics of the fourteenth century

happy new year comrades
and us
          where are we now
land of contrasts
                    golden apples and legends
oh these damned jaffa oranges
a stampede toward the sun
                              native rocks-palm trees-snakes
pretty-cushion-jewel-jellaba   berber   it's more authentic
open repression
                    a 500,000 km² bazaar
anthropometric card
                    police record
mercenaries on every street
our people brought down by volleys of exploitative feudal systems
silence is in order

see see see we don't have enough to eat we don't work we don't
understand we don't speak we don't fuck we don't live
   help
   who gets the first bullet?
shush shush don't mind me
omo is here if you want to move in blue drink fanta kodak
plus the battery that only runs down around the red square drawn by
the ball point pen all this thanks to the special bomb roaches ants of
the laughing cow
the comedian fernand raynaud smiling havas media advertisement
a little exuberant moroccan reporter africa-film thanks
underdeveloped humor summary midnight Opinion
soccer spanish cards and teddy-television
sleep sleep well
                    your guilt-free nightmare
sleep sleep well

dear crowd
from jerusalem to granada

happy new year comrades
comrade you are consuming
you are stuffing yourself
morocco is the world's biggest consumer of whisky
proclaim radio-medina radio-shantytowns
comrade you turn
you turn up for the show
you don't disdain the finished-products of the somaca automobile
factory
you collect
you make yourself comfortable
you are suspicious of the heroism
adventurism
terrorism
of poets
bizarre race with a curiously high suicide rate
all these detours smell bad
don't they
all this organic-physiological-erotic-lyrical-badly   oriented
with so few quotations
refrains
so few references
you enjoy your petty revolutionary life between two weekends
and meals for ten
you respect the stop signs
the transitions
the do-not-pass signs
within speeding limits
following the rules of the road
you consult the tables of the law
of our times of course
sure of yourself
sure of yourselves
comrades

here comes the 1st of may
and in waves throats slit with a laser cry
rational masses regenerating speech
with irrevocable diagnoses
                              dictating to us
you can take your american flour back
                              Ho ho hochiminh
workers and students
power to the people now
                              che che guevara
in waves memorandum
banners forum blank books
in ripe slogans motor force
                              ho ho
vacillating tongue fire mask
                              che che
balance sheet translated in collective dialogue

1st of may spring of speech
3 hours for 365 days of aphasia
it's very little so little even to describe a nightmare it's very little so little
even for a resolution to commit suicide it's very little so little the time it takes
to plead to save the head of a condemned man
yet today we are almost 15 million
let's tally up the illiterate the pariahs the exiled the unemployed the prisoners
the marginals the druggies the whores the syphilitic the paralytic the
underfed the uprooted the alcoholics the jailors the fanatics
what will be left?

3 hours for 365 days of aphasia
it's very little so little to don liberty and pummel the dead with it to puke up
anesthetic and jump over the hospital wall to force open the 77 padlocks that
clamp our lips
i curse this freedom
timed drip-fed reprieve

this is the balance sheet
                    we must hand in
                              we must hand in

until the day the dog dies

comrade

i am addressing the man in you No not the castrated man from moral tales not the man in your textbooks or the speeches of the U.N.

i am addressing the man in you   The rooted man   the man who has demented visions   the orgasmic man   the man who has fists that don't chew on their fingers   the man who has an untamed lancet wrapped up in layers of magnetic rancor ready to vitriol the face of genocide.

i am addressing the man in you   The man who has fissions of actions the titan who has long strides of history. I care about your dream. I care about your frenetic sprints mired in quick sands. I care as much about your missteps as about your steady steps toward a total man and your obsessions. And about your wandering of course. Your doubts. Your certainties.

Your wild nomadic freedom.

I share salt and bread with you when I ejaculate a poem and we all know what that means superstitious or not. We intervein ourselves so that blood be between us the only border of necessity.

The poem. Sharing. Silence will kill us. All private life is a scandal. Here I am. Bareheaded. Provocative. Yes to provoke the creator in you   All the creators in you. Public announcer in posters of neurons plastered to the wall of silence. Speleologist of the coming uprising.

spectators

            do not accept the silence
to each his own silence
HE WHO ACCEPTS THE SILENCE IS NOT A MAN
cadavers cadavers

                    oil rigs

                        minarets of cadavers
candidates for daily suicide
you commit suicide every day when you accept the silence
you become stiff

                    corpse-like

                            yellow

            every day when you nail shut your throat and your fists

every assembly is a demonstration
                          or else it's a cemetery
i tell you
          MAN WILL SPEAK
                          HIS KINGDOM WILL COME

REVIEW OF ABDELKEBIR KHATIBI'S *LE ROMAN MAGHRÉBIN*

Tahar Ben Jelloun

Translated from the French by Claudia Esposito

A clarification of this essay will allow us to determine in broad strokes the goals Khatibi has set for himself.

— First of all *Le roman maghrébin* [The Maghrebi novel] is a non-exhaustive[16] expository essay that develops only a limited number of themes and does not in any way claim to have mapped out all the questions relevant to Maghrebi literature and its writers.[17]

— The second point is that, without compromising the content or diminishing the importance and urgency of the ideas it defends, this essay is intended for the general public.[18]

In order to describe this essay, we have decided to focus on one of the themes developed by Khatibi, one that we consider to be among the most important given that it encompasses and subtends all the others: the problem of acculturation.

"To ask ourselves what the novel means to us Maghrebis, now in 1968, that is to say during the period of decolonization," entails tracing a functional outline that defines its method and demystifies the system.[19] Although the author addresses this question on a number of levels, it is the issue of acculturation that should have been analyzed in more detail.

To be sure, Khatibi analyzed acculturation in the Maghrebi novel by way of several categories: the sexualized perception of the West and the failure of irony, uprooting, a systematic revolt against familial and colonial alienation.[20] Nevertheless, his analysis lacks theoretical development.

The concept of acculturation alone fully defines the sick and weakened makeup of the Maghrebi writer's status. This situation is defined by the perception of the Other (as an alternative for the desired identity). As Abdallah Laroui writes in *L'idéologie arabe contemporaine*, "to think is, first and foremost, to think the other . . . the Other of the Arabs is the West."[21]

Khatibi proposes three ways of thinking the Other:

— a sexualized perspective (in the works of the Tunisian Ali al-Duaji)

— the perspective of the dominated man (the case of Albert Memmi)[22]

— a psychoanalytic perspective of the Other through the figure of the sacralized father (the case of Driss Chraïbi).[23]

Of interest to us is the question of whether Khatibi's methodology adequately deals with the problematic of acculturation.

The conceptual apparatus Khatibi deploys often comes under the sway of psychoanalysis. But why doesn't his analysis go all the way in bringing together the sociological dimension and the model of psychoanalytic interpretation?

Al-Duaji's case is rather typical in this regard. To be sure, he obviously deploys an eroticized space, but only as one of several ways of apprehending the other. This eroticization is also a concrete projection of the self in which narcissism can thrive. Even when he tries to distance himself through irony, the writer is bound to his own image. His dis-alienation occurs not through the other—even if the Other is a woman—but through his own self as mediator.

In Khatibi's analysis of Memmi we find ethno-psychoanalytic concepts such as "uprooting" and "splitting."[24] The Other is first and foremost the person who has sequestered his identity, who is the cause of "the loss of a fundamental unity." Hatred produces a dominated and rebellious writer; his novel becomes autobiography. Once again we find an unresolved narcissistic process since, contrary to what Khatibi believes, there is no "deciphering of alienation and questioning of the colonial universe."[25] The analysis of the self becomes a spectacle, a total projection of the self in writing, a doubling of the person and a sublimation of conflicts. A sociology of oppression, and therefore a denunciation of acculturation, can only be undertaken by the self (this might in fact be another effective level of analysis).

Acculturation occurs at the level of experience, of course. But we need to consider this experience in all its dimensions.

The third case, which, as Khatibi emphasizes, offers a psychoanalytic model, is that of Chraïbi. It is here that a more developed analysis would have allowed us to go beyond the particular in order to attain the universal, culminating in a challenge to the traditional and patriarchal system in place. Khatibi gestures toward this possibility, but he does not go far enough in his psychoanalytic approach. . . .[26] In order fully to define Chraïbi's revolt, it would have been necessary to operate a hermeneutic reading, analyzing, for instance, the triangular father-mother-son relationship in terms of conflict and then of signs.

The "sacralized," "deified," omnipresent, and omnipotent father is the very image of the patriarch and of charisma, the subject of a form of hatred that Khatibi calls "sadistic."[27] "I am also sadistic," writes Chraïbi, but his is a conscious and responsible sadism that is still incomprehensible to the father. One cannot speak of identification with the father here. Chraïbi devotes only hatred and hostility to his father. The murder of the father does not come from the opposition between admiration and hostility. The dissolution of the Oedipus complex remains suspended. He has substituted his mother, who could not be a woman given how "difficult he [the father] made life for her,"[28] with a real woman. As Khatibi rightly notes: "liberation is carried out through Eros. Unbridled virility is a means to combat the Father, and the brothel is the first education of a free man."[29]

These three Maghrebi cases thus illustrate and express the phenomenon of acculturation, under the sign of the edification of an authentic national culture, that is to say, a decolonized national culture. Precisely because of the phenomenon of acculturation, the Maghrebi writer's existential difficulties lead to even more serious problems, those pertaining to communication. Laroui notes the distinct separation between the intellectual and other social strata: "being out of touch with the totality of society, the intellectual sees the social dialectic from the outside. That is to say, he sees it in abstract terms and can thus resort indiscriminately to classical Arabic or to a foreign language because his only public is composed of himself and of his intellectual brethren."[30]

Whether the voice of the writer only reaches an elite or is reflected back on itself as if in echo, we cannot in the specific case of the Maghreb believe in the illusion of communication with all social strata. Above all the writer expresses himself. This may be to fulfill a narcissistic need rather than to commit an act of generosity. We won't go as far as Laroui however in claiming that a "significant part of French North African literature is transitional, circumstantial, and scarcely expressive since it conceives of itself as a regionalist branch of a culture whose center is elsewhere, and which is alone authorized to approve or disapprove of it."[31]

Khatibi did not think twice about denouncing the kind of literature that accompanied colonialism (his expository essay is first and foremost a position-taking and a denunciation) or of exploding the unilateral relationships that bound the métropole to its former colonies.

A BEGINNING BUT NO END
(EXCERPTED FROM *ONLY THE FIRE REMAINS*)

Ahmed al-Madini

Translated from the Arabic by Ghenwa Hayek

Yesterday you were that clown wandering the city streets and the path-ways of neighboring villages, children behind you running, being play-ful. Only yesterday your lips were burning with fire. And today the fire is consuming everything, burning the atoms of past glories, breaking the backs of horses, lacerating secrets, and today this fire pours from your mouth, from all the darkened caves consumed by cobwebs, to roast the bones of the city and eject it into the pits of hell. You see there is no other end, and from the burning flames emerge the rhinoceroses and the dwarves and those with sewers for mouths, new creatures. The tour hasn't ended and the ring is clouded with smoke. Inside it the heroes are in the midst of struggle and battle, a million wounded, a million killed.

But you have gathered your breath and blown out voracity and abandonment through the streets. Will you stand or will you continue to drink from the eyes that have been paralyzed and left behind?

This is the question bitterly dogging your footsteps. The first breaths were a furnace that removed the blur and dust of hypocrisy but will you stand, your wheezing, and the knowledge of those im-migrants scurrying off into the corners of the world worrying your mind? Your hair stands on end, becoming a war that bursts through the gates of heaven, fucking angels and maidens and young boys in the alleys of longing and sorrow where they mix, those immigrants from ages and ages ago.

Everything is covered in smoke, the tiles are burning, the brass stat-ues are tickled by flames. But . . . are you there gathering all this vio-lence into your arms, collecting a long file in the eye of the firestorm?

There you are walking, cold everywhere, the shameful rites occur-ring daily and the cycles of the stupid seasons becoming ever more intransigent. There you are, headed into the stupid cities, setting off to fuck the innocent.

Like any vortex, like any vortex, like any vortex, like any storm.

PART FOUR

SOUFFLES 15—ANFAS 7–8 (1969–1972)

SOUFFLES 15, titled "For the Palestinian Revolution," marks a shift in the journal's layout (fig. 15), rubrics (fig. 16) and editorial line, particularly concerning developments in the Middle East: Arab-Israeli politics, the Palestinian question, and the Eritrean, Dhofari, and western Sahara independence movements. We have included an article by the Moroccan Jewish leftist militant Abraham Serfaty, which accuses French colonial divide-and-rule politics (including the French-language schools of the Alliance Israélite Universelle, a Paris-based institution devoted to the "enlightenment" of Mediterranean Jews) and Zionism of fomenting discord between Jews and Arabs, and calls on his coreligionists to condemn the Israeli state. Though the Palestine issue also features artwork, cartoons (figs. 11–14), and poetry celebrating the Palestinian resistance (including a poem by the Lebanese writer Etel Adnan, the only female poet published in *Souffles*), subsequent issues, including the eight issues of *Anfas*, the Arabic-language journal founded in 1971, focus on political analysis and leftist commentary. One exception is a poem by the Sudanese poet Muhammad al-Fayturi, published in the final issue of *Anfas* in honor of the failed communist rebellion of 1971 ("Witness Statements," fig. 23). The *Souffles-Anfas* team did not neglect the realm of culture during this final period, however. On the contrary, it became even more explicit in its cultural politics, publishing an "Appeal to Maghrebi Writers" that articulated the struggle against French neocolonialism (and, implicitly, the autocratic postcolonial state) to Palestinian resistance against Israeli imperialism, and called on Maghrebi poets to take even bolder risks in their formal and linguistic experimentation. *Souffles* sent reporters to the first Pan-African Cultural Festival, held in Algiers in 1969 (fig. 15), and published an interview with the Senegalese novelist and filmmaker Ousmane Sembène as well as the Black Panthers' "Ten Point Program" alongside one of Emory Douglas's famous Panther posters (fig. 17). The nineteenth issue of *Souffles* further attests to the journal's pan-Africanism, featuring a poster of the iconic Congolese anticolonial leader Patrice Lumumba (fig. 18), a special dossier on the anticolonial struggles in Portugal's African colonies (figs. 20 and 21), and cartoons illustrating the common struggles of Arab and African peoples (figs. 19 and 22).

During this final phase the journal also changed course in terms of language use. Though as late as 1970 Laâbi defended a "terrorist" use of the French language ("Contemporary Maghrebi Literature"), in what was to be the final issue of *Souffles* he acknowledged that the journal had paradoxically attempted to decolonize Moroccan culture in the colonial tongue ("Foreword"). The editorial team's increasing suspicion vis-à-vis *francophonie*—the use of French as well as the institutions supporting it, from the myriad international organizations listed by Laâbi in his 1970 editorial to the publishing and critical apparatus he denounced in his review of the Algerian writer Rachid Boudjedra's first novel—led the journal to advocate for the use of the Arabic language, though it continued to publish *Souffles* for a French-language public. The penultimate text included here, a 1971 *Anfas* editorial condemning Arab regimes' complacency vis-à-vis Palestine and calling in thinly veiled terms for leftist revolution across the Arab world, might have been written at the dawn of the Tunisian and Egyptian uprisings, were it not for a Marxist-Leninist and pan-Arab lexicon that feels dated today. The editorial also makes allusion to a text on Egyptian class struggles by "Mahmoud Hussein," the pseudonym used by the Egyptian leftists Bahgat Elnadi and Adel Rifaat, published in the second issue of *Anfas*. As demonstrated by transnational intellectual affiliations such as these, *Souffles-Anfas* was part of vibrant global radical leftist tradition, one that was violently repressed in Morocco. A year after the *Anfas* 2 editorial the *Souffles-Anfas* team was imprisoned, putting an abrupt end to the leftist tribune and forum of cultural decolonization.

FIGURE 11. Front cover of "For the Palestinian Revolution," special issue of *Souffles* (no. 15; Rabat, 1969), by Mohamed Chebaa. Reprinted with permission.

FIGURE 12. "Palestine," poster by Mohamed Melehi. *Souffles* 15 (Rabat, 1969), p. 4. Reprinted with permission.

JEBU (EXCERPT)

Etel Adnan
Translated from the French by Etel Adnan

o dead cities of the XXIst century
Beirut and Tel Aviv!

these days you should learn to count
in order to survive count the tortures
of Sarafand

> in the geological cliffs of Western
> Asia vultures thank the sky for the
> abundance of their food: more dead
> Arabs than stone in this desert!

We had learned sorrow in Algiers
lived a happy moment and now
it has to be started again . . .

Noises . . .

We shall atomize the mountains so that
there shall be no more Revelations
truth will emerge from a well

Jebu commands the ghosts that are following
him to disappear in the gasoline of
our neighborhood drugstores
the wind is coming . . .

> Sitting in humid movie houses
> we have seen slummy Christs bless
> electric screens
> we have loved . . .

> We have now to crucify
> the Crucified

his age-long treason has sickened us

Ra   Shamash   Marduk
the astronauts have invaded the moon
so that in the grandeur of your
loneliness
you come back alone in your boats
o geometric monotheism announced by Jebu

Sun of the Past
     hunger
     shame
          thirst
          fear
          sickness
     isolation
     madness

cargoes of solar boats
in the free zone of Beirut harbor
our ships are armored cars
that our men lead on the roads of the
sky   the sky is an ocean where they
drown   doom is a jazz trumpet
howling on the Place des Canons

On the return (the Moon–Earth trajectory)
in the cosmic railway
Jebu says:

I have seen the earth   magnetic ball
burn at its edges   radioactive   primordial
solar   in a language atomic
electric
magnetic

she said:
I am a cosmic vessel
and my blood-brothers (the primordial bedu)
on the mercurial altars where they are slaughtered

will be born again they are my essence.

Jebu Canaanite   founder of Jerusalem
tells the Crucified:

you have suffered three days
I have suffered for three millennia

(the fedayi is a writing glued to the ground
and pushing ahead   wounded   his saliva
heals the open earth in his agony he
sees a rain of meteors

in death he forgets that they dried the
cisterns so that we eat worms and
consider happiness to be a funerary oration

                  but we have displaced the sky . . .

they do not know that the wind
is a bird which flies)

Darkly our children were drowning
in our peaceful rivers   the people
were in a swamp and we called for liberation

now do I announce:

      napalm
      hunger
      the cunning of the enemy
      the slow flying airplanes   the dynamite
      torture
      and more corpses than larvae in a rotten
      pond
      we are guilty of innocence

and also:

      the backward movement of the dead
      the guns carried by ghosts
      plants growing only in winter
      a tank made of jelly which will break the front

and soldiers of the year two thousand

creative disorder
is our divine stubbornness.

He will mount an attack on the
Fifth Ocean   give Venus the investiture
of his breath   inhabit Uranus

the people will come out of their ratty sewers
and discover the immensity of the world. Let a
single piece of bread feed the tribe. The father
will call his son: his brother . . .

Jebu has millions of roots innumerable heads
a proliferation of bodies   he is the whole and
each one of us since the first break of Time
he is the people on the space-time equation

I have seen the women-sounding villages
of my generation: Samua   Kuneitra   Kalkilya

rapacious foreigners   drinkers of
bitumen   you have in abundance but
hatred and on roads where serpents
can't feed   you forced the women of
Jericho to chew diamonds   Arabs are
but a mirage which persists . . .

In the beginning Jebu had been killed
but his eyes are the Tigris and the Euphrates
his belly is Syria his penis is the Jordan
his long leg is the Nile Valley
one foot in Marrakech
his bleeding heart encased in Mecca
his hair is still growing on the Sannine

The X-ray of his being on the day of Hiroshima
like a sweat appeared on the Jerusalem Wall.

I know
the total moon

the slow-motion sadness
the poisoned rainbows
betrayed faces filling newstime screens   turned
towards vultures as if there was any other
messiah to wait for than the bomber
the total exile.

I know the coffins walking to the mosque
in a city where roses are watered with
gasoline
the foreign capitals who like dying bees
secrete lies
and the total moon
closing its claws on the tribe.

The torrid heat of the first king of
Jerusalem—astronaut coming back from
the moon that he inhabited and on whose
craters he left his sacred writings—the
heat is still glued upon the face of a
cosmic snow

> drinkers of blood   drinkers
> of petroleum   newcomers to napalm   nouveauxriches
> of torture   Gilgamesh shall plant his sword
> between your eyes

the City covered by the wind   by tears   by ultraviolet
rays   is trembling . . .

Palestine   mother of nations   is a glorified pestilence
with solar tumors on the face and repeated rapes in the
belly

MOROCCAN JEWRY AND ZIONISM (EXCERPTS)

Abraham Serfaty

Translated from the French by Lia Brozgal and Olivia C. Harrison

I will be asked, I have been asked: why should anyone continue to be concerned with Moroccan Jewry today? Let this community dwindle down with emigration; the last holdouts will no longer pose a problem.[1]

This study concerns the entirety of Moroccan Jews: those who have remained here; those who have been dispersed and uprooted in the West; those who have been transplanted to a state whose name was so symbolically charged for all Jews, and who discover today that this name hides an enterprise of proletarization, of cultural annihilation, and a militaristic and racist adventure.

This enterprise, which, within the framework of a general mystification of Jewry, mystified Moroccan Jews, was the crowning achievement of the colonial uprooting that began a century ago.

We would like to summarize this process in order to share our conviction—a conviction that has only grown stronger with the study of documents past and present—that this mystification will inevitably become known, that Jews from the Arab world, prisoners of Zionism, will gain consciousness of their solidarity with the Arab revolution and will help to shatter the last historical attempt to lock Jews up in a ghetto—and what a ghetto . . . of global proportions!

[. . .]

I. Moroccan Jewry Before Its Uprooting

Let us be clear. This uprooting did not occur on any given date. It is an ongoing process. Today what remains of Moroccan Jewry lives closed in on itself, and is increasingly concentrated in Casablanca, a city that typifies uprooting. But the era of flourishing, lively communities is still very recent. The celebrations in the Jewish quarters [*mellahs*] of Fes, Sefrou, Salé, among others, the symbiosis of communities from the Atlas and the South were still dazzling ten years ago, despite a century of colonial efforts relayed and developed by Zionism!

Everything has been said about this past, and yet everything remains to be said. All those who studied it took the West as their reference point. Colonizers or Zionists did so in order to distort this past, most often intentionally. Patriots as well as more objective observers did so in order to situate it in an historical impasse that was nonetheless presented as a "golden era," with no connection—other than sentimental—to the future.

Only by questioning this Western reference point and by formulating a specific vision for the future—a task that the Arab world has taken on since June 1967—can we resituate this past, revive it, and connect it to the future.

That being said, we must also cast aside colonial and Zionist lies, and with them, the liars.

André Chouraqui, former secretary general of the Alliance Israélite Universelle, wrote several books on North African and Moroccan Jewry. Under cover of juridical objectivity one of his books allowed the Zionist newspaper *Noar*, which poisoned Jewish Moroccan youth from 1945 to 1952, to proclaim in January 1951 that thanks to France "the Jew has been liberated from the limitless arbitrary rule that continued to subject him to his master's will."[2]

Mr. Chouraqui is well positioned in the Zionist state, but what will those he helped mislead think when they remember the 1947 speech by the vice president of the Alliance, who declared that if it desired a Jewish home for the survivors of Nazism, "the Alliance also wonders what the future of Palestine will look like. It cannot be sure, but it is convinced that things will 'work out.' For if they didn't, stressed M. Brunschwig [sic], it would be an absolute catastrophe . . . "[3]

Let us return to this "arbitrary rule," which curiously allowed isolated communities in the mountains and the South to perpetuate themselves through the centuries intact, with their customs, their goods, and their rights.

Judeo-Arab symbiosis was not only that of a dazzling civilization, leading a contemporary Jewish author to write:

> Islam, however, is from the very flesh and bone of Judaism. It is, so to say, a recast, an enlargement of the latter, just as Arabic is closely related to Hebrew. Therefore, Judaism could draw freely and copiously from Muslim civilization and, at the same time, preserve its independence and integrity far more completely than it was able do in the modern world or in the Hellenistic society of Alexandria. . . . Never has Judaism encountered such a close and fructitious symbiosis as that with the medieval civilization of Arab Islam.[4]

Although Judeo-Arab culture experienced the retreat of the entire Arab world, stifled as it was by the expansion of capitalism, daily life within the communities nonetheless perpetuated this symbiosis.

Here it is necessary to explain *dhimmi*, or protected, status. Two communities coexisted, both of them based on an organic conception according to which men were completely integrated in their communities. Established structures organized this coexistence based on mutual respect, with one notable difference, it is true: the dominant, Muslim community held the responsibility of the state or of the tribe in political and military terms, a responsibility that included respect for the minority community. Of course, the reconstruction of Judeo-Arab symbiosis will have to prohibit every kind of discrimination, including the political kind, but this cannot be done according to the mechanistic conception of a sterile, Western-style secularism. A secular Palestine, rejecting the West in order to participate in the construction of the Arab world, is meaningful and promising only within the framework of the "democratic state" discussed by Marx in his *On the Jewish Question*, not the "political state" of bourgeois democracy.[5]

To come back to the history of Judeo-Arab symbiosis, historians of colonization and colonial assimilation—from the ideologues of the colonial administration,[6] to those that a son of the heyday of colonialism called, with characteristic racist disdain, the "advanced, ambitious, and alarming elements" of the Jewish community[7]—sought out texts that would prove their colonial theses and singled out the excesses of local adventurers or bloodthirsty sovereigns, forgetting, as does the book of a former president of Casablanca's Israelite community,[8] that these excesses also targeted Muslims, who themselves condemned these excesses.[9]

But how can we prove that our thesis is more accurate than theirs? By comparing one series of texts to another, by comparing facts that are made discrete by the process of historical research to other discrete facts? No. Moroccan Jews who experienced this symbiosis, their children who were culturally and ideologically sundered from the nation by Zionist organizations, will be able to unearth the concrete facts of daily life and lasting friendships once their eyes have been opened to the reality of Zionism.

We will ask people of good faith who did not experience this friendship to reflect upon the significance of the following facts:

The origins of *dhimmi* status can be best apprehended not through the analysis of legal documents, but through the analysis of the facts at hand before they are distorted by capitalist structures and colonization or destroyed by Zionism. Take for example the case of rural communities, the home of twenty-five percent of Moroccan Jews who were dispersed in the mountainous regions of the South, the High Atlas, and the plateaus of the Sahel. In these villages, relations between Jews and Muslims developed without external obstacles, within the cultural framework of these rural communities. One of the rare studies of these communities analyzes customary law in the Tafilalet region. It shows that if each Jew in these ancient peasant communities sought, not a "Lord" as it has been claimed, nor "a protector, nor exactly a tutor, but a 'respondent' in the full sense of the word," it was for precise reasons linked to the juridical traditions of both communities.[10] Litigation in particular was based on oath-taking by Jews in the synagogue and by Muslims before a judge [*qadi*]. In the case of conflicts between Jews and Muslims, the Muslim respondent of the Jew would take an oath before the *qadi* in the Jew's stead. This respondent was expected to take up arms to defend or avenge the Jew in the event of a crime.

Jews were also allowed to "borrow, buy, or sell goods and property, dwellings, and tribal land," exactly like Muslims. In some cases they even enjoyed a right of preemption "in cases of willful alienation of property by one of their Jewish relatives."[11]

The life of these two communities was thus organized in these "pre-capitalist" structures, where, to paraphrase Marx, production was organized for man, not man for production. European Jewish travelers, who were still attached to the human content of Judaism and not alienated by Western civilization, discovered the same feeling of "fullness" in the life of urban communities, which were steeped in the same cultural origins, the same fraternal symbiosis with the Muslim community, and finally understood the concept of "nostalgia for the *mellah*."[12]

This life was at once closed and in symbiosis with the Muslim community. It was not a ghetto encircled by a hostile world. To what we have already said let us add that this friendship and affection between Jews and Muslims still manifests itself during religious festivities, particularly during the gift-giving ceremonies on the night of Mimouna, and the fact, noted by surprised Europeans observers, that Muslims worship Jewish saints.[13]

Let us be clear. This was a comprehensive Judaism. It also included the ideal of the "return to Israel," and the Passover prayer, "next year in Jerusalem." Zionism coopted the ambiguity of this ideal and prayer. It is true that the negative aspects of this ambiguity were able to take shape in European society, distorted by capitalism and colonial ideology, giving rise to Zionist ideology.[14] But still, quite apart from all personal conviction, the fact remains that this ideal and prayer take root in the universalist and humanist aspects of Judaism. The ideal of "Israel" belongs to the sons of God, who were burdened by suffering and were promised that the Kingdom of God would come about in this world. "Next year in Jerusalem" is linked to the conception of the Messiah and the advent of this Kingdom for all men.[15]

We are not talking about the reign of the Golden Calf and of the Rothschild Bank, nor about taking Moshe Dayan for the Messiah. Zionism understood this so well that it tried to uproot the belief in the Messiah. In 1944 one of the Zionist organizers in Morocco, Prosper Cohen, who continues his work in the Zionist state today, wrote a kind of exhortation for the community to give up hope in the Messiah and in humanity. "What is the Messiah? In fact, you know no better than any other people what the Messiah is or will be. . . . Will this Jewish king come? Will this era of happiness open up for the Jews? You know it will not, headstrong people! You know that humanity is forever lost."[16]

The very same prophet of Zionism exhaled his disdain for the Jewish masses after the fiasco of the communal elections, organized in 1948 under the double aegis of Zionism and the French General Residency: "After the ridiculous fiasco of the past elections, can we still formulate an appeal for any kind of action? Indeed it seems that the torpor of a great number of our coreligionists is congenital, and that there is no remedy that can redress it."[17]

Indeed Zionism, racism, colonialism, and the disdain for men are all one and the same!

But the masses, Muslims and Jews alike, felt in their flesh a common hope in the Kingdom of God. This was given living expression in the shared friendships and celebrations of Mimouna on the last night of Passover, symbolizing the shared end of the desert of injustice men must traverse.

All of this, which requires further development, research, and reflection, is not only history. We must begin building a future, a society where once again production will be organized for man, a society where man will once again find the fullness that has been disarticulated by capitalism and Western culture, a society of creators where men will once again express their cultural values to imagine the future.

II. From the Uprooting of the "Elites" to Zionist Control

European capitalism first formulated the goal of conquering the Arab world when it began its turn toward modern imperialism. This goal was predicated from the outset upon an attempt to separate Jews and Muslims. Prefiguring both the European "left" and imperialism, Napoleon's call to African and Asian Jews—launched from Gaza in 1799—was officially grounded in the "ideals" of the French Revolution while appealing tacitly and more realistically to the bourgeoisie's appetite for conquest.

In the second half of the nineteenth century this effort to separate Jews and Muslims, aided by the eager and calculating participation of the great Jewish bankers, helped consolidate the colonial project. Edmond de Rothschild (already!) created the first colonial settlement in Palestine, to which—in a new version of the slave trade—he imported 5,000 Russian Jews. At the same time and also bankrolled by the Rothschild fortune, the Alliance Israélite Universelle was founded and opened its first schools in the Mediterranean basin, most notably in Morocco. The English banker Sir Moses Montefiore undertook a "philanthropic" trip to Morocco, making known his "concern"—which has since been widely reiterated by European colonialism—for the well-being of Jewish communities in the Arab world.

Let's listen to our previously cited Mouillefarine:

> It would be a singular mistake to think that the Protectorate is purely and simply a result of military conquest; it represents the logical conclusion of a patient, intelligent, and methodical policy that has been justly termed "peaceful penetration." Military force has simply consecrated and consolidated a possession that had already been acquired through the long work of shoring up the economic

ties created with the Sharifian authorities and the leaders of the Berber tribes. The principal architects of this merger, however, were French officers and businessmen, assisted by Moroccan Israelites whose acumen came from the new training they received from the Alliance.[18]

Of course this racist scholar was conflating a few Jewish collaborators with the general Jewish population. For while it is true that one of the first students of the first Alliance school (the school at Tétouan) became the father of Moroccan Zionism, the Jewish artisans of the Rif Mountains worked to provide munitions to Abdelkrim el-Khattabi's troupes.

But it is true that beginning in the 1920s, the few thousand Moroccan Jews who received this training constituted the only "elite," the only public face of the Jewish community.

Traditional society had to move beyond its limitations in order to brave the impact of colonization. National resistance, which emerged from the hearts of the people, was indeed a form of "resistance," yet in spite of certain undefined aspirations it never became a "revolution" that would reject the colonial impact and move beyond traditional society. This more or less developed national ideology constantly oscillated between a return to tradition and the adoption of Western bourgeois values. Even the socialist movement, including its most recent efforts, never offered anything beyond a technocratic perspective.

Uprooted from the beginning, subsumed into Western culture by virtue of its lifestyle and interests, it is hardly surprising that this Jewish "elite" either—in the best case scenario—failed to offer the Moroccan Jewish community a concrete national perspective or, quite simply, steered it directly toward Zionism. In a social structure where cultural autonomy was already very strong, this community thus found itself given over to a particular breed of "elites." Certain Moroccan Jews, quite numerous at one time, came to the nationalist movement from within the ranks of the only party that considered the national struggle as part and parcel of the future goal of the construction of socialism. By virtue of a mechanistic application of scientific socialism, these Jews underestimated or even ignored the need to undertake a specific struggle within the Jewish community, thus contributing to their alienation.

The events of June 1967 thus crowned a century of colonial penetration and division, and a quarter of a century of Zionist control over the Moroccan Jewish community. . . .

But June '67 constituted for the Arab world—and, in the end, as History will show and is already beginning to show, for Jews in the Arab world—the beginning of the end of the racist nightmare of Zionism.

III. June '67: New Prospects

We will not provide here a detailed sociopolitical analysis of June 1967, although such an analysis would be warranted. Well beyond any intellectual construction, the reality of the concept of the Arab nation has emerged in living color. For Morocco, June 1967 will be a second August 1953.

People will ask us: if the "Arab nation" exists, why not the "Jewish people"? We propose to take up these themes in a serious manner at a later date. For now let us retain the following notion, even if it is not yet clear to everyone: the reality of a sociological fact is constituted by its future.

The concept of an "Arab nation" is to be understood within the historical context of national liberation movements and the liquidation of imperialism. The concept of "a Jewish people," however, tends to evoke a tribal attitude. This attitude in its most basic form has been rendered null and void by the philosophy of Judaism itself, which through the Prophets puts forth a universalist conception of Man.[19]

It remains clear that, like the future of the Moroccan nation itself, the future of Moroccan Jewry cannot be disassociated from the future of Palestine. The failed "elite" that established Zionism in Morocco directly or indirectly and that has been silent since June 1967 would undoubtedly like to see this reality forgotten, as would other false elites. But everyone knows that this is no longer possible.

To all those Moroccan Jews, here or elsewhere, who consciously or subconsciously feel the anguish of isolation and uprooting; to all those who have begun to deliberate in the face of the true nature and impasse of Zionism, we ask you to seek knowledge and destroy, first and foremost within yourselves, the monopoly of Zionist information and the mystification brought about by the imperialist West.[20]

Read about the reality of the State of Israel in this text written by a

Zionist author who is searching, in vain, for a way out of the dead end of Zionism.[21]

Discover the crumbling of the humanist dream of Jews tricked by Zionism through another author who nonetheless affirms that the "Jewish people" is a "sui generis" notion.[22]

Reflect, through the work of Emmanuel Lévyne, on the permanent crime committed against Judaism and the combat that he has waged ever since he discovered, on board the *Exodus*, the reality of Zionism.[23]

The reality of the Moroccan Jew in the Zionist state is apparent in the stark objectivity of studies such as the one proposed by this Moroccan Jewish sociologist, even if she has not managed to go beyond the "Western" perspective.[24]

The reality of racism in the Zionist state is brought into dramatic relief in the combined studies conducted by two of its citizens, one Muslim, one Jewish.[25]

All those who are unable to understand through an examination of the facts on the ground today that Zionism is an imperialist enterprise, an enterprise built by adventurers who *never* intended to create a homeland for persecuted Jews,[26] but who sought instead to create a racist, expansionist state and an imperialist enclave should read Maxime Rodinson's study[27] and Nathan Weinstock's important work.[28]

The reality of the fascist nature of the Zionist heads of state is apparent in the frightening self-portrait Moshe Dayan has offered in his interview published in *L'Express* last May, and in the letter addressed to him by a Jewish mother, Miriam Galili.[29]

The reality of "Western culture," of its "tactics," is being blown up into tiny fragments by the will of the people, first by the Vietnamese and increasingly in the Arab world by Palestinian combatants.

How does the reality of the "blooming desert" differ from the colonial and neocolonial reality that we know so well? How does it differ from the orange groves of the Sous Valley? For those who forget that the land of Canaan was the land of milk and honey well before the advent of Western tactics, for those who attach value to the new orange groves planted only twenty years ago, let them think about the words of Roger Benhaïm, the Algerian Jew who is currently living the anguish of his deracination in France: "ON THE LAND THAT BELONGS TO GOD, MOSES, THE PROPHETS, JESUS; ON THIS LAND WHERE

MILK AND HONEY FLOW, WHERE ORANGE TREES AND GRAPE-FRUITS GROW, A MAN DIED UNDER TORTURE AND HIS TOR-TURERS WERE JEWS, MY BROTHERS." (Second speech in the desert, dedicated to Kassem Abou Akar, tortured to death by Zionists.)[30]

Faced with an impasse such as this one, before these crimes committed in the name of Judaism, stands the perspective of a fraternal Arab world of tomorrow. In the Palestinian people's struggle for a secular, unified, democratic Palestine stands amongst others the figure of the Palestinian William Nassar, commander of the Al-Assifah sector of Jerusalem, tortured by Zionists, son of a Christian father and a Jewish mother.

June–July 1969

FIGURE 13. "Palestine," poster of fedayee with Kalashnikov by Abdallah El Hariri. *Souffles* 15 (Rabat, 1969), p. 79. Reprinted with permission.

WE ARE ALL PALESTINIAN REFUGEES
Abdellatif Laâbi
Translated from the French by Olivia C. Harrison

at last I reemerge from my body
I come out of it bearing essential questions   My scream
ready   Carried high cutting through the Scandal   Dismantled
mechanisms
          I am armed from head to toe
my armor is strong to oppose any erosion   my memory is long to
force any embargo   My laughter inextinguishable   I am new   Scars
and grafts have moved toward the plants   They weigh down my step
but no longer stop my expansion
for a long time I dreamed   It was nightmares   Slow motion
races of repetitive executions   Whirling eyes   Opium-burned
demonstrations   It was cannoned temples   Erotic and pagan
crowds practicing obsessive rituals   It was nights pregnant with
moons   Unlit stars   Glimmering deserts   Swastika-engraved
domes   Branded faces   Cataclysmic winds   The Atlas erupting in a
deluge of collective memory
memory you saved me from the deception of books   You dictated
to me the itinerary of violence   You led me to the source of decisive
interrogations   You plugged me into the pulsations and tremors of
my people   From a terrorized humanity relegated to the hibernation
of caves guarded by the Cyclopes Scientist-Kings of Barbary, I carved
along their crimes and your signs my arcs and my arrows   There I
made the Weapon and the Word   There I nomadized across killing
fields and illuminations   Savors of freedom projected to the confines
of the future
          swell of conquests

at last I remerge from my body
it was neither the ghetto nor hell nor a seawall to flee the world   It
was not the call of the void education by emptiness   I am not very
contemplative even if it had to be a touchstone of what one might call
my "soul"
I no longer respond to obsessive calls   To any call
I choose my touchstones my obsessions and my targets

I choose my age my victories and my defeats
I am the Arab man in History set in motion built anew by the
vanguard of Palestinian guerrilla fighters

Arab   Arabs   Arab
a name to be remembered
great voices
            of my seismic deserts
a people marches on
through 8,000 kilometers raises tents
command bases
how many are we
yes how many gentlemen statisticians of pain
advance a number
and the prophetic masses retort
with infallible equations
today

WE
    ARE
        ALL
            PALESTINIAN
                        REFUGEES
tomorrow
we will create
            TWO . . .   THREE . . .   FIFTEEN   PALESTINES

APPEAL TO MAGHREBI WRITERS

Translated from the French by Anne-Marie McManus

The Maghrebi writers who have gathered around the journal *Souffles* and who have signed this appeal,

— conscious of the increasingly grave danger that Zionist colonization poses for the Palestinian people, a danger evident in the terrorist campaign for the national and cultural annihilation of this people as well as in desperate efforts to bring about its depersonalization and uprooting

— conscious of the avant-garde role that the Palestinian revolution (an integral part of the movement for world revolution) plays in the liberation of Arab peoples and their anti-imperial struggle

— conscious of the current impact of this revolution on the Arab masses of the Mashriq and Maghreb and its capacity to accelerate history by clarifying, ideologically and politically, the possibilities for struggle in the Arab world

— conscious that this revolution is a driving force and that it affirms the foundations on which the Arab nation will be built

— conscious of the inseparable nature of the Arab Palestinian people's struggle and the struggle of the peoples of the Maghreb.

— conscious of the upheavals that this revolution has provoked and will continue to provoke in terms of the status of contemporary Arab culture as well as its role and the responsibilities of Arab artists and intellectuals

— aware of the dramatic conditions in which Arab writers in Palestine live and the numerous forms of repression they must endure

are above all convinced that THE PALESTINIAN REVOLUTION WILL TRIUMPH

We affirm

— that the implications of this revolution for us Maghrebi writers are decisive. This revolution

— forces us, today, to radicalize our choices and our engagements. We believe that from this moment forth every piece of writing and every act, every silence and every form of indifference from a Maghrebi writer strengthens reactionary ideas in our countries and is directed against the liberation of our peoples, definitively placing them, in our view, within the very framework of repression. The sole and unambiguous way forward is participation in national combat alongside truly progressive forces and the exploited masses

— demands that we newly call into question our creative work and our methods of action and communication and that we find new ways to make our writings fulfill their true function, that is to vitalize culture

— reveals the urgent need to redouble the struggle against neocolonialism (in all its forms, notably cultural), which deploys the same methods, albeit in more subtle ways, as imperial-Zionist colonization in Palestine to bring about the deculturation of our peoples

— confirms the need that we have long proclaimed to call into question the ossified contents and forms of our traditional culture and the mystifying reasoning of bourgeois Western culture that have constituted, to the present day, the primary elements of intellectual and psychic obstacles in the Maghreb

— makes us feel better armed to lay the foundations of a radically new literature that can contribute to the emergence and the strengthening of our national cultures and to unleashing the creative potential of our peoples

— requires, particularly from Maghrebi writers of French expression (if it has not already been achieved), a radical geo-cultural reorientation: the development of dialogue and a confrontation with the creators of the Arab Mashriq in order to establish that in reality our literature, regardless of its language of expression and in this precise phase of decolonization, is an integral part of Arabic literature, to which its fate is in every way tied.

We note
— that Maghrebi literature as a whole has made little headway since our countries achieved national independence. The current situation is characterized:

— by the proliferation of bastard literary currents that confine themselves to complacent mimicry of imported literary modes without any real attachment to our countries' profound cultural realities

— by significant literary epidermism and conformism, the majority still viewing literature as a recreational or transcendent activity or as the privilege of the enlightened

— by a nearly generalized impotence that stems from a visceral fear of the creative adventure due to its potential to negate and transform

— by a "brain drain" owing to the fact that many writers continue to be fascinated with the colonizing métropoles because of their insecurities or simply because they prefer an easy—or scandalous—path.

On this point we repeat that the solution of exile will in most cases lead the Maghrebi writer to be out of touch, manipulated by foreign publishing trusts and assimilated to the tastes and obsessions of a Western intelligentsia that can't get past its exoticism and can barely mask its outdated paternalism and interventionism.

We affirm that the writer must act from within our countries and regardless of the conditions. It must be clear that creative work that does not grow from a daily praxis cannot but lead to its own marginalization and to the mystified vocations of "solitary geniuses" and "nomadic writers."

We further note
that the ideological and cultural links between Maghrebi literary production and the realities of the Arab world and the exigencies of the Palestinian revolution are still seen in an emotional and romantic light: literature concerning Palestine has become entangled in the worst ambiguities ever since the first days of nostalgia for a new Andalus, lost to defeatist jeremiads and morbid prayers.

On this note we believe that it will not be a smattering of poems or new texts by Maghrebi writers that will in any way change the facts of the Palestinian problem or the balance of power on the ground. In any case, Palestinian writers are better placed than anyone else to express the realities and aspirations of their people. Following the example of the guerilla fighters, they are already taking on, with talent and depth, this epic of national self-affirmation.

But if we reject the occasional literature that has become a literary genre with its own rhetorical forms, we believe that our new literature will have to integrate the Palestinian revolution in all its breadth, as an example, a seismograph, and a path to the Arab revolution for which the Maghrebi writer must endeavor.

What is more, the best contribution we can make to fortify the struggle for liberation in Palestine is activism here, in our countries, to accelerate the popular masses' coming to consciousness so that they may take on this struggle, principally against imperialism.

The signatories to this text CALL on Maghrebi writers:

(1) to struggle in our countries on all fronts in order to guarantee total freedom of expression and to put in place the conditions for this freedom of expression and its exercise (authentically national forms of publishing and distribution, circulation amongst countries of the Maghreb, the Arab world, Africa, the Third World, etc.)

(2) to denounce on all levels neocolonial control over the means of cultural expression and communication in the Maghreb

(3) to participate actively in the clarification of the Palestinian problem and to develop support for the Palestinian struggle for liberation

(4) to circulate information on the barbaric project of cultural annihilation of the Palestinian people by Zionist colonization for the benefit of the national and international press.

(5) to denounce new currents of anti-Arab racism in whatever forms they appear and to lead an ideological and cultural battle to demystify prejudices against Arab realities and the Arab man

(6) to maintain extreme vigilance concerning the terminology used to analyze the Palestinian problem and to denounce all uses of the Palestinian people's struggle in order to mask national problems as well as their true links with this struggle, specifically: the liberation of our exploited masses and anti-imperial combat.

(7) to spread by all means, at home as well as abroad, Palestinian thought and the revolutionary culture that has sprung from the liberation struggle.

PALESTINE WILL OVERCOME

Rabat, October 1969

Tahar Ben Jelloun   Ahmed al-Madini

Bensalem Himmich   Abdelaziz Mansouri

Abdelkebir Khatibi   Ahmad Mejjati

Abdellatif Laâbi   Mostafa Nissabouri

Azeddine Madani

This appeal is open. We hope to receive other signatures.

FIGURE 14. Palestine cartoons by George Wolinski. *Souffles* 15 (Rabat, 1969), pp. 127–28. Reprinted with permission.

Left-hand cartoon:

"You're a German. You must support Nazism."

"You're a Frenchman. You must support Pétainism."

"You're a Jew. You must support Zionism."

Right-hand cartoon:

"I'm a Palestinian."

"Impossible! You don't exist."

"Could you hold this for me for a minute?"

"Whoa! A grenade!"

"I don't understand how you can be afraid of something that doesn't exist."

"My problem is my existence, not yours."

FIGURE 15. Front cover of *Souffles* 16–17 by Mohamed Chebaa. *Souffles* 16–17 (Rabat, 1969–70). Reprinted with permission.

nation arabe

Déjà l'ombre commence à se dissiper.

L'horizon s'embrase. Les premières lueurs de l'aube chassent devant elles les ténèbres épaisses d'une nuit gluante; et avec elles, montent vers le ciel les premières clameurs audibles : des cris de liberté - de dignité - des appels à la fraternité.

Déjà l'éblouissant soleil de l'ennemi perd de son éclat. Dans ce halo annonciateur de grandes mutations, où les nuances intermédiaires diluent la lumière et l'obscurité dans lequel notre personnalité dissoute à notre ombre son droit naturel d'exister, se dessinent petit à petit les contours de notre visage, invisibles pendant des années, nous nous surprenons soudain à regarder le soleil en face.

Certes, nous ne sommes guère présentables : une vraie cohue. Tout relief et toute allure nous ont quittés. Usées ou tranchant des années, nos peaux sont des guenilles. Nos voix ne portent plus. Mais si aujourd'hui notre chair, qui pèse tant à l'adversité, n'est plus maintenue par sa carcasse, elle l'est par l'espérance et la colère. Une colère qui nous pousse à exhumer notre généalogie ; à y puiser la force de résister et de combattre comme avant nous l'ont fait tant d'autres peuples. Car, dans nos laideurs et dans

nos plaies, demeure radieux et stimulant le souvenir de la vie qu'on nous a volée.

Sans doute l'Occident aurait préféré payer pour que nous demeurions des mendiants. Car Voilà que la marée de nos clameurs menace d'emporter ses digues de retenue.

Voilà que la forêt de nos poings levés envahit les terres incultes de son univers y faisant naître un écho insoupçonnable il y a quelques années.

Voilà que l'esclave, au mépris de Dieu et au mépris de l'Histoire, décide de se prendre pour le maître.

Quelle chaleur, mes frères, se dégage de cette fusion du peuple avec ses harmonies ! Quelle incandescence rassurante sur l'avenir !

PALESTINE, DHOFAR, HADRAMAOUT, ERYTHREE.

Voilà que ces noms, aux résonances barbares hier encore, synonymes d'encens, de clou de girofle et de gomme arabique, deviennent sur les lèvres de nos peuples symboles de liberté et de justice sociale.

Peuples en luttes,
Aphrodisiaque de notre impuissance,
Etendard de nos espérances,
Baume de nos chairs meurtries ;

Vous êtes notre lune dans toute sa plénitude, mais vous êtes aussi la corde de notre arc et le tranchant de nos glaives.

Nos ennemis savent-ils tout cela ? Etrange société où la vérité est devenue à ce point problématique que la foi elle-même en est atteinte jusqu'au plus profond d'elle-même.

Qui sait ? Mais qui ne sait donc aujourd'hui que les valeurs réelles de l'Humanité doivent être défendues par l'énergie de ses enfants et le sacrifice des fils de chaque nation ;

Qui ne sait que nos souffrances, tempérées par des mégatonnes de patience, sont devenues des bouillons surchauffés ;

Que nos tentes de l'errance et de la solitude se gonflent du vent de l'espérance ;

Que notre sang enfin se refournit en sel et en fer, prêt à se répandre pour que fleurisse la terre de nos ancêtres.

Et s'il est vrai que nous sommes les descendants des pharaons du Nil et des Bédouins du Hedjaz, les héritiers de Jugurtha et de Massinissa, un jour le monde saura que nous sommes aussi la dernière génération des damnés de la terre.

Chaque nuit, un jour a son aurore. Déjà à l'horizon, pointe telle une victoire notre visage de demain. Irrésistiblement, la remontée s'opère. Nous avons lesté le passé.

LA FORET EST EN MARCHE. QUI PEUT L'ARRETER ?

J. L.

FIGURE 16. "Arab nation," rubric with image of fedayee by Mohamed Chebaa. *Souffles* 16–17 (Rabat, 1969–70), p. 5. Reprinted with permission.

FIGURE 17. "Only on the bones of the oppressors can the people's freedom be founded. Only the blood of the oppressors can fertilize the soil for the people's self-rule," poster by Black Panther Emory Douglas. *Souffles* 16–17 (Rabat, 1969–70), p. 34. Reprinted with permission.

INTERVIEW WITH OUSMANE SEMBÈNE

Translated from the French by Laura Reeck

Ousmane Sembène is Senegalese. Before making films, he worked as a dockworker at the port of Marseille and wrote several novels, including *Le mandat*. He moved from literature to cinema after having studied filmmaking in Moscow. He continues to promote a cooperative of Senegalese filmmakers and to act on behalf of African culture. Some of his best-known films include:

Borom sarret

Niaye

La noire de . . . [*Black Girl*]

Mandabi/Le mandat [The money order]

Souffles: In your view how should we define African cinema, which tends to rebel against Western culture?

O. Sembène: Let's not talk about the West. Let's talk about us. First of all we have to have the courage to face reality; seeing it is one thing and understanding it quite another. We have to begin by knowing our own country, all the while understanding its place within the international revolutionary movement. Our country may either be a part of the movement or stand outside it, but all art must be defined in relation to it. African cinema is filmmaking defined by the authenticity of the reality it shows.

Souffles: What weight do you give to the struggle waged by African cinema compared to other art forms such as theater, the plastic arts, etc.?

Sembène: Lenin said, "Of all the arts, cinema is the most important." But let's not forget that ninety percent of our population is illiterate. Cinema shows and compels thought. A truly revolutionary culture, a culture of the people, can and must be transmitted through cinema: that's why we have to count on the committed work that can be undertaken in cinémathèques and cinema clubs. This work can and must contribute to the general public's awareness.

Souffles: But let's not forget that cinémathèques and cinema clubs only serve (at least in their current structure) a small set of privileged elites. As long as the screen is absent from the streets and fields, we can't talk about popular culture.

Sembène: For the time being, we still cannot show *Le mandat* in movie theaters in Africa (except in Tunisia at the Carthage Film Festival and in Algeria in the context of this festival). How then can we even begin to imagine showing it in the streets! Of course that would be ideal. In fact it's because a film might affect the masses that it gets banned; it represents a threat. In Africa, we're still at the stage where we have to struggle to instill a culture devoid of discrimination.

Souffles: What is your view of the African artist? What is the role of the African creator?

Sembène: For me, he's a political man in all that the term implies. He's totally committed and perpetually denounces what is unjust. His role is to be an activist, a fighter. Art can be a weapon. In fact, all culture is political.

Souffles: In your opinion what should the relationship between the artist and the people look like, especially when the latter are predominantly illiterate?

Sembène: First of all we have to trust our people. We cannot define ourselves with respect to them through a hierarchical approach. In order to claim to express their aspirations we have to be a part of the people. For instance, I can say that all Senegalese created *Le mandat*. We worked twenty-four hours a day; it was a celebration, a joy for all. The story in *Le mandat* is true: an elderly neighbor came to see me and told me all the trials and tribulations of his life story. Not only is it a true story but it's also an accurate reflection of the political and social situation that currently prevails in African countries where the regime is profoundly neocolonialist.

Souffles: Can you tell us how Senegalese filmmaking came about?

Sembène: I've always been concerned with my country's political and social problems, and I've always been led to express, reveal, and denounce them. I was a unionist; I organized among my coworkers when I was a dockworker at the port of Marseille and then among Senegalese students. I started writing novels. But I realized it was necessary to go further than literature, and then I opted for film because I felt I could communicate better through film. That's why my filmmaking is political. I've never received any governmental assistance. With *Le mandat*, a Franco-Senegalese coproduction, I managed to get an advance of 300,000 CFA Francs. But ten or so of us created our own production company. It's entirely independent so that our filmmaking can truly be committed, revolutionary, and depend upon no official organization—no organization of any nature. If we were working with the state, we would not be able to express our ideas. But as I said yesterday during the screening of *Le mandat*, our team knows the reality and problems facing our country better than any politician in the government. We live the reality of a people subjected to the reactionary forces of neocolonialism on a daily basis.

Souffles: Tell us a bit about your cooperative.

Sembène: Initially we started the cooperative because we shared similar views on independent cinema. We're a group of ten or so filmmakers at odds with the state-run system. We're not trying to make money; the money that we make goes back to our shared account and we each get a salary. To the extent that we can, we're trying not to use the money in the account. We're saving it as a last resort.

Souffles: What advice would you give to young African filmmakers who want to create a cooperative?

Sembène: First of all they have to be prepared to break completely with the system. They have to be willing to go the full distance—to fight for a new and authentic cinema. No compromises, no concessions. I would like to meet Moroccan counterparts who refuse to make films like *Vaincre pour vivre* (Win to live). I saw the film at the Carthage Film Festival, where it was booed. I hope it isn't representative of what is being made in Morocco.

Souffles: What did you think of the discussion that took place at the Cinémathèque after the screening of Le mandat?

Sembène: There was a lot of emotion and little logic. But it's rather revealing of the prevailing tensions at this event. It's to be expected given that this is the first time Africans are convening, and some of them are still clinging to their illusions and refusing to be self-critical. We were there to judge the film. It just so happens that the film is African and that it describes a situation that is purely and authentically African, the very situation of postindependence Africa. For most African countries the colonial system was replaced by the neocolonialist political system as represented by bourgeois capitalists (of Western inspiration), feudalists, or bureaucrats. The African people continue to suffer from the same evils. In Senegal this is obvious. A farmer or a worker in need of an official document will never be able to get it if he follows the normal course of action. The bureaucratic apparatus is so overwhelming that all this man will come away with is the realization that he belongs to a particular social class and that he is a man at the mercy of all forms of humiliation. He has to cheat the system to get his identity papers for example. This is a very common and scandalous occurrence in our countries. I don't understand why some viewers were shocked by the film. But what is still stranger is that they weren't shocked to see the production of the film about the festival handed over to an American, and not to an African.

Souffles: How do you explain the fact that William Klein was chosen to direct the film?

Sembène: It's a contradiction. I know that an African filmmaker was offered three million CFA Francs, and he turned it down, and I can understand why. Klein got eighteen million!

Souffles: Another contradiction is the way the city has been decorated. The result is incredibly mediocre: it's Africa as seen by colonialist Europe at the beginning of the century. To return to the film about the festival, it's worth noting that there are Algerians who support Klein, such as Slim Riad for example.

Sembène: It's not a question of Algerians doling out their support, but rather a question of principle. The festival is about African culture, so it should be an African who gets the honor of filming the festival. We're capable of taking a critical look at ourselves.

Souffles: Laughter is a revolutionary weapon, a sign of maturity. How do you use it in cinema?

Sembène: For us laughter is always more powerful. Dramatization is bound to fail. You have to be able to laugh at yourself; it's a way of knowing oneself. There's nothing better than laughing at our situation in order to be able to better control and act on it.

Souffles: You studied in Moscow, where you were Mark Donskoy's assistant. And yet you make a very different type of cinema, more like cinema-novo (Glauber Rocha, Joachim dos Santos, Paulo César, . . .) Do you agree?

Sembène: Yes, you're right. I feel closer to those filmmakers because we're leading the same struggle. That's why our filmmaking is similar. In any case, the Brazilian experience is of huge importance.

Interviewed by Tahar Ben Jelloun

REVIEW OF *THE REPUDIATION* BY RACHID BOUDJEDRA[31]

Abdellatif Laâbi

Translated from the French by Anne-Marie McManus

Rachid Boudjedra's *La répudiation* is one of those books from which the reader emerges in pain, at the limit of asphyxia. How can we not empathize with this bitter, festering, delirious, harassing, provocative voice?

In its merciless lucidity our generation could not care less about morals, whether shaky or imported, as it furiously tramples the limits of the permissible and the nameable.

This novel dares to lay bare, better yet to scrutinize, a swarm of realities and truths under the most powerful of microscopes, then throws them unapologetically in the face of readers of all stripes. Let those of us implicated in this terrorist-realism, this Maghrebi realism, give up our last ties with the bourgeois-intimate literature of yesteryear. We will only be more honest with ourselves. And may the paternalist playboys of North African French-language literature mourn for our worn-out, so-called need for understanding. Let them take stock of their ethnocentrism and their alienations if they want to keep up.

This work must therefore be read after closing our dictionaries and defusing all connections to references, memories, literature-novels, academies-schools—in short, all of this museology that automatically arises in every self-respecting intellectual when he opens a new and, in regard to our subject, Maghrebi work of literature.

I will say it again. Enough! Read us according to what we are, according to the project whose foundations we are patiently, modestly, and freely trying to lay, and which we invite you to debate and enrich. In recent years Maghrebi literature has broken through the wall of silence. Since then it has energetically refused to be an ethnographic, moralizing literature of decalcomania. This literature has assumed responsibility for the necessary step of clearing, dynamiting, and reconstruction that is coursing through our culture.

Many will feel confused, will cry hermeticism, in the face of the effort to which they must consent. We will respond, stop ruminating; "open the windows of your heart," of your imagination, participate, through your active, adventurous reading, in the work. Recreate it.

Do not judge our literature based on your accumulated culture. Think of it as a new culture to be built, which emerges, feels, defines itself in these works and in other works to come, the signifying hiero-glyphs of the pyramid that is bursting forth. Every construction (the example of Egyptian pyramids speaks volumes) requires both a rig-orous rationality, a real understanding of the laws of physics, and a capacity for adventure, a sense of excess. That is to say, a challenge to ordinary, mechanical rationality, bounded rationality. Otherwise there is no real renewal, which is to say, no creation.

Boudjedra's novel is in this respect a serious contribution to the rec-reation of the Maghrebi universe and the laying bare of its essential contradictions. The author of *La répudiation* does not mince words. He pours them out in a torrent, charging them with the sum of his knowl-edge and rebellion and all the energy of his moral, intellectual, and po-litical courage.

This is of course a work that calls for others of its kind. And since there is a project, we must, if we want it to be even truer to ourselves and lead us forward, demonstrate which of its paths may turn into dead ends. In Boudjedra, we can find the residues of that which we haven't stopped denouncing in our predecessors, notably the obses-sion with the Other. I personally find the character device of the French lover, to whom the novel is narrated, to be superfluous and annoying. Likewise, the novel's way of casting a somewhat specialized adult eye (in this case, specialized in the social sciences, specifically psychiatry) on childhood and adolescence is also annoying. And I find the constant rants on all aspects of family life of the milieu described by Boudjedra to be too systematic.

The fact that we are told that the novel's critique is aimed at the Al-gerian bourgeoisie does not in any way make its intention more "pro-gressive." I also find it unconvincing that Boudjedra does not always succeed in isolating (and perhaps eliminating) issues arising from indi-vidual psycho-emotional problems.

Finally, I must say how irritated I was by the publisher's presenta-tion of the book. There is nothing more false and more commercial than this kind of auctioning of anger. We see that, as in the good old days, the Parisian publisher earns his money and prestige as a discoverer of rebels and thus as a defender of the freedom of expression.

The publisher does not refrain from saying (and we can feel a sense of self-satisfaction and vengeful spirit) about *La répudiation*: "Refusing to make colonialism responsible for all the problems his country suffers, he takes a passionate stand against stifling ancestral traditions."

Obviously I am not about to hold a congress to defend these stifling ancestral traditions, but it's a long way between doing that and granting any kind of reprieve, any semblance of rehabilitation, to the colonial system.

All of this to say that the patronage of Maghrebi and African works, unfortunately still published abroad, is extremely debilitating and always leads our writers into compromising situations.

I will not quibble too much over the Grand Prix des Enfants Terribles or the book's candidacy for the Prix Goncourt and the Prix Hassan II des Quatre Jurys. I hope that Rachid Boudjedra will be wise enough to say NO to all these attempts to recoup and integrate his work into the ideological and economic system that is all too familiar to him, at the moment when he himself will feel the urgency of such an act.

In any case read Boudjedra's book. I promise you great disgust, great tension but especially a great breath of truth and justice.

CONTEMPORARY MAGHREBI LITERATURE AND *FRANCOPHONIE*

Abdellatif Laâbi

Translated from the French by Lucy R. McNair

Framing the Debate

For the new generation of Maghrebi writers of French expression, the moment has come to define rigorously their attitude towards the language in which they write.

Note that the present contribution to this debate should not be understood as a manifesto. We can only speak in our own name; that is to say, in the name of a few Moroccan writers who have contributed substantially to the journal *Souffles*. And though we think that many of our Algerian and Tunisian colleagues share our general ideas in principle, we do not claim the right to speak in their name or to declaim anything they have not themselves elaborated and approved with us. In sum, we invite them to participate in this debate on their own terms.

Over and over we have been told, "We do not understand why young, consciously aware writers like yourselves, activists for a culture of liberation, have written and continue to write in French."

We have also heard, "What you write in French cannot enrich our national culture and can only be marginal."

Others have occasionally implied, "You are products of colonialism and can only be accomplices to neocolonialism."

Praise being of little interest to us here, we have insisted on citing these criticisms as faithfully as possible. We will however take into account the rigorous and objective analyses that have been written on our work in our own future analyses.

Let us state from the outset that we have never tried to avoid these questions or bury ourselves in silence. Except for those criticisms coming from ill-intentioned individuals or organizations attempting to mask their reactionary positions or their mediocrity through distasteful actions against a literary production whose profound demands make them uncomfortable, cornering them in choices they cannot live up to, the above-mentioned questions constitute for the most part legitimate interrogations, based on demands we often support. Each time the occasion has presented itself we have not hesitated (as in the present case) to define and redefine ourselves and to underscore the nature of the kinds of questions we feel are necessary in order to overcome ambiguous attitudes and offer clarification.

Today, five years after the publication of our first texts and under circumstances that render, more than ever before, the problem posed by this debate of acute significance, we intend to take stock of our experience and clarify where we stand.

Let us remember that this debate, inherent to Maghrebi literature written in French, is not new. The problem has been posed ever since the appearance of these works in the 1950s. Since then it has become one of the constant themes of any study devoted to this literature.

Some of the writers concerned here have themselves perceived the nature of the ambiguities that can weigh on their work and have attempted, with more or less success and effectiveness, to confront them.

But it would take too long, within the limits of this essay, to summarize the history of this subject. We hope to return to it at a later date.[32]

Our fundamental attitude is captured by the term *coexistence*, but a *non-pacifist coexistence*, marked with vigilance. We are constantly on guard. Taking provisional responsibility for French as our instrument of communication, we remain permanently aware of the dangers we risk, which consist in taking this language on as an instrument of culture. The tension of this situation is palpable and one can imagine the exhausting labor (akin to a magic trick) that we must undertake to redress all the mental and cultural mechanisms of the language we write in.

Ultimately in order to write in French a writer who is aware of these issues must invert the process of writing or, to put it in other terms, go through a series of filters and categorizations. The project can be envisaged as follows:

— We must convey a national, popular, Arab aesthetic and ideological heritage, that is to say our cultural *specificities* and our *solidarities*.

— The linguistic tool we use conveys a culture and class ideology belonging to a French, Western reality.

— The operation consists on the one hand of neutralizing—on the level of terminology and cultural models—the negative elements promoted by the foreign tongue and on the other hand of forcing this language to absorb other terms and models specific to our culture.[33]

This is how one achieves an operation of transculturation without transforming the desired goal (expressing our totality) into a kind of cultural synthesis. This is why it is often said that Maghrebi or Negro-African literature of French expression is nothing short of a terrorist literature, i.e. a literature that on all levels (syntactic, phonetic, morphological, graphical, symbolic, etc.) shatters the original logic of the French language.

This is also why many Third World fans take a certain kind of pleasure in this literature. Indeed, we have seen critics delight in exclaiming how much this literature enriches the French language. Others simply enjoy a sense of foreignness, folklore, and revitalization. Obviously these statements, reflective of a more-or-less subtle paternalism-vampirism, do not concern us. But we must note that they still move many of our writers who see in them a consecration of their efforts. What pride and glory for these people when they see a short column of *Le Monde* or another newspaper devoted to the "encouragement" of their work. The consequences are even greater when writers develop the aspects of their work that the foreign press has emphasized, those aspects it particularly savors.

We should underscore that it does not suffice to master the project we discussed above in theoretical or intellectual terms. This project is achieved, or not, within a work of literature. It is to the works themselves that we need to turn in order to take stock of its success.

Let us take the example of two Algerian writers of the previous generation: Kateb Yacine and Malek Haddad. Of the two, Haddad has no doubt analyzed the issues we treat here more fully. In "Les zéros tournent en rond" [The zeroes go round in circles] he developed an in-depth (though contestable) analysis of the colonial writer's linguistic drama. Yet when we consider his work, we find a type of writing that is extremely dependent on French literature both in its aesthetic forms and in its expressive logic.

In contrast it is hard not to feel the deep stirrings of the Algerian nation and people in the work of Kateb Yacine, who rarely addressed the issue of writing in French or did so in a rather clumsy manner in our view. For the moment (whatever one thinks of the ultimate evolution of its author), *Nedjma* remains one of the most beautiful and strongest expressions of the Maghrebi spirit. This is just a quick example to show that it is the result that matters, not the abstract reasoning preceding a work of art.

The authenticity of a work, its degree of participation in the project of liberation on the cultural level depend on the writer's sensibility, lucidity, and multifarious engagement in his people's struggle.

Overcoming Bilingualism

We want to state clearly that the literature we envisage for tomorrow must definitively overcome bilingualism for the sake of its future effectiveness, coherence, and aesthetic appeal.

There can be no doubting this vision. Any attempt to persist in gambling on the future can only arise from the bad faith of those who find comfort in the French language and live exclusively for the French public. What we say here involves no bravado. This vision is a normal component of the project of decolonization and total liberation of our culture. What we need to decide is whether we are for or against this project. Its success can only be achieved, in the long term, in our national and popular languages.

In the meantime, and during this precise stage of decolonization and anti-imperialist struggle on the cultural level, everything that can advance our position, clarify it, illuminate it, make it known, as much within as outside our borders, can only be positive. Contemporary Maghrebi literature in French should situate itself within this particular context and it is here that we can objectively appreciate its demands and possibilities.

Let us note in this respect that if we can be the critics of our work written in French, this does not mean we should lose the least degree of vigilance with regards to Maghrebi literature written in Arabic. We consider that our national language should not be *an alibi* for the writer who believes he has paid his dues in terms of "authenticity" or "realism" when he expresses himself in Arabic. This conceit is just as dangerous as that mentioned above.

It is true that the problem of literary nationality is not a question of identity or passport. Nor can it be resolved by the sole use of a national language. The content of a work, and this goes for works written in the national language as much as those written in French, is once again the decisive criterion.

Frantz Fanon wrote *The Wretched of the Earth* (which is as much a theoretical work as a piece of literature) in French. We doubt this can serve as a source of pride for "activists" of *francophonie*. Likewise, we doubt that the fact this text was written in a foreign language has disturbed or delayed the growth of Caribbean culture one bit. Like others, Fanon was a true activist for the culture of his people. He took up the weapons at hand or those that were imposed on him and he turned them against his people's enemies.

To return to our situation and to conclude, one can say that a large part of Maghrebi literature today:

— is an essential part of the project of building a national culture whose epicenter (its site of radiation) remains the history, culture, and struggle of our people.

— makes provisional use of French as a means of communication.

— is indeed a literature of decolonization insofar as it explodes imperialist forms of cultural and ideological alienation from within and with the very weapons of former and neocolonialists.

— is a literature of renewal to the degree that it challenges (and progressively stakes out other paths) within a national and Arab context all forms of academic, aristocratic, and bourgeois expression existing in our culture or imported from the West.

— lastly, is a work in progress that enjoys the advantage of moving forward through a constant self-questioning.

Appendix

The Institutions of Francophonie[34]

— **Cultural and Technical Cooperation Agency**, founded in Niamey with a treaty signed by twenty-one states on March 21, 1970.

— **U.N. Francophone Group**, (thirty member states under the presidency of the chief of the Tunisian delegation).

— **Conference of the Ministers of Education of French-speaking**

countries, uniting French, African, and Malagasy ministers biennially since 1962 (The Dakar Conference).

— **Conference of Ministers of Youth and Sports of Countries Using French in Common**, which gathered for the first time on December 5, 1969, and shall gather alternately in Africa, Madagascar, and France every year.

Special Organizations

— **The Association of Partially or Entirely French-speaking Universities** is one of the oldest French-speaking organizations (1961). It has fifty-six universities in eighteen countries as well as thirteen associate members.

— **Community of French-language Radio Stations**, members are currently only European and Canadian organizations.

— **International Association of French-speaking Parliamentarians**, founded on May 18, 1967 in Luxembourg. It has twenty-seven national parliaments and six regional legislative assemblies.

— **International Association of French-speaking Historians and Geographers** (founded in 1969).

— **International Association of French-speaking or French-inspired Lawyers and Jurist** (created in 1969).

— **Association of Partially or Fully French-speaking Public Servants** (AFOPELF).

— **International Association of French-speaking Sociologists**, 17 rue de la Sorbonne, Paris. Presidents: Henri Janne (Brussels) and Georges Balandier (Sorbonne). Founded in 1958 by Gurvitch.

— **Association of Francophone Solidarity**. This association was founded in November 1966. Honorary presidents: Jean de Broglie and Jean Charbonnel, former secretaries of state in foreign affairs. President: Bousquet, former ambassador, UDR deputy for Paris. The A. S. F. unites all the organizations founded on the basis of the solidarity created by the use of the French language.

Organizations for the Defense and Illustration of the French Language

— **International Council of the French Language**. Founded in September 1967 and presided over by Joseph Hanse (Royal Academy of Belgium), this organization proposes to "maintain the unity of French in the world" and has twenty francophone member countries.

— **High Committee for the Defense and Expansion of the French Language**. This exclusively French organization was created in March 1966 by the prime minister to advise the government and suggest "concrete measures in favor of the language."

— Without constituting "francophone" organizations per se, the Associations of Franco-Quebec, Franco-Belgian, and Franco-Tunisian Friendship enlarge the audience of activists for *francophonie*.

FUNERAL PRAYER

Ahmed Janati

Translated from the French by Anne George

the grindstone turns
heavy
from our embittered vomiting
vomiting in our Night of ewes
         where, in the shadow of our fear,
heavy
from our toothless jaws
biting in the dust of the vast arena
        of our underdevelopment.
We will make our bread AGAIN
from the morphine-flour of our torturers.
Heavy from our dried-up skins
minarets of skeletons upon skeletons
muezzin-scarecrow.
Heavy from our six-meter turbans
           SOILED
no longer used to hide the shame of our bent brows
and we DARE display upon our asses in the wind
the pride of these primary schools, our Morocco.
The grindstone turns
grindstone of oppression and repression.
   No matter there is no longer water in your streams
knights from quixotic crusades
shoe the guide baptized corruption
and draw from the desert of our thirst
        the tears and the sweat
of fifteen million minus several hundreds.
No my child
there will be no spring this year, again
the path is long to pick the smile
in our tripes hardened
        by ululations. Equality. Progress.
mikes
rattlesnakes.

No my child
you will not walk on their boulevards

burial grounds of neon lights and imported shrouds
swell the crowd paying to dig its own grave.
Our ancestors carried rifles and made the powder speak
we believed the vultures had been chased away
                    by the flag of the Christians
but it was to be our thousand and second night.

And I came back towards you
                    earth my mother
looking anew for my roots in your suffering anonymity
digging up my family tree
bond you gave birth to under torn sheets
tirelessly sewn back with the golden thread of a lethal fatalism
washing myself of the word at the bitter spring of your despair
sharing the coldness of your uncharted tourist night
Yet around you a people ignoring you
a people of pagans
                    building altar upon altar to bloodsuckers
waiting for the miracle from the heavens
or the crumbs from the monsters
people
your knees are rocks to crawl upon
flocks bludgeoned with promises
upon paths where ALREADY suns are dying
and the blindfold does not even weigh on
it has embraced your bones
for they left you only a skeleton to desensitize your hunger
your tongue is freezing
they show you the Jew to be insulted
                    and you insult him
and the West
new kaaba for the prayers of your unsettled soul
for the evil is within Us
and we spit on our eyes the baraka of the devil
to the beat of the drums
for a millennial amnesia.

FIGURE 18. Front cover of "Africa, a Single Struggle," special issue of *Souffles* (no. 19; Rabat, 1970), with poster of Patrice Lumumba by Mohamed Chebaa. Reprinted with permission.

FIGURE 19. Cartoon by Siné. *Souffles* 19 (Rabat, 1970), p. 16. Reprinted with permission.

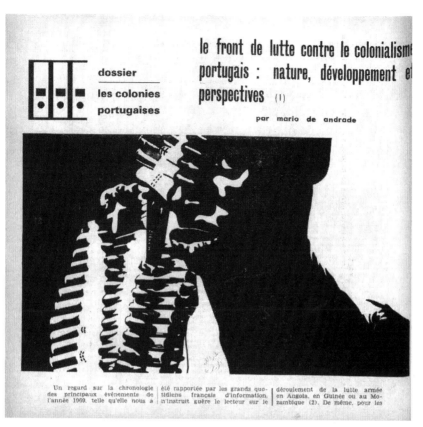

FIGURE 20. Poster of armed Angolan militant by Mohamed Chebaa, illustrating a text by Mario de Andrade. *Souffles* 19 (Rabat, 1970), p. 22. Reprinted with permission.

FIGURE 21. "Angola Day of Solidarity," poster. *Souffles* 19 (Rabat, 1970), p. 43. Reprinted with permission.

concerne ces programmes israéliens n'est pas leurs dimensions, mais leur concentration stratégique dans l'édification de sections d'élite, dans les institutions militaires, de plus en plus importantes. Le fait que ces institutions se trouvent aussi dans des pays où il y a une grande pénétration nord-américaine (par exemple l'Ethiopie et le Congo-K) n'est pas une coïncidence.

Ces programmes permettent aux Israéliens et aux Etats-Unis, à travers les Israéliens, d'exercer des influences intimes sur le développement intérieur de ces pays respectifs « La concession d'aide — militaire ou autre — est aussi une invitation ouverte pour celui qui l'accorde, à établir solidement ses intérêts nationaux dans le pays qui la reçoit, ce qui peut aller jusqu'à inclure l'incitation à la révolte et à la rébellion, bien que de manière couverte », admet Silverburg (6).

Etant donné que sa participation est motivée aussi bien par les intérêts internationaux de l'impérialisme yankee que par ses propres intérêts nationaux, Israël se donne beaucoup de mal pour travailler en étroite collaboration avec le pays amphytrion afin d'éviter tout « malentendu ». En même temps, les programmes israéliens sont rattachés à une opération de renseignements de la CIA et de l'Occident bien plus vaste.

Etant donné la nature même de l'aide dans le domaine du renseignement que les agents israéliens apportent aux Tanzaniens, aux Ethiopiens et aux Congolais, Israël est profondément mêlé au

donné une étude : « Witchcraft, Sorcery, Magic and Other Psychological Phenomena and Their Implications on Military and Paramilitary Operations in the Congo » (« Fétichisme, sorcellerie, magie et autres phénomènes psychologiques et leurs implications dans les opérations militaires et paramilitaires au Congo »), 1964, qui a été élaborée par les universitaires du Counterinsurgency Analysis Center financé par l'armée, à l'American University. Les conclusions de ce rapport ont directement trait au rôle qu'Israël est arrivé à jouer : « A la lumière de l'expérience belge,

ainsi que de celle de Tshombé au Katanga (disait-il) il semble qu'un point de vue plus souple du problème militaire pourrait se trouver dans la conception des troupes d'élite : troupes ayant été entraînées et soigneusement formées à la discipline et bien commandées ». Ce conseil militaire a été accepté : en vue de diminuer le rôle nord-américain, déjà trop visible, trop étendu et politiquement embarrassant, on a fait appel aux Israéliens, qui ont assumé la tâche de former l'escadron de paracommandos, troupe d'élite du Congo.

Le résultat définitif en ce qui

(6) S. Silverburg, Israeli Military and Paramilitary Assistance to Sub-Saharan Africa : A Harbinger for the Role of the Military in Developing States, thèse de doctorat, Americain University, 1968.

FIGURE 22. "African Revolution, Arab Revolution," cartoon by JB. *Souffles* 19 (Rabat, 1970), p. 74. Reprinted with permission.

FOREWORD

Translated from the French by Olivia C. Harrison

Souffles resumes publication today after a few months' interruption due to the material difficulties we discussed in our "appeal for a support fund" for our journal. We took advantage of this interruption to reflect upon our project as a whole and to clarify the role *Souffles* can play in the context of new developments in Morocco and the Arab world.

There is no doubt that one of the grave ambiguities we faced from the outset, increasingly burdensome as our focus extended beyond culture, was that, despite our ideological and cultural commitment to the anti-imperialist struggle, our ideals were flagrantly compromised by the fact that we expressed them in a foreign language. Indeed we affirmed that the struggle against imperialist and bourgeois culture in Morocco and in the rest of the Maghreb would inevitably and necessarily involve taking possession of our culture, which is definitively possible only through the suppression of the most basic alienation, that is to say, linguistic alienation. Yet our actions contradicted our words.

Today more than ever before—and particularly in a country like ours whose historical destiny, whose destiny of struggle and liberation, is permanently linked to the destiny of the entire Arab nation—the struggle against imperialist *francophonie* and the use of the Arabic language in all domains of thought and expression are one of the fundamental conditions of our disalienation and of our true commitment to the liberation struggle.

This is why we did not wait be caught off guard before this inevitable dead-end and its disastrous consequences, be they aphasia or complacency and bad faith. We have long worked to end this ambiguity and the only way to do so is to create an instrument of expression and struggle in Arabic.

Today we have such an instrument: *Anfas* was born last May. Its frequency (monthly), its content (more focused on national and Arab realities), its style (more accessible), and, as a result, the larger public it reaches, lend *Anfas*, in our view, an important role in the national struggle as well as in the confrontation and dialogue between progressive Moroccan thinkers and liberation movements and social struggles in other Arab countries.

People will ask us, why then a French-language journal? Without going into too much detail, we will answer that *Souffles* will not duplicate the content of *Anfas* and will in no way supplant the Arabic journal or its objectives. This is to say that the role of *Souffles* is first of all more modest without being negligible.

On the one hand *Souffles* will address those amongst our national intellectuals who, because of their education or because of their complexes vis-à-vis Western culture, do not read Arabic. Our aim is to vigorously introduce the necessary ideological struggle in these circles, to make them discover the vitality and rigor of Moroccan and progressive Arab thinkers who write in Arabic, and thus invite those who have not totally succumbed to depersonalization to acknowledge their contradictions and the necessity of their reconversion.

On the other hand *Souffles* will address a progressive foreign public, Western for the most part. Indeed we believe that by virtue of our geographic position and our linguistic capacities we have the duty to enlighten and inform those among them who have sided with Arab peoples and supported their cause. In addition we believe that this cause will gain more support if this public is informed from within about Arab realities and progressive Arab militant thought.

It is true that several progressive press venues in France and elsewhere have reported on these realities and ideas, particularly in the last few years. But the fact is that these reports come mostly from professional journalists and militants who live outside the Arab world.

Less well known are the opinions of those on the ground, whether or not they are relayed in the Arab press, and even more importantly the foundational texts of revolutionary Arab organizations (Palestine, Dhofar, Eritrea, . . .) which are rarely translated into foreign languages in spite of their importance.

We have set ourselves the goal of translating these texts in a sustained fashion so that they may be disseminated as widely as possible.

From these few observations it should be obvious that *Souffles* is no longer a journal of French expression, a sort of progressive yet forced tribune of *francophonie*, but rather a journal of liaison and information in which the use of French is practical and neutral.[35]

Finally, given material limitations and considering also the need to be more concise and efficient, we are forced to limit ourselves (with some exceptions) to texts relating to the Maghreb and the Arab world. Not that we are less concerned with the African and tricontinental struggle, but we consider that others are better positioned to bring this task to fruition and deem our choice to be perfectly comprehensible.

This is the meaning of our new struggle. We invite all those who are cognizant of the urgency of the task to participate in it.

OPENING EDITORIAL—
ON THE ANNIVERSARY OF JUNE 5: THE AFTERMATH OF DEFEAT
Translated from the Arabic by Robyn Creswell

For four years, since June 5, 1967, Zionist aggression has tyrannized Arab lands. The defeat shook every Arab to his core along with liberation fighters all over the world. It also aroused a popular force of millions, whom the dominant classes made sure to keep far away from the front lines, allowing them no role beyond the production of surplus value to keep the bourgeoisie and feudalists living in style. Popular forces rose up in protest to throw off these chains, having had enough of idol worship and impotence. They demanded arms for a radical and unified response to Zionist-imperialist aggression, with the goal of total liberation. (Here we refer to the demonstrations of June 9–15 in Egypt, the protests all over the Arab homeland, and the spread of the armed revolution in the Gulf.)

The barbaric aggression represents a significant advance in the Zionist plan to build "greater Israel" by means of destruction and genocide. Its brutal armies have again seized Arab territories of great strategic and economic importance: the east bank of the Suez Canal, the Sinai, the Gulf of Aqaba, the Golan Heights, and the West Bank of the River Jordan. Meanwhile American imperialism has pursued its own strategy of aggression to extremes, lending its unconditional support to Israel and guaranteeing overwhelming military superiority, thereby proving again that "those who are behind Israel" are linked to it by innumerable and unbreakable ties of interest. For its part the Soviet Union has advocated the withdrawal of troops, a ceasefire, and negotiations at the U.N. to "eliminate residual traces of hostility."

As for Arab regimes and their armies, they have suffered a ruinous defeat after twenty years of empty talk about "a jihad to liberate the holy places from filth," and bold rhetoric about "the work of war" and "the gathering of forces to sweep away Israel and those behind Israel and liberate the stolen lands of Palestine." Now they are back, with hardly a pause since the defeat, brandishing the same slogans from the lecterns of their summit meetings, declaring that there will be "no rec-onciliation, no negotiation, and no peace with Israel."

In reality the defeat represents a gruesome, historic exposure of the inability of these regimes—along with the class structures that support them—to liberate a single inch of Arab territory. The fact that their pol-icy since the defeat of "facing up to the enemy" has in fact been a policy of retreat merely confirms this (in the present issue we present "The Class Struggle in Egypt," the précis of a book by the Egyptian resistance fighter Mahmoud Hussein).

The core strategy of these regimes has been to pursue "a peaceful solution," which means in practice the recognition of Zionism, the ta-bling of Palestinian liberation, and even cooperation when it comes to "other" occupied territories.

The first step of the Arab regimes' strategy was to accept (by way of rhetorical refusal) U.N. Security Council Resolution 242, passed on No-vember 22, 1967, and then the Rogers Plan, which aimed at "both the elimination of hostilities and the Palestinian issue at the same time." On the basis of this position the defeated regimes went along with Spe-cial Envoy Jarring's "shuttle diplomacy," which lasted for years and whose success was delayed by Israeli foot-dragging over the conditions of withdrawal rather than the rhetorical refusal of the defeated side to negotiate. So the "no negotiations" position gradually deteriorated into actual negotiations, while the position of "liberation for every inch of Arab land" deteriorated into the suggestion that Israel withdraw from one or two inches (the latest Egyptian suggestion was to open the Suez Canal in exchange for the occupying Zionist army taking a few steps backward).

It may not be long before the diplomats of the defeated surrender altogether and hand over a sizable portion of occupied lands or con-cede the right of Zionist ships to sail the Canal. What is the latest Egyp-tian volte-face but one more step toward the liquidation of that faction still loyal to the principle of military liberation for occupied lands and the necessity of shutting out American interests (though even this faction would of course maintain the established class structure that gives power to the national bourgeoisie). In this context the slogan "strengthen the interior front" means in practice the protection of the ruling class in its efforts to eliminate a faction that doesn't accept this shameful surrender. (By "faction" we mean the leadership group of the Socialist Union rather than the various schismatics within that ruling clique.) The same developments have taken place in Syria with the rise of Hafez al-Assad.

On the military front Arab regimes have brandished their slogans of "an ingathering of powers" and "rebuilding the armed forces" in anticipation of "the decisive and final combat." Meaning they haven't strayed from the classical strategy of using organized troops—i.e. the same strategy that led to their defeat. But the policy of "military confrontation" has become a defensive posture: it complements the policy of negotiating a peaceful solution rather than opposing it. For the international balance of forces established by the United States and the Soviet Union means that the latter strictly confines its support for the defeated regimes to ensuring their defensive capabilities, whereas the U.S. works to ensure absolute military superiority for Israel. Because of their class structure the Arab regimes are essentially opposed to the idea of fighting the enemy through a long-term popular war à la Vietnam. And so the position of "no peace with Israel" degenerates into a war of attrition, the sole purpose of which is to put pressure on Israel to drop its childish posturing regarding the conditions for a ceasefire. And after the farcical failure of this war (with Israeli airstrikes deep in Egyptian territory) the ceasefire agreement became, in practical terms, permanent.

As for the Palestinian revolution, its abandonment by bourgeois regimes is now grossly evident. These same regimes initially cheered the revolution on, since it allowed them to wash their hands of the liberation struggle their own populations demanded, and to put pressure on Israel. At the same time, they spared no ruse in seeking to impose their own political and economic authority over the resistance, the better to suffocate it at the appropriate time, whether through international alliances or by training their guns on it. So a pro-resistance position quickly slides into a position of complete silence and tactical support for the horrifying massacres carried out by the reactionary Jordanian regime—as well as for "those who are behind those who are behind Israel"—against the Palestinian fedayeen. And in this way the goal of liberating the Palestinian people is transformed into a mild acknowledgment of "the legitimate rights of the Palestinian people," who are subsequently abandoned to a bloodbath.

The defeat has made clear the impotence of these bourgeois nation-alist regimes to advance the Arab masses' desire for liberation from Zionism and imperialism and the establishment of socialism and Arab unity. Such regimes place their own exploitative interests and selfish comforts above the demand for national liberation. The ruling classes that came to power on the basis of such slogans have staged a retreat from their few achievements, suspending the struggle against Arab regimes cooperating with imperialists and Zionists, enforcing a quick march toward bourgeois respectability, repressing popular forces, and transforming calls for unity into a series of clumsy experiments. The re-cent alliance of Egypt, Syria, and Libya is not an anomaly in this line of retreat. Beyond its class character, beyond its tactic of substituting a su-perficial success in unification for a real failure in the practice of libera-tion, beyond its merely tactical aim of pushing the enemy to modify the size of his demands—beyond all this it represents a merely temporary unity that would fall apart in the case of a peaceful resolution (this is so because of the real contradictions between established and rising bour-geoisies, and between those who believe in war while living far from the front and those close to the front who believe in reconciliation).

The ruling classes of the Arab world have joined together in their march toward a humiliating reconciliation and in their determination to establish a dictatorship over popular forces. They repress all popular movements and progressive struggles and plot shamefully against all revolutionary movements (they massacre the Palestinian resistance, ar-rest and torture freedom fighters, provoke and then stifle the Dhofar rebellion).

Here the question of a revolutionary alternative poses itself. In the wake of the June War, "the Palestinian resistance represents the sole bright spot in the Arab world," while the revolution in the occupied Arabian Gulf has quickly become a model for the kind of radicalism demanded by liberation. (The present issue features a document by the Popular Front for the Liberation of the Occupied Arabian Gulf concern-ing social conditions in Dhofar.)

The efforts by the agents of imperialism to "suffocate and eliminate" the Palestinian resistance is a sharp reminder of the degree to which the fate of that revolution is tied to the fate of the Arab revolution more gen-erally, particularly in those countries bordering Israel. The liberation of

Palestine goes hand in hand with the advance of the revolution in all Arab countries, under the leadership of the radical class: poor peasants and workers who demand nothing less than complete independence from imperialism and the construction of a class-based front, both military and economic, aimed at unity and liberation.

The emergence of a popular struggle against imperialism, class exploitation, and repression, and against the policy of reconciliation is the most realistic and radical method of routing the enemy and his agents.

Let this anniversary spur us to draw appropriate lessons and gather a revolutionary spirit for the task of uprooting the forces of settler Zionism, imperialist oppression, and a ruling class of traitors and defeatists.

Anfas

أقــوال شــاهــد اثـبــات

محمد الفيتـوري

لقـد اهـتـز الرأي العام العربي والعالمي للـمـجـازر التي نظمت بعد فشل الانقلاب العسكري فـي السودان ضد العناصر الوطنية والثورية المقبلة وارتفعت كـل الاصوات الشريفة للتنديد بهذه الجرائم .

وصمتت في نفس الوقت الاقلام الذهبية التي سالـت منها اطنان الدموع بعد هـزيمة انظمة بورجوازيـة الدولة وجيوشها النظامية في حزيران ١٩٦٧

هكذا ازالت النخبة العربية المفكرة والمبدعة قناعـا جديدا عن وجهها وظهـرت عنترياتها الكـلامية علـى حقيقتها ، اي في الواقع ثرثرة تغطي في العمق خنوعها امام الامر الواقع البورجوازي وحرصها على المحافظة على امتيازاتها داخل المجتمع العربـي

صوت من بين الاصوات القليلة عبر بوضوح عـن رفضه لكل التباس وعن التحامه بقضايا ونضال الشعوب العربية وبالقوى الديموقراطية والثورية الحقة التـي تكافح ضد الاستغلال الامبريالي والطبقي . هذا الصوت هو صوت الشاعر السوداني محمد الفيتوري .

1

مشيت محكوما ٠٠٠ تعريت من الذكرى ٠٠ رقصت رقصتي القاسية الحزينة (كان دمي منذنة وجسدي مدينـة) غنيت للجنون مثلما اشاء

عبر الدهاليز الطويلـة ٠٠٠ التي تختال في قاعاتها الضيقة السوداء الهـة المـوت صفوفـا ناشرات خلفها الصمت والانطفاء

FIGURE 23. "Witness Statements," poem by Muhammad al-Fayturi. *Anfas* 7–8 (Rabat, 1971), p. 98. Reprinted with permission.

WITNESS STATEMENTS

Muhammad al-Fayturi

Translated from the Arabic by Ghenwa Hayek

Arab and global public opinion has been deeply affected by the massacres of the nationalist and truly revolutionary individuals following
the failed military coup in Sudan, and all honorable voices have risen
in condemnation of these crimes.

Meanwhile, the ink has run dry from the golden pens that gushed
rivers of tears after the 1967 defeats of the bourgeois nationalist regimes
and their armies.

The Arab intellectual elite and vanguard has removed its latest
mask, revealing its words for the chatter that they really are, a chatter
that profoundly obscures their fawning obeisance to the bourgeois reality and their desire to protect their privileges in Arab society.

Only one voice among the few has clearly expressed its rejection of
all this hypocrisy and its commitment to the causes and struggles of the
Arab people, and to the forces of just democracy and revolution that are
struggling against imperial and class exploitation. This voice belongs to
the Sudanese poet Muhammad al-Fayturi.

1.

through the long labyrinths . . .
in whose narrow dark hallways
swagger the gods of death
strewing behind them silence and darkness
I walked, condemned . . . stripping off memory..
I danced my strong, sad dance
(my blood a minaret, my body a city)
I sang to madness, as I wanted to
I listened, as I wanted to
I was as one who doesn't care..
myself, and history . . .

and the fire that bursts from my skull..
rising upwards to the sky.

2.

there is something . . .
I admit it now..
I saw them..
I saw the killers..
they passed before my eyes..
shivering like wounded falcons
they were judges with weapons,
gnawing at sacred books
I almost misunderstood what had happened..
so terrible it is to understand what is happening..
and so, they approached
the dawn rained gray, rained bullets and blood
the trees bowed down in the garden of God
and the sky covered its face
—they did not kill the seed.. they did not uproot
the stone . . . I said approach,
and so, they approached . . .
defeat unmasked itself
and they approached..
they hung their crosses around my neck
I almost misunderstood what happened..
so terrible it is to understand what is happening..
 . . . then they set fire to my funeral
and one by one, circled, smearing themselves with ashes
the crime and the revolution merged before me
they gestured at the sky with soles and knives
—another crime in vain
it stains their hands, they who have not yet washed off
the older crimes.
I prophesy that you will not extricate yourself tomorrow
from your fate of an excruciating birth
from the labor pangs of the great nation.

3.

the screams have stuck in my mouth:
—-the invaders . . . the Tatars..
the victims.. the weapons . . .
revolutionary banners in the mud..
the sinners have raped the regime..
not even coffins have survived the curse.
oh, my nation..
not even the sanctity of coffins has survived.
I confess.. to you who will come tomorrow
I stood by, moving neither a lip nor a hand
and in the glare of the afternoon, I witnessed the slaughter.

INTRODUCTION

1. Abdellatif Laâbi, "Prologue," *Souffles* 1 (1966): 6. Translated in this anthology as "Prologue" by Teresa Villa-Ignacio [Part One, 17–21].

2. HTML versions of *Souffles* may be consulted at: http://web.archive.org/web/20070403020406/http://www.seattleu.edu/souffles/. PDF versions of *Souffles* may be consulted at: http://bnm.bnrm.ma:86/ListeVol.aspx?IDC=3; those of *Anfas* at http://bnm.bnrm.ma:86/ListeVol.aspx?IDC=4

3. We use the hyphenated expression *Souffles-Anfas* to refer to the journal as a whole, and *Souffles* or *Anfas* when discussing individual issues or the journals separately.

4. Frantz Fanon, *The Wretched of the Earth*, translated by Richard Philcox (New York: Grove Press, 2004), 236.

5. Abdellatif Laâbi, "Réalités et dilemmes de la culture nationale," *Souffles* 4 (1966): 5. Translated in this anthology as "Realities and Dilemmas of National Culture" by Olivia C. Harrison and Teresa Villa-Ignacio [Part Two, 61–73].

6. Kenza Sefrioui, *La revue* Souffles *(1966–1973): Espoirs de révolution culturelle au Maroc* [The journal *Souffles* (1966–1973): Hope for cultural revolution in Morocco] (Rabat: Sirocco, 2013), 101.

7. Including the poets Mostafa Nissabouri and Tahar Ben Jelloun, who joined *Intégral*, a journal founded in 1971 by *Souffles* pioneer Mohamed Melehi as a forum entirely devoted to the arts.

8. Ilal Amam and 23 Mars disagreed on several questions, including the fate of the western Sahara, annexed by the Kingdom of Morocco in 1974. Ilal Amam advocated for self-determination while 23 Mars was in favor of Moroccan rule.

9. Other notable post-independence journals founded in the decade following Moroccan independence include *Lamalif* (published in French, the journal's title spells out the letters "N-O" in Arabic) and, in Arabic, *Afaq* [Horizons] and *Al-thaqafa al-jadida* [The new culture].

10. Mohamed Cherif Sahli, *Décoloniser l'histoire: Introduction à l'histoire du Maghreb* [Decolonizing history: Introduction to the history of the Maghreb] (Paris: Maspero, 1965).

11. Laâbi, "Realities" [Part Two, 72].

12. Abdelaziz Mansouri, "Un mot sur Adonis" [A word on Adonis], *Souffles* 18 (1970): 90–92.

13. Marc Gontard, *La violence du texte: Étude sur la littérature marocaine de langue française* [The violence of the text: Studies in French-language Moroccan literature] (Paris: L'Harmattan, 1981).

14. Abdellatif Laâbi, "Littérature maghrébine actuelle et francophonie,"

Souffles 18 (1970): 36. Translated in this anthology as "Contemporary Maghrebi Literature and *Francophonie*" by Lucy R. McNair [Part Four, 226–32].

15. Abdellatif Laâbi, "Le gâchis" [Waste], *Souffles* 7–8 (1967): 3.

16. Safoi Babana-Hampton, *Refléxions littéraires sur l'espace public marocain dans l'œuvre d'Abdellatif Laâbi* [Literary reflections on Moroccan public space in the work of Abdellatif Laâbi] (Birmingham, AL: Summa Publications, 2008), 90.

17. Laâbi, "Contemporary Maghrebi Literature" [Part Four, 228].

18. Abdellatif Laâbi, "La répudiation de Rachid Boudjedra," *Souffles* 16–17 (1969–1970): 55. Translated in this anthology as "Review of *The Repudiation* by Rachid Boudjedra" by Anne-Marie McManus [Part Four, 223–25].

19. Noured Ayouch, "Entrevue avec Jean-Marie Serreau," *Souffles* 13–14 (1967): 16–22. Translated in this anthology as "An Interview with Jean-Marie Serreau" by Edwige Tamalet Talbayev [Part Three, 162–71].

20. Abdellatif Laâbi, "Avant-Propos," *Souffles* 22 (1971): 4. Translated in this anthology as "Foreword" by Olivia C. Harrison [Part Four, 240–42].

21. Muhammad al-Fayturi, "Aqwal shahid athbat," *Anfas* 7–8 (1971): 98–99. Translated in this anthology as "Witness Statements" by Ghenwa Hayek [Part Four, 249–51].

22. Sefrioui, *La revue* Souffles, 109.

23. The term *Berber* derives from the ancient Greek *bárbaros*, which signifies and onamatopoetically portrays someone who speaks a language not understood by the Greeks. We use this term to refer to the Berber movements of the latter half of the twentieth century, as this is the terminology used in the historiography of these movements, but otherwise use Amazigh/Imazighen (singular/plural) for the people who speak Tamazight.

24. Abraham Serfaty, "Le judaïsme marocain et le sionisme," *Souffles* 15 (1969): 24–37. Translated in this anthology as "Moroccan Jewry and Zionism (excerpts)" by Lia Brozgal and Olivia C. Harrison [Part Four, 196–205].

25. Etel Adnan, "Jébu (extraits)," *Souffles* 15 (1969): 20–23. Translated in this anthology as "Jebu (excerpts)" by Etel Adnan [Part Four, 191–95]. Jeanne-Paule Fabre, "Réflexions sur une bibliographie de la femme maghrébine" [Reflections on a bibliography of Moroccan woman], *Souffles* 4 (1966): 41–44. Toni Maraini, "Situation de la peinture marocaine," *Souffles* 7–8 (1967): 15–19. Translated in this anthology as "Moroccan Painting Today" by Addie Leak [Part Two, 105–9].

26. Abdellatif Laâbi, "Questionnaire," *Souffles* 5 (1967): 8. Translated in this anthology as "Driss Chraïbi and Us (Interview)" by Safoi Babana-Hampton [Part Two, 74–80].

27. Sefrioui, *La revue* Souffles. Susan Slyomovics, *The Performance of Human Rights in Morocco* (Philadelphia: University of Pennsylvania Press, 2005).

28. Babana-Hampton, *Réflexions littéraires*, xv–xvii.

29. Tazmamart was a secret prison located in the Atlas mountains where Hassan II's regime held political prisoners from 1972 to 1991. Survivors of Tazmamart have detailed the frequent torture and inhumane living condi-

tions at the prison. See for example Ahmed Marzouki, *Tazmamart, cellule 10* [Tazmamart, cell number 10] (Casablanca: Tarik, 2000).

30. Valérie Orlando, *Francophone Voices of the "New" Morocco in Film and Print: (Re)presenting a Society in Transition* (New York: Palgrave Macmillan, 2009), xii, 10, 14.

31. Abdellatif Laâbi, *The World's Embrace: Selected Poems* (San Francisco: City Lights, 2003). *Aufgabe* 5: Featuring Moroccan poetry guest edited by Guy Bennett and Jalal El Hakmaoui (2005). Pierre Joris and Habib Tengour, eds., *Poems for the Millennium: The University of California Book of North African Literature, Volume Four* (Berkeley: University of California Press, 2012).

32. René Despestre, "Les aventures de la négritude," *Souffles* 9 (1969): 42–46. Translated in this anthology as "The Winding Course of Negritude" by Laura Reeck [Part Three, 120–25].

33. Jennifer Moxley, e-mail communication to Olivia C. Harrison and Teresa Villa-Ignacio, March 6, 2013.

34. Abdellatif Laâbi, preface to Sefrioui, *La revue* Souffles.

35. For an appreciation of Abdelahad Sebti's role in the February 20 movement, see Fadma Aït Mous and Driss Ksikes, *Le métier d'intellectuel: Dialogues avec quinze penseurs du Maroc* [The work of the intellectual: Dialogues with fifteen Moroccan thinkers] (Casablanca: En Toutes Lettres, 2014), 183. Laâbi's support for the movement is noteworthy given that writers such as Ben Jelloun and Fouad Laroui have publicly distanced themselves from street protests in favor of constitutional reforms spearheaded by the king. Other figures from the radical left have remained skeptical, no doubt due to the movement's lack of a political program. Merouan Mekouar, "Morocco" in Paul Amar and Vijay Prashad, eds., *Dispatches from the Arab Spring: Understanding the New Middle East* (Minneapolis: University of Minnesota Press, 2013), 147.

36. Abdellatif Laâbi, "Et le Maroc?" ["What about Morocco?"], http://www.laabi.net/ (accessed May 12, 2014).

37. Gilbert Achcar, *The People Want: A Radical Exploration of the Arab Uprising* (Berkeley: University of California Press, 2013), Chapters 1 and 2.

38. Mekouar, "Morocco."

PART ONE

1. See Malek Haddad, "Les zéros tournent en rond" [The zeroes go round in circles] in *Écoute et je t'appelle* [Listen and I'll call you] (Paris: Maspero, 1961), and Albert Memmi, "Portrait du colonisé" in *Portrait du colonisé, précédé de Portait du colonisateur* (Paris: Buchet-Chastel 1957). Translated as *The Colonizer and the Colonized* by Howard Greenfeld (Boston: Beacon Press, 1991).

2. Memmi, *The Colonizer and the Colonized*, 130.

3. The Senghor citation was not found. The Euripides quotation is from his play *Helen*; our English translation is from *Women On the Edge: Four Plays*, edited by Ruby Blondell (New York: Routledge, 1999), 239.

4. Frantz Fanon, *Toward the African Revolution*, translated by Haakon Chevalier (New York: Monthly Review Press, 1967), 35.

5. Aimé Césaire, "Discours sur l'art africain (1966)" [Speech on African art (1966)], *Études littéraires* 6:1 (1973): 99–109.

6. Léopold Sedar Senghor, *Liberté 1, Négritude et humanisme* [Liberty I: Negritude and humanism] (Paris: Seuil, 1964), 9.

7. Frantz Fanon, *Toward the African Revolution*, 18.

8. Here we will leave aside one of the most important genres of this poetry, the malhun, a genre that would require several studies all of its own.

9. Cf. Henri Basset, *Essai sur la littérature des Berbères* [Study of the literature of the Berbers] (Paris: Ibis Press, 2001; Algiers: Carbonel, 1920). Citations refer to the Ibis edition.

10. Ibid., 193.

11. The Ibn Khaldun citation was not found.

12. The translation of Sidi Hammou and the accompanying commentary (from "After a long absence" to "and quickly") is adapted from R. L. N. Johnson's "*Fadma Tagurramt* par Sidi Hammou or G'zgrouz" [*Fadma the sanctuary* by Sidi Hammou *dit* G'zgrouz] in *Actes du XIVe congrès international des orientalistes, Alger 1905* (Paris: Ernest Ledoux, 1907), 100–111.

PART TWO

1. See Abdellatif Laâbi, "Réalités et dilemmes de la culture nationale II," *Souffles* 6 (1967): 29–35. Translated in this anthology as "Realities and Dilemmas of National Culture II" by Safoi Babana-Hampton [Part Two, 95–103].

2. See Mostefa Lacheraf, "Colonialisme et féodalités indigènes en Algérie" [Colonialism and indigenous feudal systems in Algeria], *Esprit* (1954): 523–42. Reprinted in *L'Algérie: Nation et société* [Algeria: Nation and society] (Paris: Maspero, 1965), 47–68.

3. Fanon, *The Wretched of the Earth*, 149. See Introduction, n. 4. Translation slightly modified.

4. The first sentence of this quotation combines the following two sentences: "Reclaiming the past does not only rehabilitate or justify the promise of a national culture. It triggers a change of fundamental importance in the colonized's psycho-affective equilibrium." Fanon, *The Wretched of the Earth*, 148–49. The remainder of the quotation is a loose paraphrase of the surrounding paragraphs.

5. The introduction and first sentence of this quotation is an adaptation of "colonial bilingualism cannot be compared to just any linguistic dualism." Albert Memmi, *The Colonizer and the Colonized*, 107 (see Part One, n. 2).

6. Haddad, "Les zéros tournent en rond," 35–34 (see Part One, n. 1).

7. Ibid., 36.

8. Ibid., 11.

9. Pre-independence literature has been the object of a great number of

studies in Moroccan journals, in particular *Da'wat Al Haq, Al Iman, Afaq, Al Baïnah*. Most of these articles, unfortunately, lavish a kind of excessive praise on this literature. Furthermore, the authors compile interminable lists of names and often omit the titles of works or literary excerpts. They rarely provide any biographical elements or, more importantly, bibliographies. In this respect it is utterly preposterous that some individuals should retain numerous manuscripts in their possession and not give the public access to them, and that no one should have set out to collect and publish these texts. For this entire period, only works by Mohamed El Haloui and Mustafa Ma'dawi have recently been collected in anthologies [*diwans*].

10. Ahmed Sefrioui, *Le chapelet d'ambre* [Amber prayer beads] (Paris: Seuil, 1949); *La boîte à merveilles* [The chest of wonders] (Paris: Seuil, 1951).

11. Pierre Loti, *Into Morocco*, translated by E. P. Robbins (Chicago: Rand McNally, and Co., 1892); *Le désert* (Paris: Calman-Lévy, 1895), translated by Jay Paul Minn as *The Desert* (Salt Lake City: University of Utah Press, 1993).

12. Memmi, "Portrait of the Colonized" in *The Colonizer and the Colonized* (see Part One, n. 1).

13. Aimé Césaire, "Letter to Maurice Thorez," translated by Chike Jeffers, *Social Text* 103 (2010): 149–50. Originally published as *Lettre à Maurice Thorez* (Paris: Présence Africaine, 1956).

14. The bibliography of this autopsy is growing progressively. As for the bibliography of the Jewish question, everyone knows that it has been a bookstore success and that it assiduously fills the pages of the majority of periodicals with relentless testimonies and special reports. The masochism of this acute awareness is certainly not fortuitous.

15. Frantz Fanon gives a psychiatrist's account of this phenomenon of dehumanization in *Peaux noires, masques blancs* (Paris: Seuil, 1952). Translated as *Black Skin, White Masks* by Charles Lam Markmann (New York: Grove Press, 1967). D. Boukman's play, published in this issue of *Souffles*, admirably illustrates the same phenomenon (see the passage on "the madman's dream," for example.)

16. This class of intellectuals does not stop there. Sometimes, it enrolls in the school of the Third World. The European intellectual "goes Negro" for instance. Safaris, tam-tams, and African flora fill his texts. There is nothing new in this phenomenon. Even though he cuts a more intellectual figure, and even though his motives are different, this is the same figure we find, in a more naive and spontaneous form, if you will, in the vast corpus of European exoticist literature from the turn of the century. Yet the latter appears to us more normal, since exoticist authors content themselves with offering a feeling of estrangement to their readers by describing the so-called "overseas" countries.

17. On this topic see J. Mathias, "L'artisanat marocain," *Bulletin Économique et Social du Maroc* 27: 96–97 (1963): 55–109.

18. See for example Herbert Read, Chapter 2 in *Icon and Idea: The Function of Art in the Development of Human Consciousness* (Cambridge, MA: Harvard

University Press, 1955), which deals with the question of the development of popular art by analyzing its psychological (gestalt) laws and its visual (iconographic) laws.

19. By using graphic art and modern advertisement in their teaching and outside it. In this sense they have done their utmost to accompany didactic or personal exhibitions with posters and artistically drawn catalogs, whereas in the past the graphic aspect never seemed to interest painters in general—those who should have been the most sensitive to it. It would perhaps be interesting here—to give an idea of the seriousness of these new investigations—to cite the example of the poster drawn by M. Melehi for a group exhibit in Rabat, and chosen by New York's Museum of Modern Art as one of the best international posters of 1966.

PART THREE

1. Tahar Ben Jelloun, preface to *Poésie complète 1965–1995* [Collected poems 1965–1995] (Paris: Seuil, 1995), 9–10.

2. Aimé Césaire, *Aimé Césaire: The Collected Poetry*, translated by Clayton Eshleman and Annette Smith (Berkeley: University of California Press, 1984), 47.

3. Jean-Paul Sartre, *Black Orpheus*, translated by John MacCombie, *The Massachusetts Review* 6:1 (1964–65): 13.

4. Léopold Sédar Senghor, *Liberté I, Négritude et humanisme* (Paris: Seuil, 1964), 24 (see Part One, n. 6).

5. Lilyan Kesteloot, *Black Writers in French: A Literary History of Negritude*, translated by Ellen Conroy Kennedy (Philadelphia: Temple University Press, 1974), 107.

6. Sartre, *Black Orpheus*, 52.

7. Albert Camus, *The Plague*, translated by Stuart Gilbert (Vintage Books, 1972), 3. Originally published as *La peste* (Paris: Gallimard, 1947).

8. Ibid., 4.

9. Ibid., 5.

10. Ibid., 36.

11. Ibid.

12. Ibid., 41.

13. Ibid., 54–55. Translation modified: "Arab" substituted for "Algerian."

14. Serreau directed "La femme sauvage" at the Théâtre Récamier in Paris in December 1962 and January 1963.

15. Aimé Césaire famously called for *la négraille* ("nigger scum") to rise up against colonial oppression in *Cahier d'un retour au pays natal* (Paris: Présence Africaine, 1983), 61. Translated as *Notebook of a Return to the Native Land* by Clayton Eshleman and Annette Smith (Middletown, CT: Wesleyan University Press, 2001), 47.

16. He analyzes contemporary postwar Maghrebi literature from 1945 to 1962, a time period that corresponds to the struggle against the colonial system.

17. *Le roman maghrébin* is being translated into Arabic by M. Barrada in collaboration with the author. In fact it is more than a translation, because a number of themes will be expanded upon and several writers will be studied, in particular writers of Arabic expression such as 'Abdeljalil Ben Jalloun.

18. Khatibi will soon publish a study of the sociology of literature where theoretical developments will be foregrounded.

19. Abdelkebir Khatibi, *Le roman maghrébin* [The Maghrebi novel] (Paris: Maspero, 1968), 17.

20. Ibid., 67–82.

21. Abdallah Laroui, *L'idéologie arabe contemporaine* [Contemporary Arab ideology] (Paris: Maspero, 1967), 15.

22. Memmi has just published an essay entitled "L'homme dominé." Albert Memmi, *Dominated Man: Notes Toward a Portrait* (New York: Orion Press, 1968).

23. See our Chraïbi dossier, *Souffles* 5 (1967): 3–21.

24. All uprooting is but a moment, a crisis that is meant to be overcome. We can only participate in totalizing knowledge (aspire to universality) by succeeding in going beyond a number of issues. The alienation of the writer is overcome through writing, but this is not just any writing when it comes to the colonized man (or during the period of decolonization). Form is no longer a simple means, it acquires all the aspects of revolutionary demands. The signifier has an autonomy that allows it to operate on different levels; it is simultaneously a vehicular object and a signified expression. Only Kateb Yacine masters this remarkable technique, which Khatibi calls "terrorist, [as it] explodes the structure of the novel and creates a scintillating language shooting out in all directions and outdoing itself indefinitely." Khatibi, *Le roman maghrébin*, 103.

25. Ibid., 73.

26. Ibid., 78–80.

27. Ibid., 79.

28. See our interview with Chraïbi, *Souffles* 5 (1967): 5 (a second edition of *Le passé simple* is underway). See Introduction, n. 26.

29. Khatibi, *Le roman maghrébin*, 80.

30. Laroui, *L'idéologie arabe contemporaine*, 182.

31. Ibid., 176.

PART FOUR

1. Among these, two categories: those who simply want to live at home, here. This is their right, and no one can deny it to them. Those who aspire to be conscientious, responsible men can no longer ignore that their first duty as Jewish Moroccans is to wage a struggle against Zionism within the Jewish Moroccan community.

2. André Chouraqui, "La condition de l'israélite marocain est celle d'un être inférieur aux autres sujets de l'Empire Chérifien. Telle est la conclusion de

l'ouvrage édité en France par M. Chouraqui sous l'égide de l'Alliance Israélite Universelle" [The condition of the Moroccan Jew is that of being inferior to the other subjects of the Cherifian Empire. This is the conclusion of the book by Mr. Chouraqui published in France by the Alliance Israélite Universelle], *Noar: Journal d'Information Juive au Maroc* 29 (January 12, 1951): 1–2. André Chouraqui, *La condition juridique de l'israélite marocain* [The juridical condition of the Moroccan Jew] (Paris: Presses du Livre Français, 1950), 198.

3. "L'Alliance en face des problèmes actuels: Conférence de M. Jules Braunschwig" [The Alliance before today's problems: A talk by Mr. Jules Braunschwig], *Noar* 9 (May 1947): 16.

4. S. D. Goitein, *Jews and Arabs: Their Contact Through the Ages* (New York: Schocken Books, 1955), 130.

5. Let us recall that Marx criticized the bourgeois conception of the secular state, thus opposing mechanistic interpretations of socialism: "But the religious spirit cannot be *really* secularized. For what is it but the *non-secular* form of a stage in the development of the human spirit? The religious spirit can only be realized if the stage of development of the human spirit which it expresses in religious form, manifests and constitutes itself in its *secular* form. This is what happens in the *democratic* state. The basis of this state is not Christianity but the *human basis* of Christianity. Religion remains the ideal, non-secular consciousness of its members, because it is the ideal form of the *stage of human development* which has been attained." Robert C. Tucker, ed., *The Marx-Engels Reader*, 2nd ed. (New York: Norton, 1978), 39. Original italics. How can we fail to see that this objective also corresponds to an aspiration common to both Judaism and Islam: the realization on earth of the Kingdom of God?

6. And their contemporary avatars at the Center for Research on Mediterranean Africa at the University of Aix-en-Provence, such as André Adam and Robert Mantran. André Adam, *Casablanca: Essai sur la transformation de la société marocaine au contact de l'Occident* [Casablanca: Essay on the transformation of Moroccan society in contact with the West] (Paris: CNRS, 1968). Robert Mantran, *L'expansion musulmane: VIIe–XIe siècles* [Muslim expansion from the seventh to the eleventh century] (Paris: PUF, 1969).

7. Edouard Mouillefarine, "Étude historique sur la condition juridique des Juifs au Maroc" [Historical study of the juridical condition of Jews in Morocco] (PhD diss., Université de Paris, Faculté de Droit, 1941), 190.

8. Is. D. Abbou, *Musulmans andalous et judéo-espagnols* [Andalusian Muslims and the Judeo-Spanish] (Casablanca: Antar, 1952).

9. Compelling proof of this popular condemnation is found in the fact that the tomb of Saint Solica, a Jewish saint adored for risking her life to keep the faith rather than ceding to a sovereign, was also worshipped by Muslims.

10. Le Capitaine des A. M. M. Molinari, "Observations sur la condition juridique des juifs en tribu de droit coutumier berbère, dans le territoire du Tafilalet" [Observations on the juridical condition of Jews in a tribe of Berber

customary law in the territory of the Tafilalet], *Revue de la Justice Coutumière* 1 (1955): 13.

11. Ibid., 12.

12. E. S. and H. L., "La revanche du Mellah: Chavouot à Sefrou" [The revenge of the Mellah: Shavouat in Sefrou], *Noar* 10–11 (1947): 15. See also "Réflexions d'un visiteur au Maroc" [Reflections of a visitor to Morocco], *Noar* 14 (1948): 8–9, 24. When citing the first article, Serfaty substitutes the Arabic term designating the Jewish quarters in Morocco, *mellah*, for its more negatively inflected Eastern European equivalent, *ghetto*.

13. Louis Voinot cites thirty-one cases of saints worshipped by both Jews and Muslims, fourteen cases of Muslim saints worshipped by Jews, and fifty cases of Jewish saints worshipped by Muslims. Louis Voinot, *Pèlerinages judéo-musulmans du Maroc* [Judeo-Muslim pilgrimages in Morocco] (Paris: Larose, 1948), 85.

14. The Israeli Socialist Organization Matzpen summarizes this process as follows: "Western civilization produced anti-Semitism as its legitimate offspring, Nazism as its illegitimate one. European Jewry, unable to recognize anti-Semitism as a product of a civilization of which it was part, elevated it to the rank of a 'law of Human nature' and produced Zionism to cope with that alienation." Israeli Socialist Organization (Matzpen), *The Other Israel: Israeli Critique of Zionist History and Policy* (Tel Aviv: Israeli Socialist Organization, 1968), 10. (Naturally, it is neither my role nor my place to discuss the position of this or that Israeli anti-Zionist organization, though I would like to acknowledge their courage here. Revolutionary praxis already—and increasingly—allows us to move beyond misleading debates about theory and practice through the shared revolutionary armed struggle of tomorrow's unified Palestine.)

15. As noted by Emmanuel Lévyne, today the Biblical conception of Israel befits the Palestinians, who can indeed say "next year in Jerusalem." Emmanuel Lévyne, "Le judaïsme et la libération de la Palestine" [Judaism and the liberation of Palestine] in "Le peuple palestinien," special issue of *Hertyem: Critique politique de la vie quotidienne* 1 (1969): 10.

16. Prosper Cohen, *Congrès juif mondial: Conférence extraordinaire de guerre, 26–30 novembre, 1944* [World Jewish Congress: War Emergency Conference, November 26–30, 1944] (Casablanca: SIPEF, 1946), 213.

17. Prosper Cohen, "Après la bataille" [After the battle], *Noar* 14 (1948): 4.

18. Mouillefarine, *Étude historique*. Page not found.

19. Those wishing better to understand the "Jewish problem," insofar as it has its roots in the development of capitalism, must read Abraham Léon's book, written in hiding in 1941 before the author was arrested by the Nazis and killed at Auschwitz. The new edition of the book features a preface written by Maxime Rodinson that offers an historical synthesis. Abraham Léon, *La conception matérialiste de la question juive* [A materialist understanding of the Jewish question] (Paris: Études et Documentation Internationales, 1968).

20. It must be said that conditions on the ground make this nearly impossible to accomplish. None of the works mentioned here are imported or sold in Morocco; this is the double effect produced by censors and the foreign network of bookstores. The French language press in Morocco is either Zionist or dripping with racism. The foreign press boils down to the Zionism of *France-Soir* and the so-called objectivity of *Le Monde*. The first duty of patriots is thus to organize this information.

21. Marc Hillel, *Israël en danger de paix* [Israel in danger of peace] (Paris: Fayard, 1968).

22. Saül Friedlander, *Réflexions sur l'avenir d'Israël* [Reflections on the future of Israel] (Paris: Seuil, 1969).

23. Emmanuel Lévyne, *Judaïsme contre sionisme* [Judaism against Zionism] (Paris: Cujas, 1969).

24. Doris Bensimon-Donath. "Développement et sous-développement en Israël: Aspects socio-culturels" [Development and underdevelopment in Israel: Sociocultural aspects], *Revue Française de Sociologie* 9:4 (1968): 522–36.

25. Sabri Gerics, *Les Arabes en Israël, précédé de Les Juifs et la Palestine par Eli Löbel* [Arabs in Israel, preceded by The Jews and Palestine by Eli Löbel] (Paris: Maspero, 1969).

26. The role played by Zionism in the Nazi massacre is clearly established by the following letter, addressed by Ben Gurion to the Zionist executive branch on December 17, 1938, when the Anglo-Saxon countries proposed to open their doors to the Jews of Germany and Central Europe: "The Jewish problem now is not what it used to be. The fate of Jews in Germany is not an end but a beginning. Other anti-Semitic states will learn from Hitler. Millions of Jews face annihilation, the refugee problem has assumed world-wide proportions, and urgency. Britain is trying to separate the issue of the refugees from that of Palestine. It is assisted by anti-Zionist Jews. The dimensions of the refugee problem demand an immediate, territorial solution; if Palestine will not absorb them another territory will. Zionism is endangered. All other territorial solutions, certain to fail, will demand enormous sums of money. If Jews will have to choose between the refugees, saving Jews from concentration camps, and assisting a national museum in Palestine, mercy will have the upper hand and the whole energy of the people will be channeled into saving Jews from various countries. Zionism will be struck off the agenda not only in world public opinion, in Britain and U.S.A., but elsewhere in Jewish public opinion. If we allow a separation between the refugee problem and the Palestinian problem, we are risking the existence of Zionism." Cited in Israeli Socialist Organization (Matzpen), *The Other Israel: Israeli Critique of Zionist History and Policy* (Tel Aviv: Israeli Socialist Organization, 1968), 9.

27. Maxime Rodinson, *Israel: A Colonial Settler State?*, translated by David Thorstad (New York: Pathfinder Press, 1973). Originally published as "Israël fait colonial?" in "Le conflit israélo-arabe," special issue of *Les Temps Modernes* 253 bis (1967): 17–88.

28. Nathan Weinstock, *Le sionisme contre Israël* [Zionism against Israel] (Paris: Maspero, 1969).

29. Jacques Boetsch, "*L'Express* va plus loin avec Moshe Dayan" [*L'Express* goes further with Moshe Dayan], *L'Express*, May 19–25, 1969, 56–63.

30. Roger Benhaïm, *Jérusalem, Jérusalem! Israël ou l'assimilation: La foi juive en question* [Jerusalem, Jerusalem! Israel or assimilation: The Jewish faith in question] (Paris: C.E.D.A.G. Le Perreaux, 1975): 16. Original emphasis.

31. Born in 1941 in Aïn Beïda in Algeria. Teaches philosophy in France; published a collection of poems, *Pour ne plus rêver* [No longer to dream] (Algiers: SNED, 1966), and a novel, *La répudiation* (Paris: Denoël, 1969), translated by Golda Lombrova as *The Repudiation* (Colorado Springs, CO: Three Continents Press, 1995).

32. To best prepare for this debate, the reader is invited to consult the following documents:

—Malek Haddad, "Les zéros tournent en rond" (see Part One, n. 1).

—Albert Memmi, *Portrait du colonisé* (see Part One, n. 1).

—Albert Memmi, *Anthologie des écrivains maghrébins d'expression française* [Anthology of francophone Maghrebi writers] (Paris: Présence Africaine, 1964).

—Abdelkebir Khatibi, *Le roman maghrébin* (see Part Three, n. 19).

—*Confluent* 47 "Aspects de la littérature maghrébine contemporaine" [Aspects of contemporary Maghrebi literature"] (1965).

—*Orient* 5 (Paris, 1965).

—*Souffles* 1, 2, 3, 4, 5, 10/11, 13/14.

33. The opposite operation (still used by some Maghrebi authors) consists of adapting Maghrebi reality to a foreign public. The cynicism of these writers can go so far as to insert footnotes to make it even easier for their public: Hamam: Turkish bath. Derb: alley. Medina: "Arab city," etc.

34. From *Le Monde*, June 14–15, 1970.

35. In this regard we would like to make it clear that we neither want to encourage nor stifle creative writing in French. Alongside literary texts translated into Arabic we will continue to publish Moroccan and Maghrebi texts written in French insofar as they correspond to the journal's editorial policy.

MOHAMMED ISMAÏL ABDOUN was born in 1945 in Béchar, Algeria. A poet and professor of literature at the University of Algiers–Bouzaréah, he specializes in the works of Kateb Yacine and Henri Michaux. His critical works include *Lecture de Henri Michaux* (2003) [A reading of Henri Michaux], *Lecture(s) de Kateb Yacine* (2006) [Reading(s) of Kateb Yacine], and the anthology *Kateb Yacine* (1983).

Born in Beirut in 1925 and educated in France and the United States, **ETEL ADNAN** has published poetry, fiction, plays, and essays in French and English. Her works include the acclaimed novel *Sitt Marie Rose* (1977) [English translation, 1982], *L'apocalypse arabe* (1980) [*The Arab Apocalypse* (1989)], a poem dotted with graphic signs, and her meditation on war, *In the Heart of the Heart of Another Country* (2005). Adnan is also known for her brightly colored paintings and sculptures, and she often conjugates writing and painting in her artistic and poetic works. After teaching philosophy at Dominican College (now University) in San Rafael, CA, for more than a decade, Adnan was cultural editor for the Lebanese dailies *Al-Safa* and *L'Orient le Jour* until the 1975 Lebanese civil war erupted. She now lives in Paris.

Trained in Tétouan (Morocco), Seville, and Rome, **MOHAMED (ROMAIN) ATAALLAH** (b. 1939) taught at l'École des Beaux Arts in Casablanca before taking up long-term residence in France. Best known for his paintings of geometric shapes and "magic squares," Ataallah began his career painting landscapes and now works with diverse media, including video. He lives in Tangier.

NOUREDDINE (NOURED) AYOUCH (b. 1945) is a Moroccan entrepreneur and activist whose ventures include the short-lived women's magazine *Kalima*; La Fondation Zakoura, designed to combat adult and youth illiteracy; La Fondation des Arts Vivants, dedicated to the restoration of theater productions; and l'Association Daba, which encouraged citizen and particularly youth participation in the legislative elections of 2007.

MOHAMED BENNANI (1937–1995) studied law and theology at Karaouiyne University before accepting a position as director of the Cultural Center in Fes and discovering his vocation as a painter. A self-taught artist, he was invited to participate in numerous collective exhibitions in Morocco, Egypt, Europe, and the United States from 1958 onward, and held his first solo show in Rabat in 1961. In 1965 he obtained a scholarship to study art history at the École du Louvre in Paris, and relocated definitively to France, though he continued to correspond with friends in Morocco, including the *Souffles-Anfas* team. Bennani's painting style is marked by bold, abstract brushwork and the predominance of black and white. Most of his paintings were destroyed in a fire shortly after his death.

MOHAMMED BERRADA (b. 1938) is a novelist, literary critic, and translator of, among others, Abdelkebir Khatibi, Tahar Ben Jelloun, Roland Barthes, and Jean Genet into Arabic. Formerly a professor of Arabic literature at Mohammed V University in Rabat and president of the Union of Moroccan Writers, he now lives in Brussels, where he continues to write and translate. Several of Berrada's critically acclaimed novels have been translated into English, including *Luʿbat al-nisyan* (1986) [*The Game of Forgetting* (1992)], *Al-daw' al-harīb* (1993) [*Fugitive Light* (2002)], and *Mithl sayf lan yatakarrar: Mahkiyyat* (1999) [*Like a Summer Never to Be Repeated* (2009)].

Novels by the Moroccan writer **TAHAR BEN JELLOUN** (b. 1944) include *Harrouda* (1973), *L'enfant de sable* (1985) [*The Sand Child* (1987)], *La nuit sacrée* (1987) [*The Sacred Night* (1989)], for which he won the Prix Goncourt, and *Cette aveuglante absence de lumière* (2001) [*This Blinding Absence of Light* (2002)]. His poetry is collected in *Poésie complète* (1995). A long-time resident of France, he has taken on issues of discrimination against immigrants in France in such texts as *Hospitalité française* (1984) [*French Hospitality: Racism and North African Immigrants* (1999)] and *Le racisme expliqué à ma fille* (1997) [*Racism Explained to My Daughter* (2006)].

The writer, cartoonist, and filmmaker **AHMED BOUANANI** (1938–2011) is the author of three poetry collections, *Les persiennes* (1980) [The blinds], *Photogrammes* (1989) [Photograms], and *Territoires de l'instant* (2000) [Territories of the moment], and one novel, *L'hôpital: Récit en noir et blanc* (1990, 2012) [The hospital: A black-and-white tale]. Best known in Morocco as a filmmaker who lent poetry to the everyday life of ordinary Moroccans, he directed the shorts *6 et 12* (1968) and *Mémoire 14* (1971), and the feature-length *Assarab* (1979) [The mirage].

Born in Tangier and trained in Tétouan (Morocco) and Rome, **MOHAMED CHEBAA** (1935–2013) joined the faculty of l'École des Beaux Arts in Casablanca in 1966 and participated in the creation of *Souffles*, whose calligraphic logo he designed. From 1969 he was the sole artistic director of both *Souffles* and *Anfas*. Along with other artists of the Casablanca Group, such as Farid Belkahia and Mohamed Melehi, Chebaa is known as one of the founders of modern Moroccan art, which sought to break with the folkloric traditions and imitative art that flourished under French colonial rule and to make the visual arts accessible to the greater public. In 1969, Chebaa, Ataallah, Melehi, Belkahia, Mohamed Hamidi, and Mustapha Hafid launched Morocco's first public and free exhibition, at the Jamaʿa al-Fna Square in Marrakech. Chebaa's abstract painting style draws on Islamic art and Moroccan pictorial traditions in a formal exploration of form, line, color, and space.

AHMED CHERKAOUI (1934–1967) was one of the most important modern Moroccan painters, and the first to use Islamic calligraphy and Berber pictorial traditions (tattoos, ceramics, rugs, jewelry) in his explorations in abstract form and color. Trained in France and Poland, Cherkaoui was poised to return to Morocco when he died. His oeuvre had a profound influence on Moroccan painters as well as writers such as Abdelkebir Khatibi and Edmond Amran El Maleh, who authored important essays on his work.

DRISS CHRAÏBI (1926–2007) was a Moroccan author best known for his first novel, *Le passé simple* (1954) [*The Simple Past* (1990)], which, via the tale of a son's revolt against his tyrannical father, delivers a powerful critique of colonialism and sexism in 1950s bourgeois Moroccan society. Chraïbi's second novel, *Les boucs* (1955) [*The Butts* (1983)], is a startling revelation of the dire conditions in which Maghrebi immigrants were living and working in France. Chraïbi continued to address pertinent social and political issues in novels including *Succession ouverte* (1962) [*Heirs to the Past* (1971)], *La civilisation, ma mère!...* (1972) [*Mother Comes of Age* (1984)], and *La mère du printemps* (1982) [*Mother Spring* (1989)]. His Inspector Ali detective novels remain his most popular works.

RENÉ DEPESTRE (b. 1926) is a Haitian poet and activist. His first collection of poetry, *Étincelles* (1945) [Sparks], published when he was nineteen years old, was banned by the Haitian government. Depestre studied at the Sorbonne from 1946 to 1950, where he took part in decolonization protests and wrote for the celebrated pan-Africanist journal *Présence Africaine*. Expelled from Duvalier's Haiti in 1957, he moved to Cuba at Che Guevara's invitation, where he founded the publishing house Casa de las Americas and contributed to several other cultural institutions. Depestre's widely-translated publications include *Végétations de clarté* (1951) [*Vegetations of Splendor* (1980)], *Un arc-en-ciel pour l'occident chrétien, poème mystère vaudou* (1966) [*A Rainbow for the Christian West* (1972)], and the novel *Le mât de cocagne* (1979) [*The Festival of the Greasy Pole* (1990)]. He has traveled extensively, won several literary prizes and fellowships, and served as the UNESCO special envoy to Haiti.

EMORY DOUGLAS (b. 1943) was the minister of culture of the Black Panther Party and the art director for the party's tribune, *The Black Panther*, from 1967 until the party disbanded in the early 1980s. His iconic artwork has been the subject of several solo exhibitions and art books, most recently *Black Panther: The Revolutionary Art of Emory Douglas* (2007), published on the occasion of Douglas's 2007 solo show at the Museum of Contemporary Art, Los Angeles.

The Sudanese poet **MUHAMMAD AL-FAYTURI** (1936–2015) began writing poetry in the late 1940s, while studying Islamic history and literature at Al-Azhar and Cairo universities. A journalist and prolific poet, he published a number of collections, including *Aghani Ifriqiya* (1956) [Songs of Africa], *'Ashiq min Ifriqiya* (1970) [Lover from Africa], *Sharq al-shams, gharb al-qamar* (1992) [East of the sun, west of the moon], and *Aghsan al-layl 'alayk* (1997) [*Shrouded by the Branches of Night: Poems*].

Like Cherkaoui, **JILALI GHARBAOUI** (1930–1971) is one of the most important abstract painters of twentieth-century Morocco. Trained in Paris and Rome, Gharbaoui experimented with French impressionism and German expressionism before turning to abstraction in the early 1950s. His paintings are marked by forceful, nervous brushstrokes and vivid colors.

MOHAMED HAMIDI (b. 1941) studied and later taught at l'École des Beaux Arts in Casablanca alongside Melehi, Chebaa, and other artists of the Casablanca Group. Trained at l'École des Métiers d'Art and l'École Nationale Supérieure des Beaux-Arts in Paris, Hamidi spent several years in France before returning to Morocco. His paintings explore themes of sexuality and fertility, experimenting with Berber forms, Kufic calligraphy, color, and geometry.

Trained at l'École des Beaux Arts in Casablanca and then in France, Poland, and Italy, where he took courses in set design, engraving, and architecture, **ABDALLAH EL HARIRI** (b. 1949) is known for his irreverent, playful use of calligraphy, his monochromatic treatment of color and, more recently, his experiments with burnt materials. He lives in Casablanca.

A mountain climber, poet, priest, and theologian at l'Église Catholique Orthodoxe de France in Montpellier, **BERNARD JAKOBIAK** (b. 1932) spent six years teaching high school students in Morocco. His poetry collections include *Il y aurait un nous* (1969) [There would be an us], *L'enterrée vive* (1996) [The woman buried alive], *La tendresse intacte* (2010) [Tenderness intact], and *Le fardeau des orages* (2012) [The burden of storms]. *Bernard Jakobiak*, a volume dedicated to his life and work, was published in 2007 in the series Poètes trop effacés from Le Nouvel Athanor.

AHMED JANATI was born in the Berberophone city of Ahermoumou (now known as Ribat El Kheir) in 1948. He was a twenty-two-year-old student when he submitted his first poem, "Al Janaza" (Funeral prayer) to the editors of *Souffles*.

MOHAMMED KHAÏR-EDDINE (1941–1995) published numerous volumes of poetry, including *Soleil arachnide* (1969) [Arachnid sun] and *Ce Maroc!* (1975) [This Morocco!]. His novel *Agadir* (1967), which won Jean Cocteau's Grand Prix des Enfants Terribles, takes poetic inspiration from the earthquake that struck the eponymous city in 1960. Khaïr-Eddine contributed to *Les Lettres Nouvelles* and

Présence Africaine, and coauthored the manifesto "Poésie-toute" [All-poetry] with Mostafa Nissabouri.

ABDELKEBIR KHATIBI (1938–2009) trained as a sociologist and was one of Morocco's most celebrated writers, a respected critic of art and literature, and one of the twentieth century's most important theorists of cultural decolonization. Khatibi's fictional texts include *La mémoire tatouée: Autobiographie d'un décolonisé* (1971) [Tattooed memory: Autobiography of a decolonized man], *Amour bilingue* (1983) [*Love in Two Languages* (1990)], and *Triptyque de Rabat* (1993) [Rabat triptych]. Some of his most noted essays are *Le roman maghrébin* (1968) [The Maghrebi novel], *Maghreb pluriel* (1983) [The plural Maghreb], *Figures de l'étranger dans la littérature française* (1987) [Figures of the foreigner in French literature], and, with Mohamed Sijelmassi, *The Splendor of Islamic Calligraphy* (1996).

In addition to cofounding *Souffles* and *Anfas*, of which he was editor-in-chief from 1966 to 1972, **ABDELLATIF LAÂBI** (b. 1942) is a prolific poet, novelist, essayist, playwright, and children's author. He has produced numerous translations of seminal Arabic-language writers, including Mahmoud Darwish, Abdelwahab Al-Bayati, and Ghassan Kanafani. His seminal anthology *La poésie marocaine, de l'indépendance à nos jours* (2005) [Moroccan poetry from independence to the present day] was the first to bring together over fifty Francophone and Arabophone poets in a single volume. Translations of his work into English include *The World's Embrace: Selected Poems* (2003), *The Rule of Barbarism* (2012), and the autobiographical *The Bottom of the Jar* (2013).

The writer and literary critic **AHMED AL-MADINI** (b. 1949) is the author of several novels and short story collections, including *Hikayat wahm* (1992) [The story of an illusion], *Qisas min al-maghrib al-'arabi* (1996) [Short stories from the Arab Maghreb], and the collection of poems *Baqaya ghiyab* (2003) [Remainders of absence]. He holds a PhD from the Sorbonne and was awarded the Moroccan National Book Award in 2002.

TONI MARAINI (b. 1941) is an Italian art historian who specializes in Maghrebi art and culture. In the 1960s she taught art history at l'École des Beaux Arts in Casablanca and was associated with the *Souffles* poets and the Casablanca Group. She has also taught at Mohamed V University in Rabat and at l'Institut de Communication Audiovisuelle in Casablanca. Much of her work on Moroccan art has been collected in the volume *Écrits sur l'art: Choix de textes, Maroc 1967–1989* (1990) [Writings on art: Selections, Morocco 1967–1989]. Maraini has also published poetry and translated Maghrebi writers into Italian.

Born in Assilah in 1936, **MOHAMED MELEHI** was trained at l'École des Beaux-Arts in Tétouan before traveling to Spain, Hungary, Italy, and the United States, where he exhibited his work alongside Frank Stella and Piet Mondrian. He returned to Morocco in 1964 to join the faculty of l'École des Beaux Arts in Casablanca alongside other artists of the Casablanca Group. A founding member of *Souffles*, Melehi served as its artistic director and typesetter until 1969. His iconic drawing of a black sun adorns the front cover of early issues and was incorporated as the "o" of the title *Souffles* in later issues. In 1971 he founded, with Toni Maraini, Mostafa Nissabouri, and Tahar Ben Jelloun, an influential art and poetry journal, *Intégral*. An active and prolific artist, Melehi is best known for his signature wave paintings and sculptures.

The Tunisian writer **ALBERT MEMMI** (b. 1920) is best known for his first novel, *La statue de sel* (1953) [*The Pillar of Salt* (1975 [©1955])] which depicts a Jewish boy's coming of age in predominantly Muslim, French colonial Tunisia, and for his seminal essay *Portrait du colonisé, précédé du portrait du colonisateur* (1957) [*The Colonizer and the Colonized* (1965)], which analyzes the interdependent identities of colonizer and colonized and established Memmi as a founder of postcolonial theory. Beginning with *Portrait of a Jew* (1962), Memmi's critical writing has also consistently addressed issues of Jewish identity.

A cofounder of *Souffles* and *Intégral* and former director of l'École des Beaux Arts in Casablanca, **MOSTAFA NISSABOURI** (b. 1943) is the author of the poetry collections *Plus haute mémoire* (1968) [Highest memory], *La mille et deuxième nuit* (1975) [The one thousand and second night], and *Approche du désertique* (1999) [*Approach to the Desert Space* (2001)]. He lives and writes in his native Casablanca.

Born in 1939 and trained at l'École des Beaux Arts in Tétouan, where he continues to teach, as well as in Spain and France, **SAAD BEN SEFFAJ** (also known as Saad Ben Cheffaj) is equally at ease with figurative and abstract painting. He works with mixed media, incorporating ready-made objects of various textures into his paintings, and draws on the Mediterranean, and particularly on Greek mythology, for his subjects. His work has been exhibited in Morocco and in Spain.

ABRAHAM SERFATY (1926–2010) was on the editorial board of *Souffles-Anfas* from 1968 until his arrest in 1972. Serfaty was a longstanding member of the communist party, first in France, where he completed his studies in engineering, then in Morocco, where he joined in the struggle for independence from France. In 1970 Serfaty was involved in the creation of the Marxist-Leninist party Ilal-Amam (Forward). Imprisoned for seventeen years, Serfaty is the author of *Dans les prisons du roi: Écrits de Kénitra sur le Maroc* (1992) [In the prisons of the king: Writings on Morocco from Kénitra Prison], *La mémoire de l'autre* (1993) [The memory of the other] (with his wife Christine Daure-Serfaty), and *Le Maroc, du noir au gris* (1998) [Morocco, from black to gray].

Senegalese novelist and filmmaker **OUSMANE SEMBÈNE** (1923–2007) was one of the most important cultural figures of the anti- and postcolonial eras. An autodidact and a unionist who served in the French colonial army during World War II, Sembène published his first novel, *Le docker noir* (1956) [*Black Docker* (1987)], before Senegalese independence and went on to study film in the U.S.S.R. Several others of his novels have been translated into English, including *Les bouts de bois de Dieu* (1960) [*God's Bits of Wood* (1995)], *Le mandat, précédé de Vehi-Ciosane* (1966) [*The Money-Order with White Genesis* (1972)], and *Xala* (1973) [English translation, 1974]. Sembène adapted several of his novels to the silver screen with the express intention of reaching a large segment of society. His best known films include *La noire de . . .* (1966) [*Black Girl*], *Mandabi* (1970), *Xala* (1975), and *Mo;oladé* (2004).

JEAN-MARIE SERREAU (1915–1973) was a French actor and stage director. During the 1950s and 1960s he directed the Théâtre de Babylone in Paris, and in 1970 he founded the Théâtre de la Tempête à La Cartoucherie in Vincennes. In addition to staging works by postcolonial writers with actors from former French colonies, he was known for staging avant-garde works by Samuel Beckett, Jean Genet, and Eugène Ionesco.

The controversial French political cartoonist **SINÉ** (b. Maurice Sinet in 1928) was already known as an outspoken anticolonial activist when his cartoons appeared in *Souffles*, having begun his career publishing cartoons in favor of Algerian independence in the weekly magazine *L'Express*. A long-time contributor to the leftist satirical paper *Charlie Hebdo*, Siné is the author of numerous books, several of which have appeared in English, editor-in-chief of the satirical magazine *Siné Mensuel* (successor to *Siné Hebdo*), and a regular blogger (Siné déblogue).

ABDALLAH STOUKY (b. 1946) is a prominent journalist and editor in Morocco. A longstanding member of the Moroccan Communist Party, he founded *Al Maghrib*, the daily paper of the centrist party Rassemblement National des Indépendants (RNI), in 1978, and has since contributed to several media outlets, including the official news agency Maghreb Arab Press (MAP), the leftist daily *Al Bayane*, and the new weekly *L'Observateur du Maroc et d'Afrique*. In 1981 he launched his own publishing house, Éditions Stouky, devoted principally to publishing the work of Moroccan poets, including Mohammed Khaïr-Eddine and Ahmed Bouanani.

Born in Tunis in 1934 and killed in 2015 during the attack against the French satirical magazine *Charlie Hebdo*, **GEORGE WOLINSKI** was a beloved French political cartoonist. In 1968 he founded the satirical magazine *L'Enragé*, with Siné, and joined the editorial team of the communist daily *L'Humanité* in 1977. His cartoons appeared in *Libération, Le Nouvel Observateur,* and *Charlie Hebdo,* and he published numerous comic books and cartoon compilations, most recently, *Vive la France!* (2013).

Acclaimed novelist and translator **MOHAMED ZAFZAF** (1942–2001) began writing poetry and short stories in the early 1960s, and published several short story collections and novels, including *Al-Mar'a wa al-warda* (1972) [The woman and the rose], *Arsifa wa judran* (1974) [Pavements and walls], and *Al-tha'lab alladhi yazharu wa yakhtafi* (2004) [The fox that appears and disappears]. A triennial Arabic literature prize was created in his honor in 2002.

OLIVIA C. HARRISON is Assistant Professor of French at the University of Southern California. Her first book, *Transcolonial Maghreb: Imagining Palestine in the Era of Decolonization* (2016), analyzes political imaginaries of Palestine in postcolonial Maghrebi literature. Her articles have appeared in *PMLA*, *Social Text*, *Sites*, and *Modern & Contemporary France*. With Teresa Villa-Ignacio, she is guest editing "Traduire le Maghreb/Translating the Maghreb," a special issue of *Expressions maghrébines*, forthcoming in 2016.

TERESA VILLA-IGNACIO is Postdoctoral Fellow in English and Visiting Scholar in French at Tulane University. Her current book project, "Poethical Import: Translationships in Contemporary French-American Poetic Exchange," examines the centrality of ethics in relations of translation and collaboration among France- and U.S.-based contemporary poets. She is the producer of a podcast series titled "Sounding Translation" featuring interviews with poet-translators.

SAFOI BABANA-HAMPTON is Associate Professor of French at Michigan State University. Her book *Réflexions littéraires sur l'espace public marocain dans l'oeuvre d'Abdellatif Laâbi* (2008) [Literary reflections on the Moroccan public space in the work of Abdellatif Laâbi] critically examines the role of culture in the construction of civic consciousness and the formation of a modern public space in Morocco. She is also cotranslator of *Open Correspondence* (2010), a book of letters between Abdelkebir Khatibi and Rita El Khayat.

GUY BENNETT is the author of several collections of poetry, various works of non-poetry, and numerous translations. Recent publications include *View Source*, the edition/translation of Giovanna Sandri's *Only Fragments Found: Selected Poems, 1969–1998* (2014), and a translation of Mohammed Dib's *Tlemcen or Places of Writing* (2012). His writing has been featured in magazines and anthologies in the United States and abroad, and presented in poetry and arts festivals internationally. Publisher of Mindmade Books and coeditor of Seismicity Editions, he lives in Los Angeles and teaches at Otis College of Art and Design.

MAYA BOUTAGHOU is Assistant Professor of Modern Languages and Women's Studies at Florida International University. Her book *Occidentalismes, romans historiques postcoloniaux et identités nationales au dix-neuvième siècle* [Occidentalisms, postcolonial historical novels and national identities in the nineteenth century] is forthcoming from Champion. She is guest editor of "The Algerian

War of Independence and Its Legacy in Algeria, France, and Beyond," special issue of *L'Esprit Créateur* (Winter 2014), and the author of several articles on Francophone and Arabic literature.

LIA BROZGAL is Associate Professor in UCLA's Department of French and Francophone Studies, where her research focuses on cultural productions of the Francophone Maghreb; the history and culture of Maghrebi Jews; *beur* literature and cinema; and contemporary French culture. She is the author of *Against Autobiography: Albert Memmi and the Production of Theory* (2013), and her essays have appeared in *South Central Review, Contemporary French and Francophone Studies,* and *French Forum.* Her coedited volume, *Being Contemporary*, is forthcoming with Liverpool UP, and she is currently completing a monograph on the literary and visual representations of the massacre of Algerians in Paris on October 17, 1961.

ROBYN CRESWELL is the translator of Abdelfattah Kilito's *The Clash of Images* (2010) and Sonallah Ibrahim's *That Smell & Notes from Prison* (2013). He is the poetry editor of *The Paris Review* and Assistant Professor of Comparative Literature at Yale University.

HODA EL SHAKRY is Assistant Professor of Comparative Literature at Penn State University, where she specializes in modern Arab/ic and African literatures. Her research and publications explore literature and visual culture of the Middle East and North Africa, Islamic philosophy, postcolonial studies and critical theory. Her current book project investigates literary engagements with Islamic thought in twentieth century Arabophone and Francophone literature of the Maghreb.

CLAUDIA ESPOSITO is Associate Professor of French at the University of Massachusetts Boston. She is the author of *The Narrative Mediterranean: Beyond France and the Maghreb* (2014) and of several articles on French and North African writers and filmmakers published in *Studies in French Cinema, Journal of Postcolonial Writing* and *The French Review.*

ANNE GEORGE is cotranslator of Abdellatif Laâbi's *The World's Embrace: Selected Poems* (2003). In 2004 she digitized *Souffles* issues 7 through 22 and made them freely available on the Seattle University website. She currently teaches French and the humanities at Whatcom Community College, Bellingham, Washington.

GHENWA HAYEK is Assistant Professor of Arabic at the University of Chicago. She is the author of *Beirut, Imagining the City: Space and Place in Lebanese Literature* (2014). Her translations have appeared in *Banipal* and *The New York Times*, as well as in *Beirut 39* (2010), an anthology of new writing from the Arab world.

ADDIE LEAK holds an MFA in Literary Translation from the University of Iowa. She has translated poems by Mostafa Nissabouri and prose texts by Bibish Marie-Louise Mumbu and Khaled Khalifa.

ANNE-MARIE MCMANUS is Assistant Professor of Modern Arabic Literature and Culture at Washington University in Saint Louis. She received her PhD in comparative literature from Yale University, where she specialized in North African and Middle Eastern literatures. She has translated and published research on contemporary Syrian literature and is currently completing a monograph on translation and Arabic plurilingualism in the aftermath of decolonization.

LUCY R. MCNAIR is Assistant Professor of English at LaGuardia Community College/CUNY in Queens, New York. She is the translator of Mouloud Feraoun's Algerian classic, *The Poor Man's Son* (2005), Samira Bellil's inner-city memoir, *To Hell and Back* (2008), and of poetry by Andrée Chedid, Venus Khoury-Ghata, and Amina Said in Nathalie Handal, ed., *The Poetry of Arab Women* (2000). Her translation of Edmond Amran El Maleh's short story "Taksiat" appeared in Pierre Joris and Habib Tengour, ed., *Poems for the Millennium, Volume Four* (2012).

Poet, translator, and editor **ANNA MOSCHOVAKIS** is the author of two books of poetry, *You and Three Others Are Approaching a Lake* (2011), winner of the James Laughlin Award from the Academy of American Poets, and *I Have Not Been Able to Get Through to Everyone* (2006). Her translations from the French include Albert Cossery's *The Jokers* (2010), Annie Ernaux's *The Possession* (2008), and Georges Simenon's *The Engagement* (2007). Since 2002, Moschovakis has been a member of the publishing collective Ugly Duckling Presse in the capacity of editor, designer, administrator, and printer.

JENNIFER MOXLEY is the author of *The Open Secret* (2014), *Clampdown* (2009), *The Middle Room* (2008), *The Line* (2007), *Often Capital* (2005), *The Sense Record and Other Poems* (2002), and *Imagination Verses* (1996). She has translated two books by the French poet and scholar Jacqueline Risset: a book of essays, *Sleep's Powers* (2008), and a book of poems, *The Translation Begins* (1996). In 2010 her translation of Anne Portugal's *Absolute Bob* was published by Burning Deck. She was the poetry editor for *The Baffler* magazine from 1997 to 2010 and a contributing editor of *The Poker* magazine from 2003 to 2008. Moxley teaches poetry and poetics at the University of Maine.

LAURA REECK is Associate Professor of French at Allegheny College, Meadville, Pa., where her specializations include Francophone postcolonial studies, ethnic minority writing in France, and the Maghreb. She is the author of articles on these subjects, as well as of the monograph *Writerly Identities in Beur Fiction and Beyond* (2011). She has translated subtitles for Rachid Djaïdani's short documentary *La ligne brune* (2010), short fiction by Mohamed Razane, including "So Far So Close By" in *Brooklyn Rail* (July 2011), and an excerpt from Zahia Rahmani's *Moze* in the edited volume *A Practical Guide to French Harki Literature* (2014).

EDWIGE TAMALET TALBAYEV is Assistant Professor in the Department of French and Italian at Tulane University. She has published various essays on the intersection of modernity, colonialism, and transnationalism in the Maghreb. She recently coedited *Le Maghreb méditerranéen: Littératures et plurilinguisme* with Claudia Esposito and Hakim Abderrezak (2012). She is currently completing a monograph entitled "The Transcontinental Maghreb: Francophone Literature in a Mediterranean Context" and a coedited volume, "Critically Mediterranean: Aesthetics, Theory, Hermeneutics," with Yasser Elhariry. She is editor of the international journal *Expressions maghrébines*.

ANDREW ZAWACKI is the author of four books of poetry: *By Reason of Breakings*, which won the University of Georgia's 2001 Contemporary Poetry Series Award; *Anabranch* (2004); *Petals of Zero Petals of One* (2009); and *Videotape* (2013). He has translated Aleš Debeljak's *Without Anesthesia* (2011) from the Slovene and Sébastien Smirou's *My Lorenzo* (2012) from the French. Coeditor of *Verse*, Zawacki is Associate Professor of English and Director of the Creative Writing Program at the University of Georgia.

Note: Page numbers in italic type indicate illustrations.

in, 1, 3, 7, 11–12; sociopolitical critiques of, 114; as tourist destination, 115
Moussa, 47
Moxley, Jennifer, 10
Mu'allaqat, al-, 68
Musical instruments, 50

Nahda, al-, 64
N'Aït Attik, Mririda, 47
Napoleon Bonaparte, 201
Nassar, William, 205
National culture, 61–73, 95–103; acculturation and, 183; concept of, 59, 61–62; context for emergence of, 62–65; decolonization and, 62; folklore in relation to, 43; importance of, 17; language and, 4, 5, 59–60; liberation as basis of, 45, 58, 64; literature and, 66–73; the novel and, 56; promotion of, 13, 31. *See also* Cultural decolonization
Nationalism, 164
Nazism, 97, 264*n*26
Negritude, 8, 9, 14, 39–45, 60, 113, 120–25
Negro art, 40–42
Neocolonialism, 115, 187, 221
Nissabouri, Mostafa, 1, 3, 30, 213, 255*n*7; "Grotte," 117–19; "Manabboula," 60, *86*, 87–90; "Untitled," 134–37
Noar (newspaper), 197
Novels, 56–58, 181–84

"Opening Editorial–On the Anniversary of June 5: The Aftermath of Defeat," 243–47
Oral literary tradition, 46–55
Organisation Alif (A) [Ilal Amam (Forward)], 3, 255*n*8
Organisation Ba (B) [23 Mars], 3, 255*n*8

Organisation de l'Armée Secrète, 162
Orientalism, 3, 6, 59–60, 68, 115
Orlando, Valérie, 7
Orpheus, 53, 113, 115, 124–25
Ouary, Malek, 81
Ouled Hmad, Morocco, 47

Painting. *See* Moroccan painting
Palestine, 2, 113, 187, 198, 204–5, 209–13, 243–47, 264*n*26; cartoons about, *214*; front cover of *Souffles*, *189*; posters, *190*, *206*
Pan-African Cultural Festival, 188
Petit Marocain, Le [*The Little Moroccan*] (newspaper), 13
Picasso, Pablo, 40
Poets, societal role of, 49–50
Popular Front for the Liberation of the Occupied Arabian Gulf, 246
Postcolonial decolonization, 66
Pound, Ezra, 15
Présence Africaine (journal), 9
Price-Mars, Jean, 122

Qur'an, 53

Race: atavism and, 97; color as indicator of, 122–23; in Cuba, 124; essentialist conception of, 123; in Haiti, 120–21. *See also* Negritude
Revue de l'Automobile (journal), 30
Revue du Monde Noir (journal), 9
Riad, Slim, 221
Rifaat, Adel (pseudonym: Mahmoud Hussein), 188, 244
Rimbaud, Arthur, 83
Robeson, Paul, 39
Rocha, Glauber, 222
Rodinson, Maxime, 204
Rogers Plan, 244
Rothschild, Edmond de, 201
Rothschild Bank, 200
Roumain, Jacques, 122

critique of, 5, 95–103; dominance of, 31, 62; intelligentsia of, 95–97, 100, 102, 259*n*16; Maghrebi literature in relation to, 139; Third World in relation to, 101, 163–64

Wolinski, George, Palestine cartoons by, *214*

Women, status of, 7, 74, 79

World Festival of Negro Arts (Dakar, 1966), 14, 39–45

Zafzaf, Mohamed, "Afternoon, with the Sun," 114, 142–44

Zaydan, Jurji, 139

Zionism, 187, 196–205, 209, 243–46, 263*n*14, 264*n*20, 264*n*26

Made in the USA
Middletown, DE
01 June 2018